AF353556

// Annika Öhrner
// Dan Karlholm
// Anna Rådström
// Charlotte Bydler
// Oscar Svanelid
// Pamela Schultz Nybacka
// **Håkan Nilsson** (Ed.)

Renegotiations

THE ROLE OF PUBLIC ART IN THE NEW MILLENNIUM

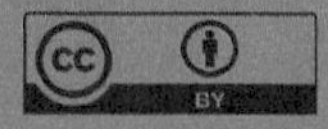

(CC BY 3.0)

The images are not included in creative commons

Södertörns högskola
(Södertörn University)
Biblioteket
SE-141 89 Huddinge

www.sh.se/publications

© the authors

....

Omslag & Grafisk form
Andreas Karperyd

Stockholm 2023

Södertörn Academic Studies 91
Södertörn Studies in Art History and Aesthetics 8

ISSN 1650-433X

ISBN 978-91-89504-09-7 (print)
ISBN 978-91-89504-10-3 (digital)

Content

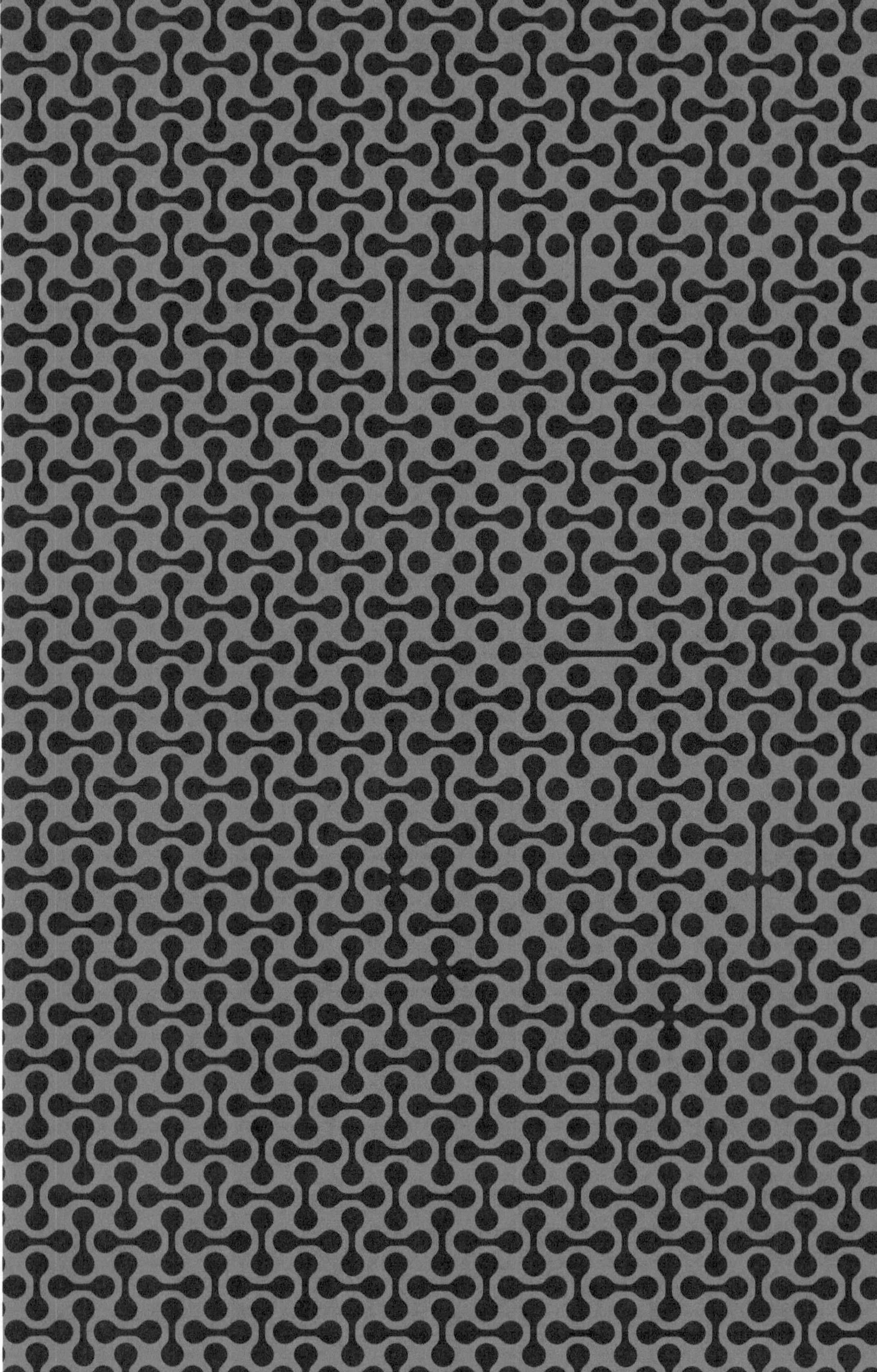

Renegotiations.
An introduction
// Håkan Nilsson

This anthology is the result of a research assignment undertaken by the department of Art History at Södertörn University, between 2018 and 2020. The project was commissioned by the Public Art Agency in Sweden, after it had been given a new mandate to create a Knowledge Hub for public art and the design of commonal spaces. An important part of the commission was to work in collaboration with universities and university colleges in the areas of education and strategic research projects.

The formal written agreement between Sweden's Public Art Agency and Södertörn University details the assignment, the purpose of which was to write an overview of the history of public art in Sweden, both publicly commissioned art and art produced by independent actors outside established art field. The assignment also included the task to identify and elucidate key concepts within public art and to develop an ethos of art critical reflection. This assignment was carried out in two phases. In the first phase, Södertörn University worked in collaboration with the Valand Academy at the University of Gothenburg to produce *The Public Art Research* review (2018); here, Södertörn University was responsible for the Nordic region.[1] The report was presented at the conference *Researching Public Art* (October 11-12, 2018), an event organized by the Public Art Agency Sweden in cooperation with the Royal Institute of Art, KTH, Södertörn University, HDK-Valand, Skissernas Museum and ArkDes. The second phase of the assignment includes this anthology, as well as the participation of individual researchers (to varying degrees) in two symposia in collaboration with Public Art Agency Sweden, which hosted both events. Within the assignment's remit, the Art History Department at Södertörn University also held the conference *Public Art in the Nordic Countries* (Feb 20-21, 2020). Researchers and other public art stakeholders, mainly from the Nordic countries, were invited to discuss the role of public art in each country.

---

1   Kjell Caminha, Håkan Nilsson, Oscar Svanelid & Mick Wilson, *The Public Art Research Report: A report on the current state of research on public art in the Nordic Countries, and in a wider international context* (2018).

The symposia featured discussions between researchers, artists and curators, either commissioned by or representing the Public Art Agency Sweden under the themes of "criticality and instrumentality" and "temporariness and permanence".[2] Issues raised during the symposia concerned artists who work in the public sphere in general, and artists commissioned by Public Art Agency Sweden in particular, as well as scholars who endeavor to describe the role and position of public art today. The conference, on the other hand, had a more clearly delineated research perspective. Structured around two keynote lectures and two round table discussions, researchers and artists from Sweden, Norway, Finland, Iceland, Denmark and the Netherlands were invited to discuss the current state of public art.[3] The focus centered on a comparison between the Nordic countries, particularly in the area of public art research. The artist's perspective featured highly in the first keynote lecture, in which the artist and architect Sandi Hilal spoke under the title "Permanent temporalities". Hilal presented her work, with a focus on the participatory art project *Al Madhafah/The Living Room*, which

---

2   Criticality and instrumentality were in focus on March 28, 2019 at Public Art Agency Sweden. The participants were Dan Karlholm, Håkan Nilsson, Oscar Svanelid and Annika Öhrner from Södertörn University (SH), the artists Éva Mag, Sam Hultin, Meriç Algün, Johanna Gustafsson Fürst and Edi Muka from Public Art Agency Sweden (PAAS). Magdalena Malm, Director of Public Art Agency Sweden, welcomed the participants, and the symposium was moderated by Rebecka Katz Thor (PAAS) and Håkan Nilsson (SH). Temporariness and permanence took place on December 4, 2019, also at Public Art Agency Sweden's office. Participants were Charlotte Bydler, Dan Karlholm, Håkan Nilsson and Oscar Svanelid from SH and the artists Malin Arnell & Åsa Elzén, Kajsa Dahlberg, Carl-Oscar Sjögren and Katarina Pirak Sikku. Rebecka Katz Thor from PAAS welcomed the audience and then moderated the discussion together with Håkan Nilsson. Dan Karlholm's speech was later published as "Evigheten, flyktigheten och den konstnärliga resiliensen" ("Eternity, transience and artistic resilience"), in *Nya Småland*, ed. Jonatan Habib Engqvist (Stockholm: Jonatan Habib Engqvist) (Stockholm: Arvinius + Orfeus Publishing & Linnaeus University Press, 2020), pp. 153-155.

3   In addition to these two keynote lectures, the conference was structured around two round table discussions. The first main theme was "Public art and public art management" with Catarina Gabrielsson (Associate Professor, KTH School of Architecture), Æsa Sigurjónsdóttir (Associate Professor of Art History, University of Iceland), Jessica Sjöholm Skrubbe (Associate Professor, Department of Culture and Aesthetics, Stockholm University), and Laura Uimonen (Ph.D. Environmental Art, M. Sc. Architecture, Finland) as a contributor. The moderator was Annika Öhrner from SH. The second main theme was "Public art and the public", with Peter Bengtsen (Associate Professor, Division of Art History and Visual Studies, Lund University), Arild Berg (Ph.D, Faculty of Technology, Art and Design at OsloMet - Oslo Metropolitan University), Trude Schjelderup Iversen (Senior Curator, KORO Kunst i Offentlige Rom), Jacob Kimvall (Ph.D. in Art History and Associate Professor at the Department of Culture and Aesthetics, Stockholm University) and Kristine Samson (urbanist, docent, and Associate Professor, Performance Design, Department of Communication and Arts, Roskilde University, Roskilde University). The discussion was moderated by Håkan Nilsson from SH.

took place in Boden 2018 under the auspices of Public Art Agency Sweden. The second presentation was given by Jeroen Boomgaard from the Netherlands. Under the title "Public Spaces as the Realm of the Possible", Boomgaard spoke about his experiences working with the Foundation for Art and Public Space (SKOR) in the Netherlands – which was discontinued in 2012 – and about the function public art serves in public spaces today, and how we can engage in a collective dialogue about this. The function of a public art funded through taxes, which at the same time is expected to critique institutions of power, is a rather rare phenomenon internationally speaking, and since the Netherlands discontinued SKOR, this currently occurs mostly in the Nordic countries.

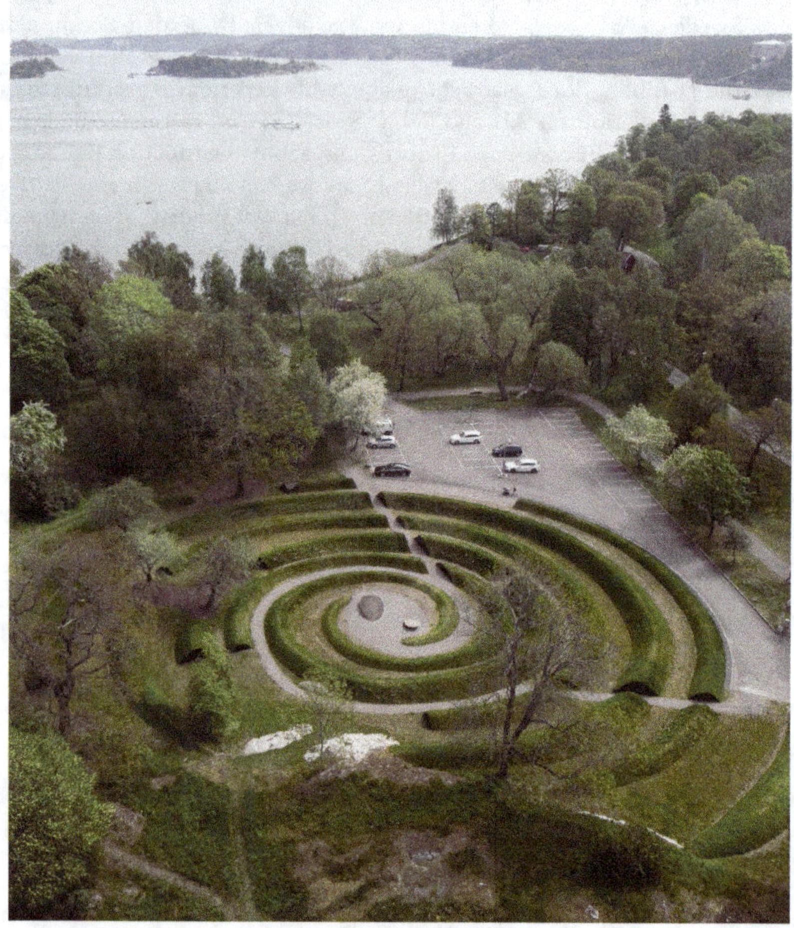

Lea Porsager, Gravitational Ripples, 2019, Phoot: Ricard Estay/Public Art Agency Sweden

The symposia and the conference were crucial in the research project's capacity to operate within a diversity of contexts; artistic perspectives intermingled with those of researchers, both of which were themselves recontextualized into a broader background. The project description served as the starting point for the research project. It posed certain questions and topics for discussion that touched on the complex relationship between the commissioning body and the art-practitioner, as well as looking beyond examples of public art specifically commissioned by the 'public.' The use of the term "renegotiation" came partly from discussions that have surrounded public art on an international level since at least the 1990s, when debate about public art (or art in public spaces) intensified. The intensification of the debate was due in part to increased polarization, pitting those who saw other possibilities for public art against those who favored more traditional expressions and values. The importance of contemplation and aesthetics was called into question by artists, critics, academics and radical institutions who argued that art is the bearer of other values and perspectives. These discussions also need to be understood in relation to the fact that in the final decades of the 20th century, the entire art world became increasingly polarized, to the extent that an embrace of aesthetic values was seen as a reactionary response to a period of progressive experimentation.

The aesthetic dimension of public art could thus symbolize two sides of the same coin. On the one hand, it meant a return to a conceptualization of art in which art was stripped of its political potential. On the other hand, it was argued that apolitical 'aesthetic' art was in actual fact often harnessed for political purposes, most evident in the public sphere where it served to conceal hidden agendas around gentrification and segregation. Aesthetic *makeovers* led to increasing property values, as well as higher rental prices for offices and apartments, which in turn forced out local vendors, alternative businesses and low-income earners. Moreover, a second, parallel dialogue, was taking place at the time, in which the entirety of public space was increasingly characterized as under threat, partly due to the privatization of the public sphere, caused by deregulation, and partly in relation to, for example, increasing digitalization. In response to this, there was a mushrooming of radical alternatives which aimed to safeguard the public sphere. Non-commissioned art – i.e., graffiti, street art and temporary works – took their place alongside sculptures in the square, thus occupying public space. Towards the end of the millennium, we also saw the emergence of a new generation of artists, designers, craftsmen and architects. Following the end of the Cold War, the IT bubble and the economic crisis, these practitioners sought independence from entrenched organizational structures by creating art outside the traditional art field, preferably in the public sphere, contributing thereby to a new round of renegotiations.

Today, the dichotomy between temporary, artist-initiated projects and commissioned "aesthetic" objects is less pronounced, and in retrospect it is clear that the discussions were not really about different artistic expressions, but about how they can be used and what role they can play. The strategies used in these alternative practices were embraced by established institutions, and thus have been applied for completely different purposes. Temporary interventions, just like traditional art objects, are used by municipalities and real estate companies as part of value creation. At the same time, many have pointed to the critical potential offered by more permanent artworks, particularly when they are seen as something more than aesthetic objects. Against the backdrop of the ever-changing, ephemeral and flexible nature of the neoliberal social order, art can be a source of repose, friction and a space for reflection. Here too, we can speak of renegotiations. The realization that the kind of artistic expression with the greatest critical potential is not self-evident has led to a complex situation, giving rise to a greater degree of diversity in public art practice. Commissioners of public art, from developers and independent curators to local municipalities, are now incorporating multiple types of artistic expression. Furthermore, there is a greater awareness in art schools as well as an increased level of activity among independent artists and art groups, who are also actively working in the public sphere.

The research project "Renegotiations: the role of public art in the new millennium" takes this complex situation as its starting point. By rooting discussions and problematizations of the role of public art, a platform for the project was formed. Starting from this platform, contributing researchers have discussed various aspects of the potential roles of art in the public sphere in present day Sweden. Limiting the discussion to Sweden is important in several ways – the country has state, regional and municipally funded public art, which is both encouraged and expected to contribute to critical reflections. While similar solutions exist in neighboring countries, they are relatively rare; indeed, organizations seemingly working in a similar way in other countries are often independently organized and thus only occasionally receive public funding. The research project does not aim to create a comprehensive picture of all art production. What it sets out to offer are examples and case studies that highlight certain key issues. Each researcher in the anthology has based his or her analysis on issues the researcher sees as particularly pertinent and urgent. While a continuous dialogue has been maintained throughout the project between all participants, each researcher has been responsible for the approach he or she has taken. Here, historically based arguments are just as important as in-depth analyses of contemporary works. Critical reflections on questions of 'utility,' on who gets to participate in the public sphere and what concepts are used are just as important as those examining the positive effects of public art.

Håkan Nilsson's introductory text "Public Art: An attempt to navigate" sets out to summarize the issue of public art from both practical and theoretical perspectives. Nilsson gives examples of what public art can be, based on the funding body commissioning the work (e.g. publicly funded or "unsolicited" and thus often illegal art), but also examines the many grey areas that arise with works of art that are either part of the public sphere but funded by private donations, or, works that are publicly funded but can only be enjoyed by a few. The text also identifies several places where we can encounter public art: biennials; festivals; sculpture parks; graffiti and street art; private and public buildings. The review invites discussions concerning art in public spaces and what purpose(s) public art actually serves. The text also reviews the many issues and concerns usually associated with public art, such as gentrification and instrumentalization, and with this, discussions pertaining to the integrity of the individual artist and the autonomy of art. Håkan Nilsson also touches on how the entire art scene has changed and how classical institutions, which manage collections and host exhibitions (e.g. museums and art galleries) are also extending beyond the white cube. Finally, consideration is given to the question of dialogue and how, in order to be effective, this is linked to active listening.

In the article "The Art of the Million Program in Today's Living Environment", Annika Öhrner discusses Gert Marcus' color compositions on the high-rise buildings in Västra Flemingsberg, which were commissioned by Huddinge municipality, in Stockholm County, and completed in 1974. Öhrner goes on to look at *Evig anställning (Eternal Employment)* by Goldin+Senneby (Simon Goldin and Jakob Senneby), which was funded by Public Art Agency Sweden and won the 2018 Västlänken (West Link) competition: *Kronotopia* for a station in Gothenburg. Siri Derkert's *Ristningar i naturbetong (Carvings in Natural Concrete)*, at Östermalmstorg metro station, commissioned by Stockholm County Council and completed in 1965, is also among the works discussed. The key perspective, however, is the question of the long-term nature of the artwork, where "permanent" works from previous eras continue to act upon their surroundings while their contextual conditions change. In the chapter, Öhrner points to the common contemporary belief in the agency of the performative artwork and its capacity to influence space, public discourse, and democracy, while parallel qualities in older works of art, and their institutional contexts, are often ignored. What abstract and concrete relations did post-war ideas and claims on behalf of art establish, and how do they relate to contemporary conditions? How does art, originating from different eras, interact with an individual viewer or resident? Öhrner shows how the same ideas prevailed in the post-war period as today; high investment in public art was matched by hopes for high impact. The generous and often politically progressive art production of the era resulted in "permanent" works that lingered in urban spaces. A greater awareness of this complex landscape, and the impact of artistic and institutional heritage in our own time, is needed.

Time is also an important factor in Dan Karlholm's text "Art Work in Public Time: A study of *Forest Calling, Ställbergs Gruva* and *Eternal Employment*. As his starting point, Karlholm takes three relatively recent projects, all of which were funded by Public Art Agency Sweden. Extended in time, these three projects are neither temporary (short-lived) nor permanent (eternal), they are instead consistent with the contemporary idea of the artwork as a project, where the start date is much easier to ascertain than the end date. Karlholm, however, sets out to problematize the notion of a shift between unique works to undefined projects. All three examples, Karlholm writes, can be said to challenge not only the accelerating ephemerality and adaptive flexibility of late modernity, but are also at odds with notions of marketization and commodification. In these works, Karlholm traces interesting crossings and thresholds that seek to problematise. They all have (at least) one foot in the past in order to implement new futures. *Skogen kallar* (*Forest Calling*) (co)works toward 'another future', a better future than the ecological devastation we face if nothing is done to prevent it, while *Ställbergs Gruva* is a collective work based on the idea that the future has already arrived. The artists behind *Eternal Employment* do not themselves work; they instead ask the question "What is work?", now and in the future, delegating to the future the task of answering that question. Karlholm's discussion coheres around different, interconnected temporalities where nothing is either present, past or future but rather present, past and future simultaneously.

In "*Listen!* A Sculpture in the Square and a #MeToo Monument" Anna Rådström analyzes the expression of "traditional" public art, i.e. the sculpture in the square and/or a monument, and its continued relevance. The chapter focuses on Camilla Akraka's *Listen!* which was placed on the newly renovated Rådhustorget in Umeå in 2019. The work was initiated by the municipality of Umeå but was also partly funded by a donation from Sparbanken and, at the time of its inauguration, was claimed to be Sweden's, or rather the world's, first monument to the #MeToo movement. The gleaming red feline raises questions about the production of meaning in public art. Rådström explores how the work addresses the contemporary #MeToo movement and feminist history and how it also functions as a reminder of the progressive character of the municipality. Through concepts such as "thoughtprints," Rådström seeks to situate and discuss different interpretative possibilities. The animal depicted in the sculpture is described as a 'cougar', often leading to the assumption that it is female, which in turn leads Rådström to reflect on the woman as animal and part of nature. The text also discusses the life of the cougar outside the square, where it has become a landmark for Umeå, and where images of the work appear in a variety of contexts.

In the chapter "The Place of Play in an Anthropocene Public Sphere. On *Vril Båt Sten/Fijfere Vanás Geaðgi* by Joar Nango and Anders Rimpi", Charlotte Bydler discusses a work whose translated English title reads *Burl Boat Stone*, and *Fijfere Vanás Geaðgi* in the three different Sámi languages that are relevant here. Joar Nango and Anders Rimpi's installation was commissioned by Public Art Agency Sweden in 2017 and is a site-specific work for the Giella preschool in Jåhkåmåhkke (in Lule Sámi) or Jokkmokk (in Swedish), as part of a language revitalization project for Sámi languages. The words mark some important differences: "Fijfer" is Southern Saemie for "burl", while "vanás" means "boat" in Lule Sámi, and "geaðgi" refers to "stone" in Northern Sámi. By using words from three different Sámi languages, the work addresses the multilingual character of the local region, represented in the group of preschool children, who speak different languages. It is therefore a site-specific work, a language revival project that must be understood against the backdrop of the historical suppression of Sámi languages, and perhaps in relation to the forced relocation of Northern Sámi to Southern Saemie territory. Thus the three languages spoken at the preschool are represented by the three words, which capture three different worlds. Bydler further asks how we should relate to public art commissioned by a nation-state that fails to recognize the rights of indigenous Sámi people. Here, questions of the "permanent" are partly understood in relation to the artwork's extension into the future, as well as to the Sámi's historical right to a territory in which they can undoubtedly show they have legitimately settled since time immemorial. With this dual perspective, Bydler goes on to define the terms "permanent" and "public" in relation to each other, such as in "permanent public artwork", a line of reasoning with further relevance for our most recent geological epoch: the Anthropocene.

In the text "Safety Art. On art as a security/safety measure for public spaces", Oscar Svanelid touches on another aspect of the "utility" of public art, namely when it is part of a context that aims to enhance the safety/security of a public space. Svanelid notes that safety, or the lack thereof, is increasingly perceived as a problem in modern society, and he explores why this issue has become part of the municipal policy agenda for several residential areas in general and specific locations, in particular. The text is based on the role played by Anders Årfelt's *Stockholmslejon* (*Stockholm Lions*) in the 2017 terrorist attack on Drottninggatan in Stockholm. He goes on to discuss some municipally commissioned light-based artworks in Gothenburg, created within the project *Trygg, vacker stad* (*Safe, Beautiful City*) (2005-2018). In analyzing a number of light-based artworks in tunnels, Svanelid discusses questions surrounding what safety and security mean and who we want to make feel secure. The notion that crime and insecurity can be 'built away' is problematized with questions about the will to eliminate 'undesirable elements' from the streetscape. The desired effect of greater mobility presupposes that only the 'right' kind of individuals should have mobility increased. The problem, Svanelid notes, is not the light art itself, rather the problem lies in the fact that it has become the standard for safety/security art. At the same time, he also sees a different "social life" for the artworks in their encounter with the public, which takes place beyond both artistic intention and municipal control.

Commissioned art can have "utility" and still retain its integrity and critical edge. In the text "The Renegotiation of Care. Contemporary art and research in a new care environment", which explores artworks at the Skandion Clinic in Uppsala, Pamela Schultz Nybacka describes how the hospital environment was planned in intimate relation with the formation of art to be installed there. In her role as participant observer, Schultz-Nybacka discovered, among other things, that the notion of what a hospital environment should be initially limited the artist Filippa Arrias in her creative process, even though the project manager Lotta Mossum was open to relaxing these invisible barriers – an important reminder of how constraints can be internalized without ever being explicitly laid out or even acknowledged. The Skandion Clinic provides an interesting example regarding two important aspects of public art, in general. The first is the question of how artists and others involved in the design of a building should relate to its intended use, in this case, care for children with cancer. The second is how and when art should enter into the process. In the case of the Skandion Clinic, art was introduced at a formative stage of the planning process and came to shape the design of the hospital.

In "Temporary Liaisons and Far-reaching Convergences. Public art under municipal auspices," Håkan Nilsson brings the volume to a close with a discussion of how temporary art came to be municipally funded as public art. The text is based on a survey of those responsible for public art in Sweden's 20 largest municipalities and touches on both the proportion that municipalities invest in temporary art and their motivation for making that investment. The responses to the survey varied, partly due to the way the questions were interpreted by respondents. Because of this, concepts such as 'temporary' and 'permanent', as well as the effects temporary artworks are often expected to produce – e.g. interaction and participation – are discussed. The text also provides an outline of the immediate background and wider context of temporary art in relation to the art world. Although several municipalities have a long history of supporting and commissioning temporary art, many report that 2015 represented a watershed year: in 2015 and after, this kind of art began to be used in earnest. The text presents a variety of ideas from respondents about why temporary art is on the rise, e.g. from the need for public art to reflect what is going on in the broader art world to notions about the viewer's ability to encounter and interact with the work. Several also point to larger societal changes, where temporary solutions are better able to meet contemporary demands for flexibility. There are also many examples of the difficulties municipalities face when implementing this kind of art, one principal reason for which is that governing documents and regulations often require the establishment of something permanent. This is also where a convergence in opinion becomes clear: temporary art must satisfy many different requirements, but the institutions commissioning the art must also act to adapt their systems to the new conditions that temporary art itself creates.

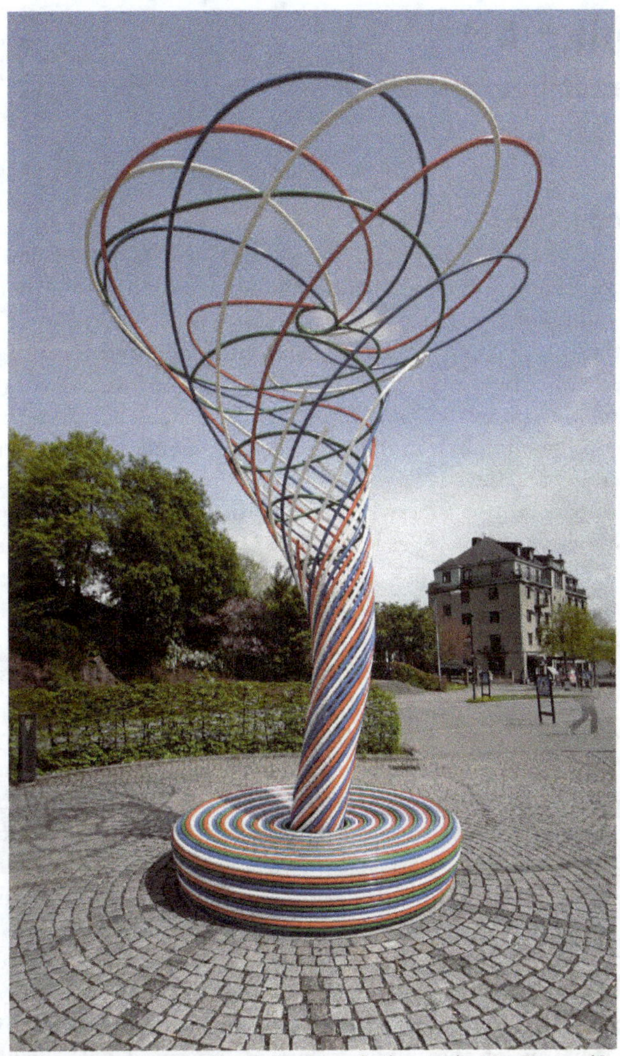

Permanent art in a temporary context. Tornado Touchdown by the artist duo Mats Bigert and Lars Bergström was commissioned by Borås municipality and was inaugurated at the opening of the Borås sculpture biennale 2010. However, in 2021 when the permanent installation was found to be in need of severe restauration, the work was replaced by another artwork. Photo: Studio Bigert & Bergström Bus
© Studio Bigert & Bergström / Bildupphovsrätt 2022

Public Art:
An attempt to navigate
//Håkan Nilsson

Introduction

Defining "public art" is easier said than done. The word "public" itself gives rise to a variety of different and sometimes conflicting interpretations. For example, do we mean "public" with respect to "the public sector" and thus, in the case of art, as something financed through public funds? This is not uncommon. In 2019, when The Swedish Arts Grants Committee conducted a survey of the so-called 1% rule, they chose to define a "public environment" as "environments owned or used by the public, i.e., the state, region or municipality."[1] Or do we mean the public space, which, since the liberalization and deregulation policies of the 1980s and 90s, relies less and less on public funds and instead is the conglomeration of private, commercial, municipal and state spaces – not forgetting today, the mixing of physical as well as virtual arenas? The aim of this text is to explore different definitions of public art and to discuss the situations and contexts in which public art exists.

The privatization of public space is a recurring theme in public discourse, which in turn largely plays out through private channels, such as the editorial pages of newspapers. This is to be expected, at least if we follow the logic of the social and critical theorist Jürgen Habermas, who has made a major contribution to this debate regarding the bourgeois public sphere. Habermas has argued that public discourse must be protected from the influence of the state, not least since it is the public that scrutinizes the activities of the state.[2]

Habermas thus points to a third definition of the public sphere, in addition to the aforementioned "state-funded" and "common" (which can, but does not have to, include the commonly owned) definitions. This third understanding of the public sphere is concerned with how public

---

1   *1% för konstnärlig gestaltning av offentlig miljö: en komparativ studie av enprocentsregeln i kommuner och regioner 2012 och 2018 [One Percent for the Artistic Design of Public Spaces: A comparative study of the one-percent rule in municipalities and regions in 2012 and 2018]*, ed. Bitte Jarl (Stockholm: The Swedish Arts Grants Committee, 2020), p. 15.

2   Jürgen Habermas, *Borgerlig offentlighet: kategorierna "privat" och "offentligt" i det moderna samhället [The Structural Transformation of the Public Sphere: An inquiry into a category of bourgeois society]*, trans. Joachim Retzlaff (Lund: Arkiv förlag, 1984).

discourse (and public space) is to be kept *open*, an essential element in the preservation of democracy. These different perspectives on the nature of the public sphere affect how we view public art. Before turning to the question of how art can act to "scrutinize", it might first be beneficial if we continue to explore the concept of the "public" in terms of the commons.

The fact that something is public does not mean it is accessible to everyone, even if we are speaking of art exhibited in a public environment and financed with public funds. The Government Offices of Sweden, prisons, and infectious disease departments are all possible sites of public art to which only a small number of people have access. The website sl.se describes the Stockholm metro as "the world's longest art exhibition", but to access it you need to buy a ticket.[3]

Furthermore, the fact that something is accessible to all does not mean that it is publicly funded. Private housing companies fund art in squares and parks; private initiators raise money to erect memorials to individuals they wish to honor; private donation boards fund public art: for example, *Eva Bonniers donnationsnämnd* (Eva Bonnier's Donation Board) works "to initiate and hold dialogues on the role of art and architecture in the public space, as well as to implement art projects."[4]

However, the fact that art is public and accessible to all does not necessarily mean that it is commissioned or paid for by either public or private actors. It is becoming increasingly common for artists and artist-led initiatives to claim space in the public domain without having been commissioned. This may be because they want to create an independent platform to discuss the public sphere (in Habermas' sense), or because they want to occupy certain spaces in order to demonstrate their potential. It may also be because there is nowhere else to act, or because the street is simply the place where they want to be seen by a wider public, as may be the case for street art and graffiti.

In other words, public art is a concept that encompasses both art commissioned by the authorities and art that opposes the very same authorities. This is just one of the many paradoxes that arise in the conversation about public art.

---

3   www.sl.se [accessed 05/10/2019].
4   https://www.evabonniersdonationsnamnd.se/sv/ [accessed 11/12/2019]

The field of public art

Public art is described and discussed in a variety of contexts, but only in exceptional cases does it appear in forums that concern "ordinary" art. Critical appraisals in newspapers and online journals mainly deal with art which finds its way into galleries and museums, even if there are occasional targeted efforts, for example, when kunstkritikk.se looked at several recently installed public works in the country.[5] The upshot is that if one wants to read more about public art, one must turn to other sources.

Larger commissioning bodies, such as Public Art Agency Sweden, county councils/regions and larger municipalities, publish books on the year's initiatives and/or volumes relating to all the art associated with any major project. Many municipalities have also put together inventories of their own holdings. These publications also include major initiatives, often based on a specific theme, such as the 2005 report by Public Art Agency Sweden on approximately 1,500 building-related artworks it has funded since 1937. This led to the further report, *Beställd konst: Fastighetsägarnas vård och underhåll av byggnadsanknuten konst (Commissioned Art: The Care and Maintenance of Building-Related Art by Property Owners)*, published in 2008.[6] The central question raised in the report from 2008 was whether public building-related art could be given the same long-term protection as historical art in churches and castles.[7] The inventory in turn laid the groundwork for the research project *Offentlig konst: Ett kulturarv (Public Art: A Cultural Heritage)* from 2014, where, in a comprehensive publication bearing the same name, several cases were discussed in greater detail.[8]

Public art can thus be studied through a variety of sources and literature. Its history and creative processes can be studied at, for example, the Skissernas Museum in Lund, which has the world's largest collection of sketches, models and preparatory work for both Swedish and international public art. Knowledge of street art and graffiti is

---

5   See, e.g., the inventory "Offentlig konst från Jokkmokk till Lund" [Public Art from Jokkmokk to Lund]: https://kunstkritikk.se/offentlig-konst-fran-jokkmokk-till-lund/ [accessed 11/25/2019].

6   Klara Wahlström red., *Beställd konst. Fastighetsägarnas vård och underhåll av byggnadsanknuten konst [Commissioned Art: Property owners' care and maintenance of building-related art]* (Stockholm: Public Art Agency Sweden, 2008).

7   Wahlström *Beställd konst [Commissioned Art]*, op.cit., p. 5.

8   Karin Hermerén & Henrik Orrje, *Offentlig konst – Ett Kulturarv – Tillsyn och förvaltning av byggnadsanknuten konst [Public Art - A Cultural Heritage - Supervision and management of building-related art]* (Stockholm: Public Art Agency Sweden, 2014).

disseminated through certain magazines and publications. The publishing house *Dokument Press*, for example, has published a large number of volumes since 2000.[9] But knowledge is also spread via social media, which is logical given the short-lived character of this art form. Writing on the subject is also prolific, with pieces functioning as much as a guide to public art as a reflection on it. *Det där är väl ingen konst? (That's not Art, is it?)* is based on a several controversial public artworks. From commissioning and jury deliberation to the often angry reactions from various quarters, the book provides a broad yet multifaceted picture.[10] Otherwise, it is common for publications on public art to function as a kind of guidebook, structured like art walks, such as *Konst på stan (Art in the City)*.[11]

Even as a field of research, "public art" shows great variety in terms of what is selected as public art and the issues that public art addresses. The research survey conducted by Södertörn University and the Valand Academy, on behalf of Public Art Agency Sweden, demonstrates this breadth. To exemplify this, one can look at the state of contemporary research on alternative art practices. Indeed, since the 2010s, four doctoral theses have been written on graffiti and street art in Sweden. Only two of these fall within the domain of art history, though neither discuss such phenomena from a strictly aesthetic perspective. The other two theses come from the disciplines of landscape architecture and media studies.[12] What this tells us is that a variety of different disciplinary fields are interested in public art. Not only art history; it is a phenomenon that involves urbanists, ethnologists, sociologists, economists, gender studies scholars, landscape architects, interior designers, architects and, of course, artists. A large number of artistic doctoral theses are also based on practices in public spaces.[13]

---

9   https://dokument.org/ [accessed 09/30/2019].

10   Brita Åsbrink & Kaj Larsson, *Det där är väl ingen konst?* [*That's Not Art, Is It?*] (Stockholm: Carlsson förlag, 2008).

11   Bo Wingren, *Konst på stan. Offentlig utsmyckning i Stockholm* [*Art in the City. Public decoration in Stockholm*] (Stockholm: Natur och Kultur, 1997).

12   Jacob Kimvall, *The G-Word: Virtuosity and violation, negotiating and transforming graffiti*, doctoral thesis (Stockholm: Stockholm University, Department of Art History, 2014) ; Peter Bengtsen, *The Street Art World*, doctoral thesis (Lund: Lund University, 2014).

13   See, for example, Roland Ljungberg, *Kunskaps- och vattenrum: Delprojekt i konstnärlig upplevelsepark för hållbar utveckling* [*Knowledge and Water Spaces: Subproject on an artistic adventure park for sustainable development*] (Stockholm: Konstfack, 2014); Lisa Torell, *Potential of the Gap*, doctoral thesis (Tromsø: Tromsø Academy of Contemporary Art and Creative Writing, 2018). Both projects demonstrate the breadth of artistic research.

The breadth of perspectives and issues arising out of "public art" raises questions about how we should view it in relation to other art. According to the philosopher and art theorist Arthur Danto, since at least the 1960s, "art" has been understood as whatever the "art world" decides it to be, that is, potentially anything.[14] Faced with such a definition, public art becomes a narrower form of art. On the other hand, looking at the practice itself and the many questions it raises, public art, with its new viewers, its commissioning bodies, its fields of research, its possible and impossible venues and its many different regulations, represents an expansion of the concept of art.

Public art/art in public space

One way of structuring what public art could possibly be is to distinguish between what is commissioned by and financed through public funds, what is commissioned by another major actor and, finally, what is created by way of other initiatives. But this is also a division that is difficult to maintain; a great deal of public art falls into grey areas. In the wake of the privatization of state-owned companies and the deregulation of the service sector, which began in the 1990s, the boundary between the private and the public has become blurred and fluid. Not least, this has contributed to the fact that art, which once fell into the category 'public,' with the sale of companies and properties, art suddenly became private, perhaps even moving from once having been accessible to the general public to now not being so .

It is not only deregulation and privatization that have changed the art world, however. As public art engages more actors, the field becomes more professionalized and specialized. "Commissioned" public art is increasingly managed and administered by private curators and art mediators, who are hired by both municipalities and private actors to handle procedures ranging from citizen dialogues to artist selection and the placement of artworks. *ArtPlatform* is an art agency that started in 2001, mainly working as a commissioning agent for private and municipal real estate and construction companies. Since 2016, there has been an increase in commissions coming from municipalities' and regions' public art departments, and today, they work much more with municipalities and regions than they do directly with private actors.[15]

---

14   Arthur Danto, "Konstvärlden" [The Artworld] in *Konsten och konstbegreppet* [*Art and the Concept of Art]* (Stockholm: Raster, 1996).

15   In an e-mail dated 11/18/2020, Åsa-Viktoria Wihlborg puts that percentage at 80-20 in favor of

Professionalization requires that actors maintain a dual perspective. As Magdalena Malm describes, the greatest challenge for the contemporary curator is the need to simultaneously understand the intended audience and the artist's working process. She described her position as a curator, shortly before she took over as director at Public Art Agency of Sweden (2012-2020), as follows:

> This ability to change position and step inside both perspectives is a continuous movement that is central to the work of most curators. My thoughts move into the artist's imagination, and immerse themselves in what shape the work could take, they move on, out to the audience and into their minds, into their bodies, trying to imagine what they will experience... [16]

On the other hand, we are also seeing the emergence of private organizations, such as the independent digital platform *konstpool*, which aims to raise artists' awareness of public calls for proposals and to help artists with the often complicated application procedure, resulting from the bureaucratization of the process when public procurement law applies.[17]

Public art can emerge in the context of art exhibitions, which take place in an art gallery or a museum, but which extend beyond the gallery space; for example, ArkDes' exhibition "Public Luxury - Architecture, Design and the Struggle for the Common" (2018) or "Acting in the City" at Norrköping Art Museum (2013-14), which sought to "use the city as a stage".[18] Public art can also emerge as part of various art school programs. At the time of writing, Valand, *Konstfack* and the Royal Institute of Art offer courses in public art, or, to use the precise wording of *Konstfack*, in the "open". Sometimes public art arises as part of other educational projects. In 2017, for example, the *ART KOD (ART CODE)* project used art to help young people influence their environment.[19]

---

the municipalities.

16   Magdalena Malm, "My Dear Friend", *Imagining the Audience: Viewing Positions in Curatorial and Artistic Practice*, ed. Malm & Annika Wik (Stockholm: Art and Theory Publishing, 2012), pp. 205-6.

17   https://www.konstpool.se/sv/home [accessed 09/28/2019].

18   Quotes from exhibition curator Susanne Ewerlöf's introduction "Acting in the City" in *Acting in the City*, ed. Johanna Uddén (Norrköping: Norrköping Art Museum, 2013), p. 6.

19   Tobias Barenthin Lindblad, *Art Kod: Demokrati, konst och det offentliga rummet* [*Art Code:*

Sometimes public art occurs through temporary exhibitions in the public space (where certain works are made permanent), such as Borås' sculpture biennial and Örebro's *Open art.* It is created through private initiatives, sometimes receiving public support such as *Umedalen's sculpture park, Konstvägen Sju Älvar, Wanås Konst, Konst på Hög* Kumla or *Pilane* at Tjörn. Sculpture parks also include municipally initiated and funded projects, such as Görvälns sculpture park in Järfälla as well as locally, artist-organized exhibitions such as *Skulpturparken* in Ängelsberg. I have already mentioned that the number of self-initiated art projects in the public space is a growing and significant part of the art world. When Public Art Agency Sweden announced the call for "Local Art Projects" in 2018, it targeted both municipalities and non-profit organizations. It received 382 applications from a wide range of applicants – municipalities, local art spaces, further education colleges, libraries and many individual artists.[20] Add to this graffiti and street art, which are a ubiquitous but not always legal part of the public streetscape. The latter examples remind us that public space as an arena for art remains a question of access. The battle over which expressions should be accepted and given space is complicated. Art historian Jacob Kimvall writes in the book *Noll tolerans (Zero Tolerance)* that the issue of graffiti is a question of definitions, where it has been important for zero tolerance proponents to make graffiti synonymous with scribbling. In a further step, this link turns all graffiti into vandalism and therefore illegal. Illegal activity, in turn, creates insecurity.[21] In the controversial mural festival, *Wall Street,* that took place in Nacka (a region outside Stockholm), in 2019, Nacka municipality tried to create a mural festival with elements of graffiti with the intention of "increasing security", of enhancing "well-being and safety in the public environment" by introducing a "program code" in which a new "DNA" would be created for the works to be exhibited. These included a cultivation of becoming a "masterful" street artist instead of the "rebel", substituting "anger" for "wisdom", "illegal" for "illegal", etc.[22] It is quite a coincidence that in Nacka, some 20 years earlier, in the

---

Democracy, art and the public space] (Stockholm: Dokument Press, 2017) .

20   Public Art Agency Sweden's local call for proposals 2018 was part of the so-called Knowledge Hub initiative.

21   Jakob Kimvall, *Noll tolerans: Kampen mot graffitti [Zero Tolerance: The fight against graffiti]* (Stockholm: Verbal förlag, 2012).

22   https://www.nacka.se/stadsutveckling-trafik/konsten-att-skapa-stad/genomforda-projekt/infor-wall-street/ [accessed 09/07/2021]

middle of the era of zero tolerance, a number of walls were opened up for legal graffiti.

To be classified as something that generates "insecurity" is doubly unfortunate when it comes to art in public spaces. Public art is often seen as something that helps to keep public space public. In many cases, it is also given the role of a "security creating" actor. In his chapter for this anthology, Oscar Svanelid problematizes how this phenomenon manifests itself at the municipal level when he discusses, among other things, the City of Gothenburg's initiative *Trygg, vacker stad (Safe, Beautiful City)*.[23] In the report *Tro, Hopp och Konst (Faith, Hope and Art)*, architect and theorist Monica Sand also describes how locally based art groups work to create security. She describes the group *Gatukraft Lindängen* like this: "...with simple and short-term artistic interventions, they work to create community, security and attention."[24] Many stress the importance of the artist's own interests in engaging in dialogue at a time when society appears more divided. Magdalena Malm, for example, senses an increased interest in the "social" where "the notion of public space has moved back into focus and aspects of the common and the civic have gained new relevance."[25]

Public space and its role in the survival of democracy is of course a highly relevant issue. Architect Catharina Gabrielsson dedicates over a hundred pages of her doctoral thesis, *To Make a Difference*, to a historical accounting of the emergence of public space in a Western context, from the time of the *Agora* in ancient Greece to the present day. This line of reasoning is essential for the discussion she later pursues regarding the role and function of art in the public sphere.[26]

The city's public spaces

Inevitably, discussions on public art must also include what characterizes public space. In these discussions, power analyses based on the

---

23   Oscar Svanelid, "Safety Art: On art as a security measure for public spaces"

24   Monica Sand, *Tro, hopp och konst - konst som politiskt verktyg: forskningsrapport om Statens konstråds satsning Konst händer 2016–2018* [*Faith, Hope and Art - Art as a political tool: research report on the Public Art Agency Sweden's initiative Art is Happening 2016-2018*] (Stockholm: ArkDes, 2019), p. 85

25   Magdalena Malm, "Introduction" in *Curating Context: Beyond the Gallery and into Other Fields*, ed. Magdalena Malm (Stockholm: Art and Theory Publishing, 2017) , p. 9.

26   Catharina Gabrielsson, *Att göra skillnad: det offentliga rummet som medium för konst, arkitektur och politiska föreställningar* [*To Make a Difference: Public space as a medium for art, architecture and concepts of the political*], doctoral thesis, (Stockholm: Royal Institute of Technology, 2006).

work of French philosophers such as Michel Foucault (1926-1984) and Gilles Deleuze (1925-1995), as well as work by their compatriots Henri Lefebvre (1901-1991) and Michel de Certeau (1926-1986), and the aforementioned Jürgen Habermas, are repeatedly referenced. The philosopher Hannah Arendt (1906-1975) is another important theorist, partly for her argument about the "social" as something that lies between the private and the public, of particular relevance today given how discussions about the position of social media in the public sphere have arisen, and partly for her argument about how the common can only exist as "a multiplicity of perspectives."[27] In a similar vein, the political theorist Chantal Mouffe, whose *On the Political* has played a major role in the art and architecture debate, argues that public space can be a place where differences meet without leading either to an oversimplified consensus or to pure conflict. Mouffe shifts the focus here from antagonism to "agonism," which provides space for disagreement without hostility. [28]

The Greek agora, the square in which democracy was born and exercised (by free men), is a kind of archetype for public space. But focusing on the square as the archetypal form can lead to a narrow understanding, the narrowness of which lies in the prioritization of the city over the suburbs and countryside, as noted by poet and architect Lars Erik Raattamaa, among others, calling it 'metronormativity.'[29] Accelerating urbanization tends to consign rural and sparsely populated areas to oblivion.

---

27 Hannah Arendt, *Människans villkor* [*The Human Condition*], trans. Joachim Retzlaff (Gothenburg: Daidalos, 1998), p. 91.

28 Chantal Mouffe, *Om det politiska* [*On the Political*], trans. Oskar Söderlind (Hägersten: Tankekraft, 2008).

29 Lars Mikael Raattamaa, "Metronormativity," *Arena*, 2006:6.

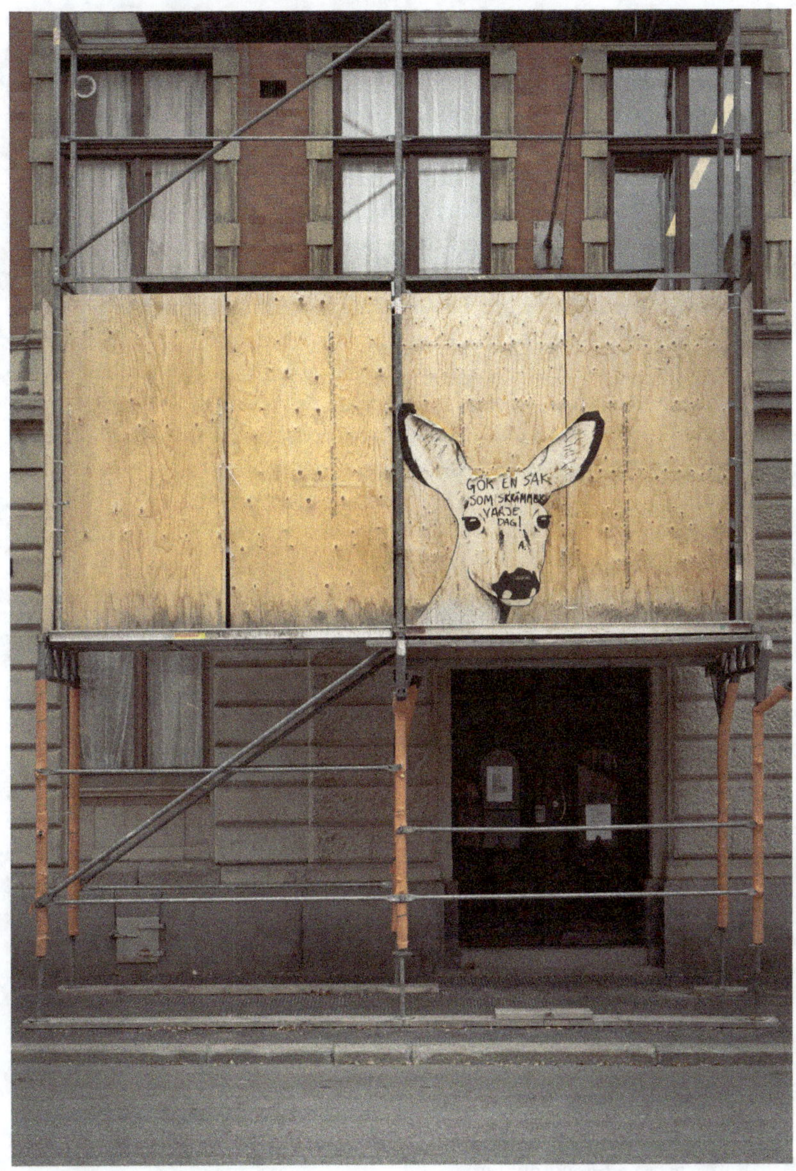

Street art by Klisterpeter, Stockholm 2021
photo: Jens Sethzman

The turn toward the city from the suburbs is a clear trend, not only in Sweden but worldwide. Concepts such as "city-branding" and "placemaking" reflect the focus in recent decades on cities, rather than regions and countries. In Sweden, urban space, with its dense buildings and supposedly rich street life, has been seen as a remedy for dull, grey suburban life. This marks a radical departure from the ideal of the 1950s and '60s, marked by the hope that the lush, sparsely built-up suburbs would be the cure for the dead concrete desert of the inner city.[30] In a similar vein, Monika Murzyn-Kupisz and Jarosław Działek note in their foreword to *The Impact of Artists on Contemporary Urban Development in Europe* that, contrary to what many anticipated, city life generally became even more attractive with the dawn of the digital age.[31] Their article, "Theorising Artists as Actors of Urban Change," from the same book, also characterizes artists as a group that populates urban spaces to a greater extent than other groups.[32]

In the city, another shift from the public to the private is also visible, as the balance of the housing stock in Sweden's major cities has shifted from municipally-owned rental housing to, at the time of writing, condominiums. Conversion policies have intensified the debate on gentrification, in which art has played many different roles.[33] Art, aesthetic objects whose actual economic value is difficult to determine, has not least proven to be, precisely, both status- and value-enhancing, notions that have been discussed and problematized in recent decades. An important resource in this discussion is the essay, "Agoraphobia", by art historian and theorist Rosalyn Deutsche.[34] Another important theorist in this context is art historian Miwon Kwon, whose "One Place After Another" addresses the issue of the "site-specific" and how this concept must be understood in relation to the history and economy of a place, where the artwork relinquishes some of its

---

30 See Tor Lindstrand & Håkan Nilsson's articles "Sous les Paves, les Paves," *Hjärnstorm*, 123-24 (2016) and "Solid Flows," *Architecture and Culture* 5:2 (2017).

31 Monika Murzyn-Kupisz & Jarosław Działek, "Preface", in *The Impact of Artists on Contemporary Urban Development in Europe*, ed. Monika Murzyn-Kupisz & Jarosław Działek Działek (Cham. Switzerland: Springer, 2017), p. v.

32 Monika Murzyn-Kupisz & Jarosław Działek, "Theorising Artists as Actors of Urban Change" in Murzyn-Kupisz & Działek (2017), p. 2.

33 The term "gentrification" comes from the British sociologist Ruth Glass, who coined it in her introduction to the anthology *London: Aspects of Change* back in 1964. The term is derived from the English word "gentry," which translates into English as "lower nobility" or "the upper middle class."

34 Rosalyn Deutsche, *Evictions: Art and Spatial Politics* (Cambridge, Massachusetts: MIT Press, 1996).

autonomy "to integrate art more directly into the realm of the social."[35] The relationship between the aesthetic/autonomous concept of art and a more process-oriented and open conception is not quite so simple, however. It is not possible to create a dichotomy between one kind of art that adds economic value and another that carries political potential. As Nato Thomson of the American organization "Creative Time" puts it: "You could basically say that any public art piece is helping gentrification."[36] But the fact that art is something more than a decoration, meaning that it can reaffirm existing power structures and act in an exclusionary way, as well as carry the capacity to engage and create debate and even effectuate positive change, characterizes the international discussion on public art.

At the same time, we see another shift that is philosophically linked to what is called New Materialism. Here, theorists such as Jane Bennett and Donna Haraway have pointed to ways of thinking about "agents" in non-human terms.[37] In the context of the expanding discussion about the Anthropocene and the climate crisis,[38] many artists have come to view rural and sparsely populated areas from very different perspectives. In this context, old dichotomies and hierarchies of city and countryside, inner city and suburb become secondary. Rather, it is a reassessment of what nature is and, from the perspective of the theme of this volume, also a question of what public space and public time can be and how they can be understood.

The role of public art

In the Social democrat government's 2018 bill *Policy for a Designed Living Environment*, it is stated that "art plays an important role in creating public spaces with long-term qualities." It is also argued that it should "be incorporated in the community building processes at an early stage."[39] Similar considerations and hopes can be found in the

---

35 Miwon Kwon, "One Place after Another: Notes on Site Specificity," *October*, Vol. 80. (Spring, 1997) p. 91.

36 Nato Thomson & Suzanne Lacy, "Perceptions of Care," *Curating Context*, Malm ed., op.cit.

37 See, for example: Jane Bennett, *Vibrant Matter: A Political Ecology of Things* (Durham & London: Duke University Press, 2010); Donna J. Haraway, *Staying with the Trouble: Making Kin in the Chthulucene* (Durham & London: Duke University Press, 2016).

38 The *Nationalencyklopedin* defines the Anthropocene as follows: "(from the Greek a nthrōpos 'man' and kaino s 'new'), the age of man, proposed geological epoch usually relating to the period after about 1800, during which man has been a significant factor in the change of the earth's geology, climate, and ecosystem."

39 Quotations taken from the abridged version of the *Policy for a Designed Living Environment* 2018

justifications for art projects in both the private and public sectors. Art is often seen as something that will add value (which may or may not entail economic value), as well as something that will increase residents' sense of place and thus their drive to care for it.

The capacity for art to generate debate and engagement raises hope. This may be the intention with the statement that the arts should "strengthen cultural and democracy-promoting activities in areas with low voter participation," which guided the government's major initiative *Äga Rum* which could be translated to both "taking place" and "owning space." The initiative was divided between two agencies and resulted in Public Art Agency Sweden's *Art is Happening* and the Swedish Arts Council's *Creative Places*. The main point of *Art is Happening* was that Public Art Agency Sweden was not tied to government-funded building projects. Instead, it could turn to civil society through an application procedure for individuals and organizations in these areas of "low voter participation." Individuals/ organizations could propose sites for art, and then (if selected) be matched with one or more artists and architects who would ultimately create a work of art in consultation with the commissioning bodies.[40]

One question raised by *Art is Happening* was whether public art is or should be instrumental; that is, whether it should serve a purpose that often lies beyond the artwork-artist-viewer. This question has many roots. While the government writes about the right to artistic independence, we also see that there is a belief that art should facilitate "democracy-promoting activities," something that, as many have pointed out, is not so straightforward. For while it is easy to sympathize with this ambition, one might wonder, as art scholar Jeff Werner does, whether art is really capable of, or even should, be burdened with such lofty expectations. In reference to *Art is Happening*, Werner writes of a paradox. When one looks at how the state, county councils, municipalities or the private sector, spend their money, culture is not a high priority. Yet the expectations of what culture is supposed to achieve with this meager budget are high: "Culture almost always comes second [...] Yet culture

---

(Ku18:05) p. 7

40 In retrospect, the process has not been easy to understand. In the subsequent analysis of the whole project, it was pointed out that the design of "[b]oth authorities have been in line with the mandates, but the design and implementation of Public Art Agency Sweden has been character- ized by greater clarity." See *Kultur I demokratins tjänst. En utvärdering av satsningen Äga rum Rapport 2019:2 [Culture in the Service of Democracy. An evaluation of the Taking Place initiative Report 2019:2]* (Stockholm: Swedish Agency for Cultural Policy Analysis, 2019), p. 9.

is accorded high hopes of fixing things that all others have failed to do."[41]

Werner describes the arts as both underfunded and overburdened with expectations. He sees this as a symptom of today's politics, which no longer drives policy issues, but is instead devoted to administration. Hence, he writes:

> [p]olitical expectations that architecture, urban planning, design, art and museums will counteract the dilution of democracy by creating new meeting places, new forms of dialogue and increased engagement among citizens. This reflects a changing view of the role of both politics and culture in society. In the post-democratic state, politics is becoming increasingly administrative in nature, and the administration of society, rather than changes or improvements, becomes the ideal.[42]

Monica Sand, who was contracted as a participant observer by Public Art Agency Sweden for *Art is Happening*, also sees obvious risks in this equation. In the aforementioned report *Faith, Hope and Art*, she reflects on the change the artistic mission undergoes when art is commissioned to act in the service of democracy: "The artistic mission thus moves from a primarily aesthetic mission to a widened social mission where art can function as a political and social instrument for change." This, Sand warns, could have "unpredictable consequences for artists and residents alike." [43]

---

41 Jeff Werner, *Postdemokratisk kultur* [*Postdemocratic Culture*] (Halmstad: Gidlunds förlag, 2018), p. 110.

42 Werner, *Postdemokratisk kultur* [*Postdemocratic Culture*], op.cit., p. 139.

43 Sand, *Tro, hopp och Konst* [*Faith, Hope and Art*], op.cit., pp. 13-14.

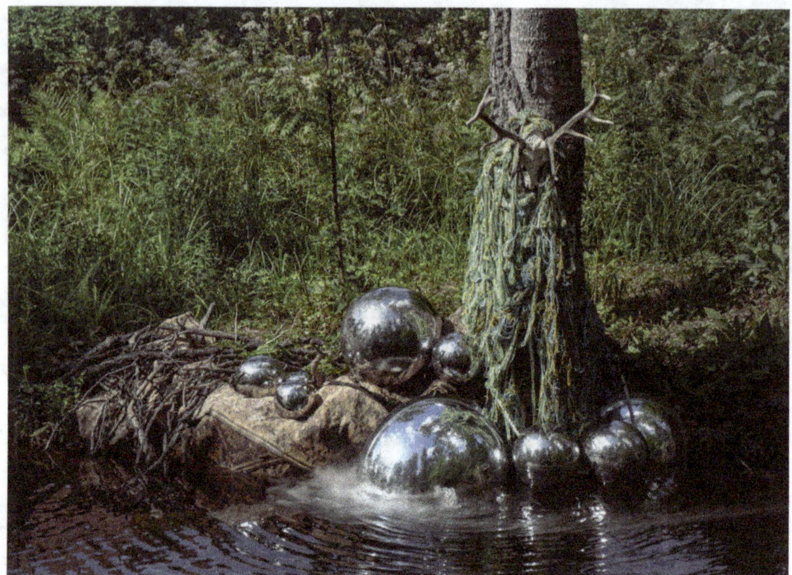

Backa Carin Ivarsdotter, Strömkarlen, 2019, Photo: Håkan Nilsson
© Backa Carin Ivarsdotter / Bildupphovsrätt 2022

On the other hand, we should also note that even the aesthetic object carries a set of values, and in many cases the values it carries are far from straightforward, with its societal-effects being also "unpredictable." It is partly a question of to whom the work of art appeals, who feels included and who is excluded. It is also about how someone is seen and/or portrayed. Jessica Sjöholm Skrubbe, for example, has discussed how the many nudes of predominantly young women, which were placed in Swedish parks during the era of *Folkhemmet*, communicate gender norms.[44] Similar arguments can be found in Gärd Folkesdotter and Anna-Karin Malmström-Ehrling's report *Spegel, gravsten eller spjutspets? (Mirror, Gravestone or Spearhead?)*. While covering a longer time span, it is limited to a narrower geographical area, including all artworks in seven towns in Gävleborg County that were placed outdoors in public spaces during the period 1920-2000. The authors

---

44 Jessica Sjöholm Skrubbe, *Skulptur i folkhemmet: den offentliga skulpturens institutionalisering, referentialitet och rumsliga situationer 1940-1975* [*Sculpture in the Swedish Welfare State. Institutionalisation, referentiality and spatial situations 1940-1975*], doctoral thesis (Gothenburg: Makadam, 2007) .

36

conclude that although the nude, passive woman is a fading presence, it is difficult to detect new trends, i.e. "any work that breaks with known themes of femininity or masculinity or that questions the heterosexual norm."[45]

From one perspective, "instrumentality" is relatively unproblematic and self-evident: the developer or municipality that invests money in art in a residential area may well do so in order to raise the status and the attitude of the inhabitants toward their local environment. The difficulty is how to do this without creating art that contributes to the gentrification and homogenization of these areas, an 'unpredictable consequence' that runs counter to the ambition of strengthening democracy.

However, the idea of art as instrumental in the sense of a democratic tool and catalyst can be described in other terms. In the abovementioned *ART CODE* project (a collaboration between the Bergslagen Art Foundation and the Örebro Regional Council, among others), the starting point was to involve children and young people in their local environment, with the aim of interlinking this with professional artists who became "tools" to realize their ideas. The book *Art Kod: Demokrati, konst och det offentliga rummet Democracy (Art Code: Democracy, Art and Public Space)* describes the need to strengthen democracy where "the method, or code, to do this is art, public space and democracy. By working with art, dialogue can be deepened, and Art Code can reveal what children and young people are looking for."[46]

This does not contradict the fact that the instrumentalization of artists/art can be driven by hidden agendas. As Monika Murzyn-Kupsiz and Jarosław Działek note, since at least the late 1980s, many researchers have pointed out the risks of artists becoming involved and instrumentalized in gentrification processes over which they have no control: "artists may therefore (consciously or unconsciously) be instrumentalized by actors with greater political and economic power."[47] A case in point is Sharon Zukin, who in *The Cultures of Cities* (1995), for example, analyzes the changes that SoHo in New York City was undergoing at the time. But Murzyn-Kupsiz and Działek also

---

45 Gärd Folkesdotter & Anna-Karin Malmström-Ehrling, *Spegel, gravsten eller spjutspets? Offentlig konst och genus* [*Mirror, Tombstone or Spearhead: Public art and gender*] (Uppsala: Centre for Gender Research, Uppsala University, 2007), p. 117.

46 Barenthin Lindblad, *Art Kod* [Art Code], op.cit.

47 Murzyn-Kupsiz & Działek, *The Impact of Artists on Contemporary Urban Development in Europe*, op.cit., pp. 23-24.

point out that many researchers highlight the opposite results within artistic practice; for example, they refer to Nick Wate's *The Community Planning Handbook* and point out the tremendous potential the author sees in locally anchored projects: "...[Wate] sees an important potential role for artists in community planning efforts including community art and art workshops...".[48]

This complex duality is one of the reasons that so many theorists and practitioners stress the importance of ensuring artists are involved early in the process. In this way, the opportunity to maintain control over one's own process is increased. For example, in Public Art Agency Sweden's report *Konsten att gestalta offentliga miljöer: Samverkan i tanke och handling (The Art of Designing Public Spaces: Collaboration in Thought and Action)* from 2015, the first lesson it seeks to advance is to "[w]ork for early and diverse collaboration between design competencies and other actors."[49] Similar conclusions are drawn by Thomas Borén and Craig Young, who discuss the merits of artists establishing an early presence and being involved in decision-making processes, as opposed to entering a process at a particular point in time without any real knowledge. They emphasize local involvement and see that the best results are achieved when the artist is involved in the place even *before* conversion or construction processes begin. The authors highlight as one such example Konsthall C in the Stockholm suburb Hökarängen, and its role in the redevelopment of the local area.[50]

The artist's own autonomy and the autonomy of the work of art

Most would agree that achieving a fully autonomous position for public art, from which it can act in isolation, is neither possible nor desirable. Art, as Marcel Duchamp has said, is created in the encounter with the viewer.[51] For art in public spaces, this encounter potentially occurs with a much more heterogeneous group of viewers than within the walls of, say, a museum or a gallery. This means that parts of the silent contracts,

---

48 Ibid., p. 25.

49 *Konsten att gestalta offentliga miljöer: Samverkan i tanke och handling [The Art of Designing Public Spaces: Collaboration in thought and action]*, ed. Henrik Orrje & Anna Lindholm (Stockholm: Public Art Agency Sweden, 2017), p. 17.

50 Thomas Borén & Craig Young, "Artists as Planners? Identifying five conceptual spaces for interactive urban development" in Murzyn-Kupisz & Działek 2017, pp. 309-312.

51 Marcel Duchamp, "The Creative Act", (1953) in *The Essential Writings of Marcel Duchamp*, ed. Elmer Peterson & Michel Sanouillet (New York: Oxford University Press, 1973).

as described by the art historian Carol Duncan has, are put out of play.[52] The artist can neither assume a certain prior understanding nor rely on the museum's ability to create an interpretation bubble with a certain deference to the work's status as art.

The question of the autonomy of the artwork and its role in a larger context is thus much more complex in the case of public art than, at first glance, it may seem. This situation can be described in terms of what Irit Rogoff has called "criticality,"[53] a concept that was discussed during one of the symposia that Södertörn University organized in collaboration with Public Art Agency Sweden in March 2019, as part of the research assignment of which this volume is itself a part. "Criticality" captures the ambivalence that characterizes the position the artist takes when taking a public commission. It implies a renunciation of the classical "critical distance" while at the same time creating space to contribute to an in-depth problematization from within.

---

52 In *Civilizing Rituals: Inside public art museums* (London: Routledge, 1995), Duncan describes how the museum space is used to educate its visitors, which has other obvious parallels with how public spaces and public art are supposed to promote democracy. The major difference lies in how Duncan depicts the way the viewer is disciplined by and within the museum space.

53 Irit Rogoff, "Smuggling – An embodied criticality, [eipcp.net: 2008]

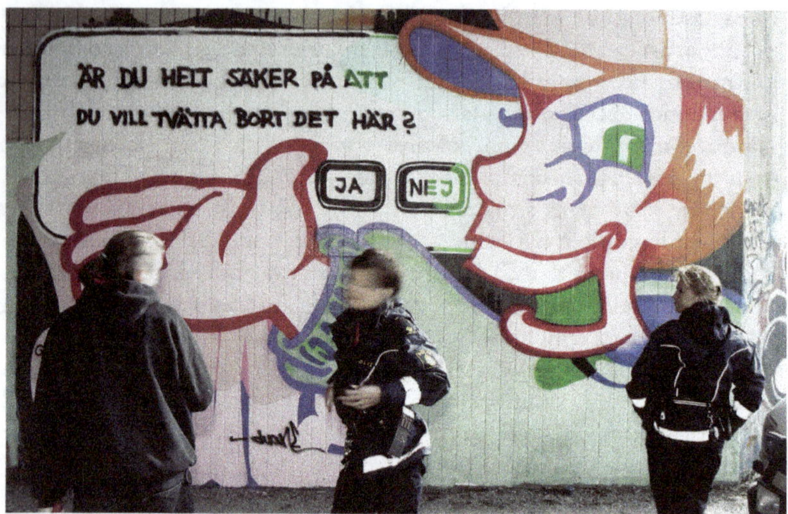

This image from 1997 shows how two police officers explain to Gunnar Nummelin that the project with legal graffiti walls in the Nacka municipality he initiated has been terminated. The painting in the background by artist Duane comments upon the event. [The text reads "Are you sure that you want to erase this?"]

As an artist, being entrenched in something while maintaining a critical distance is not an easy balancing act. It does not even have to be about explicit expectations from clients. In art critic Dan Jönsson's analysis of several different public artworks, he nevertheless sees many common aspects despite differences in expression: "The values expressed in these public works are simply those that are considered core democratic values, 'Swedish values', as Mona Sahlin [former leader of the Social Democratic Party] once put it, such as community, tolerance, openness and participation."[54] Jönsson points here to the risk of artists more or less unconsciously taking it upon themselves to portray certain values they perceive the client and/or the political situation calls for. Another complexity lies in assessing how any criticism that the artwork may convey will actually be understood. As

---

54 Dan Jönsson, "Själva verket. Några tankar kring konst och offentlighet" [The Work Itself: Some thoughts on art and the public sphere] in *Plats, poetik och politik: samtida konst i det offentliga rummet* [*Place, Poetics and Politics: Contemporary art in the public sphere*], ed. Linda Fagerström & Elisabet Haglund (Malmö: Linda Fagerström & Elisabet Haglund (Malmö: Arena, 2010), p. 28.

the artist and architectural theorist Gunnar Sandin notes, cultivating a close relationship with art in the "age of the creative industry" can create commodity-building added value, whether or not the artworks produced actually express a critique of the enterprise itself. "This, because a brand-oriented type of cultural economy, which through events, project placements, education, research programs and *you name it*, looks to cultivate, for its own profiling purposes, art as a producer of alternatives."[55]

The literature surrounding public art is full of similar warnings and insights. The artist willingly enters a situation that is both difficult to grasp and to master, and thus also risks falling into a disadvantageous position, despite having good intentions. Sometimes this leads to stranded projects where, for one reason or another, the artist is forced to terminate the collaboration. However, Borén and Young point to this scenario as one where the artist may be considered the winner: the artist stands with a finished work of art; the client is left empty-handed: "Basically, it is the city and the citizens that seem to be on the losing side in failed collaborations, whereas the artists in many cases make a work of interest anyway (for the public and/or the art scene)."[56]

In other words, art's potential for autonomy, its criticality and its ability to contribute to values that benefit both local users and the artist are questioned from a variety of positions. "Collaboration" seems to come into conflict with the "autonomy" of the artist. Yet the latter is especially valued by most actors. Artists themselves, but also art intermediaries and curators, see it as crucial to defend the integrity of art. But perhaps the paradox is nothing more than a chimera, since according to several prominent thinkers in the art world, there is no real contradiction. Theorist Claire Doherty, for example, writes that co-influence does not have to mean a sacrifice in quality: "In our experience, empowering our audiences to speak back as a part of the making and unfolding of the work does not necessarily mean the surrender of artistic integrity or artistic authorship, though the terms of engagement need careful attention."[57] Magdalena Malm even sees the very exchange and mutual respect between the artist and viewer as

55 Gunnar Sandin, "Offentlighetens spegel. Om konst, politik och poetik" [The Public Mirror: On art, politics and poetics] in Fagerström & Haglund *Plats, poetik och politik [Place, Poetics and Politics]*, op.cit.

56 Borén & Young, "Artists as Planners?," op.cit., p.302

57 Claire Doherty, "From Crystal Ball Gazing to Air Traffic Control: Art Producing in Public Context," *Curating Context*, Malm ed. , op.cit.

proof of quality: "Quality stems from consistency, both in the creation of an artwork and its contextual presentation. Quality also ensures that an artwork can be accessible to an audience."[58]

This is also a central issue in shaping the decision-making processes that accompany a public artwork's journey from the conceptual to its material realisation. The growing ranks of curators and other 'intermediaries' testify to a great deal of educational work both in terms of negotiating with commissioning bodies and dialogue with users. This also results in increased bureaucratization, with artists either relying on outside expertise or having to navigate complex systems of tendering, contracting, regulatory systems and safety regulations themselves. Many artists report increased frustration with this situation.

Renegotiated game plan: the public arts

Many of the complexities described above are related to the fact that public art is becoming less and less about "sculptures in the square." A recurring theme in books and texts on public art from recent decades is that it has simply 'changed': established expressions and art forms have been left behind, which in turn has meant that contemporary practice is not as easily captured by a more traditional concept of art. Curator Elisabeth Haglund and art historian Linda Fagerström, for example, begin the anthology *Plats, poetik och politik* (*Place, Poetics and Politics*) from 2010 as follows: "Public art is a concept that has been increasingly challenged, explored and expanded by artists in Sweden and internationally in recent decades."[59] It is hard to disagree with them. Publicly commissioned art has been transformed and expanded both in its expression and appeal. It has been quite some time since the public commissioned art to mark the significance of a place or a person; today it is the exception, as in the case with the memorial Lea Porsager, which was commissioned to remember the victims of the tsunami, and inaugurated at Blockhusudden on Djurgården in Stockholm in 2018. It is telling that it took several years for Peter Linde's statue of

---

58   Magdalena Malm, "Curatoriell metod som praktik" [Curatorial Method as Practice] in *Rörlig Konstproduktion* [*Mobile Art Production*], red. Magdalena Malm & Annika Wik (Lund: Propexus, 2010), p. 27.

59   Elisabeth Haglund, "Introduction" in Fagerström and Haglund, *Plats, poetik och politik* [*Place, Poetics and Politics*], op.cit.

the football star Zlatan Ibrahimović to find its place. The work was first intended to be placed outside the Friends Arena in Stockholm in 2017, but after several twists and turns it was unveiled in Malmö in 2019. There, the statue was vandalized after the former Malmö FF icon bought a large part of the Stockholm club Hammarby IF.

Curator Maria Mur Dean describes how the curatorial group/art producers Consonni seek to operate at the intersection between art and the public sphere with something that cannot quite be understood as "public art": "The intersection between art and public sphere does not quite fit into the category 'public art' as it does not refer to work that occupies open physical spaces addressed to a pre-existing public."[60] In the same anthology, Claire Doherty, acting as a spokesperson for the British group Situations, writes similarly about their work as something that cannot be understood with the traditional "public art concept." Instead, she describes their method as "agitations, dislocations and interventions, and new stories, which remake our sense of place."[61] We can understand why Dan Jönsson writes "[t]he world as well as art has undeniably taken a few turns since the time when a public artwork had basically two functions to choose from: memorial or decoration."[62]

---

60   Maria Mur Dean, "Survival Guide for Art Production," *Curating Context*, Malm ed, op.cit.

61· p. 21. Claire Doherty, "From Crystal Ball Gazing to Air Traffic Control: Art producing in public context," in *Curating Context*, Malm ed, op.cit., p. 85.

62   Jönsson, "Själva verket. Några tankar kring konst och offentlighet" [The Work Itself: Some thoughts on art and the public sphere] op.cit., p. 28.

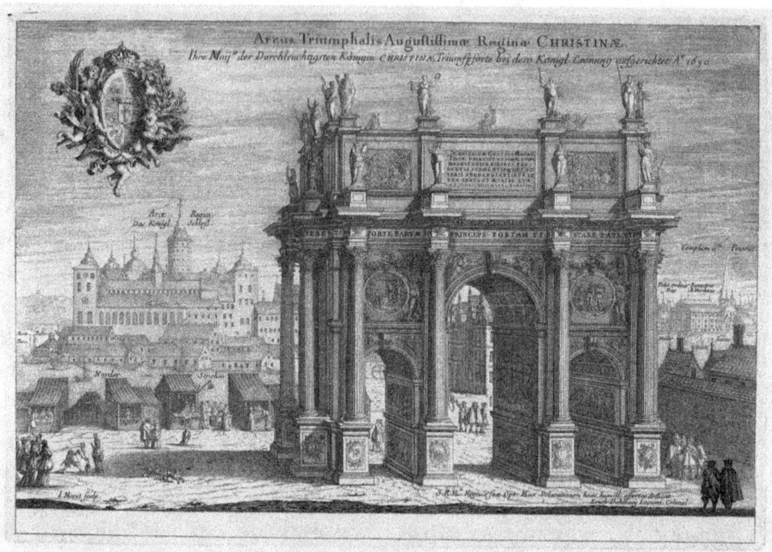

Erik Dahlberg (1625-1703), Jean Marlot (ca 1619-1679),
Queen Kristina's triumphal arch in the print of Jean Marot 1667. The Royal Library

But was this ever really true? Art historian Sten Karling describes how long before we even had an idea of a "public sphere," art could be both temporary and included in festivals. Karling describes, for example, the Triumphal Arch that was built with wooden beams, canvas and papier-mâché at Norrbro in Stockholm on the occasion of Queen Kristina's coronation (1650) and which was left there for a number of years until the weather made its deterioration more or less inevitable.[63] And in a more contemporary context, art historian Mårten Snickare reminds us that since antiquity, publicly placed works of art have had a performative character since they require the viewer to "activate" them. Snickare's example here is the Arch of Titus in Rome, erected in 81 AD.[64] These exceptions do not, of course, contradict the fact that public art has undergone radical changes in recent decades. But to

---

63   Sten Karling, "Drottning Kristinas Triumfbåge i Stockholm" [Queen Kristina's Triumphal Arch in Stockholm] *Sankt Eriks Årsbok* [*St. Erik's Annual*] (1969), pp. 63-99.

64   Mårten Snickare, "Bildhandlingar: Att skapa mening med Titusbågen" [Image Actions: Making meaning with the Arch of Titus], i *Performativitet: Teoretiska tillämpningar i konstvetenskap* [*Performativity: Theoretical applications in art history*], ed. Malin Hedlin Hayden & Mårten Snickare (Stockholm: Stockholm University Press, 2017).

understand this change, we need to look at not only the shifts in the political landscape, but also the entire art world. Sweden's art world has undergone major changes since the art scene became increasingly global toward the end of the 20th century. This has meant, among other things, that places previously on the "margins" of the art world, such as the Nordic countries, have come into sharper focus and are suddenly portrayed as "art miracles," as art theorist and curator Jonas Ekeberg has described it in his book *Postnordisk*.[65]

Globalization is one factor that in recent decades has led to changes in the art world. It has led, among other things, to a larger number of artists working with foreign actors/gallery owners and building their careers partly or entirely outside the Swedish art world. It is partly related to the fact that we now see many more graduate artists in the field. But it is also related to larger, even global structural changes. The local and the global exist side by side; as Indian Raqs Media Collective describes it: "To understand a place, any place, we have to think the world."[66]

Local art scenes have also changed since the turn of the millennium. In Stockholm, Moderna Museet long served as an obvious hub for an art scene that otherwise consisted of a network of art galleries attracting new graduates and helping them build their careers. Today, exhibition activities are offered by several different types of commercial forces. Many new art spaces, such as Artipelag, Sven Harrys and Fotografiska in Stockholm, have private owners, where funding is supplemented by conference facilities and restaurants. At the same time, several restaurants such as Wedholms and Sturehof are investing in art exhibitions. The line between art dealers, auction houses and gallery systems has been blurred by mixed forms, such as CF Hill and Arsenalsgatan 3 in Stockholm, both of which are run by former auctioneers and engage in both exhibition and valuation activities.

The boundaries of the classical art field, which has itself shifted to more alternative practices and is now shaped by various artist-driven initiatives, are also fluid. Many artists find alternative ways to shape their careers, with everything from artist-run initiatives to biennials in Sweden and abroad. Affiliation with a gallery is not a requirement or something an artist must pursue; many choose entirely different, often non-commercial paths. These shifts have led to a reassessment

---

65 Jonas Ekeberg, *Postnordisk - Den nordiske kunstscenens vekst og fall 1976-2016 [Postnordic - The rise and fall of the Nordic art scene]* (Oslo: Torpedo press, 2019).
66 Raqs Media Collective, "The Play of Protagonists," in *Curating Context*, Malm ed, op.cit. , p. 45.

of how artists view their public mission. Peter Hagdahl, an artist and curator at Public Art Agency Sweden, notes in an interview that "in the past, public art was perhaps a feeding ground that was a must, and something that was done maybe without much thought."[67] So if public art used to have an air of something not fully valued, since artists had to make compromises with respect to creative decisions and quality, today many more artists see this scene as an opportunity to create what they would otherwise never have been able to do, a unique chance to have the time and resources to develop a larger project. Though it may be a bit of a sweeping statement, Linda Fagerström describes the matter as follows: "[artists] see no difference between the expressions they use for public art and other types, nor any reason to define the difference – if there is one."[68] For the artist hoping to achieve success in his or her career, public commissions can be a key factor both in terms of funding and cultural capital.

An important prerequisite for this change is that there is now a greater breadth of artistic expression. In the conversation above, Peter Hagdahl describes how Public Art Agency Sweden has undergone major changes in recent years. This has also led to a shift in which artists and what kind of art the agency seeks out in its collaborations. Previously, there was "a group of artists who took up a lot of space on the public art scene." Hagdahl goes on to say that while these artists were talented, they were not the artists he wanted to encourage to make public art. So, they began a process of bringing these "less obvious artistries into this context."[69]

If this active rethinking has contributed to a greater variety of artistic expressions in Public Art Agency Sweden's work, similar shifts are taking place on the private, regional and municipal levels. It can also be said that as a result many artists working with more traditional expressions have felt they are less in demand. Perhaps the elevated status of public art in the art field has also led to a discussion about another kind of gentrification, where another generation of artists,

---

67   Peter Hagdahl et al., "Ett samtal om friktion på Statens konstråd" [A Conversation on Friction at Public Art Agency Sweden] in *I det gemensamma: konst, samhälle, komplexitet,* [*In the Common. Art, society and complexity*] ed. Anna Nyström & Anders Olofsson (Stockholm: Art and Theory Publishing, 2017), p. 158.

68   Elisabeth Fagerström, "Plats, poetik och politik: Samtida konst i det offentliga rummet" [Place, Poetics and Politics: Contemporary art in the public space], Fagerström & Haglund op.cit., p. 16.

69   Hagdahl, "Ett samtal om friktion på Statens konstråd" [A Conversation on Friction at Public Art Agency Sweden] p. 158.

adopting different practices, has made an older (more traditional) generation obsolete.

Today, it is not at all obvious that artists make a career out of the gallery system, or whether they even want to. Here, public art has been seen as an opportunity to explore issues with and for a completely different audience. As Claire Doherty notes, the participatory field rooted in *Community Art* has clearly broadened and been integrated into art as what she describes as a "vital working process for the democratization of art." She goes on to note that this has also had an impact on public art: "Most notable changes include the commissioning of artists from the contemporary gallery sector employing media, materials, and processes previously thought unsuitable for the public realm, the incorporation of dynamic curatorial methods and the exchange of single-sited permanent outcomes in favor of dispersed interventions or cumulative, curated programs which evolve over space and time to remarkable structures which act as gathering points for a diverse temporary community."[70]

The renegotiated game plan: the art scene

Traditional art galleries and museums have also redefined their practices and sought greater engagement outside their own walls. An example of this shift came with the so-called *New Institutionalism*, a term coined by curator and critic Jonas Ekeberg in the first issue of the journal *Verksted* in 2003. The term was an attempt to capture a trend in which a number of art galleries had begun to adopt overtly self-reflexive and self-critical practices. In an issue of the online journal *On Curating* devoted to the phenomenon, Lucie Kolb and Gabriel Flückiger describe New Institutionalism as "institutions characterized by a focus on (critical) examination of the organization and disposition of art" and point to Palais de Tokyo in Paris, Kunstverein München and Rooseum in Malmö as examples.[71]

In his doctoral thesis on artistic research, Danish curator Simon Sheikh describes New Institutionalism as an effect of the welfare state, or rather as a kind of lamentation over the dismantling of its institutions: "New Institutionalism was not only an attempt at finding new, progressive avenues for institutions to explore, rather than embracing the culture industry and the society of spectacle, but also retrospective

---

70   Claire Doherty, "Relation to citizen: Partipication beyond the 'event' of the public artwork" in *Imagining the Audience*, Malm & Wik ed, op.cit., pp. 153, 154.

71   Lucie Kolb & Gabriel Flückiger, "New Institutionalism Revisited," *Oncurating.org*, 21 (2013), p. 9.

and preserving, a cultural expression of the withering away of the welfare state."[72] There is something sad about this description, which is to some extent confirmed by the fact that many of the institutions that were considered to be the standard bearers of this new trend have disappeared or changed direction. Sheikh's former colleague from NIFCA (another institution that practiced the same kind of self-critique), Nina Möntmann, noted in 2007 that most of the institutions brought under the umbrella of the concept had been recast or closed down: "Most of the institutions seem to have been put in their place like insubordinate teenagers."[73]

At the same time, this turn toward self-critique continues to play a role outside these institutions. The semi-public museum space, which Möntmann described as a "hub for various transdisciplinary forms of collaborations," is a definition that accurately describes how several county museums and art spaces across Sweden function today.[74] We see examples of this in the long-standing involvement in urban planning. Konsthall C has already been mentioned in this regard, but one can also mention Marabouparken's four-year involvement in the ParkLek project in which artist Kerstin Bergendal worked on a participatory project in Hallonbergen and Ör, in the municipality of Sundbyberg in the Stockholm region. We also see examples of this in several exhibition projects that occupy urban spaces and engage their audiences.

The changing relationship between the public and public art

In terms of both expression and ambition, public art has in recent decades moved toward more temporary interventions and engagements with users, all as a natural part of the process and/or work. We can examine several factors in relation to this shift. As we have seen, both the concept of art and the field of art have undergone significant changes, but the expectations placed on art have also changed. The notion of what art is and can be has broadened in many respects, thanks in large part to the fact that actors in the public art world have increased in

---

72 Simon Sheikh, *Exhibition-Making and Political Imaginary*, doctoral thesis, (Lund: Lund University, 2012), p. 91.

73 Nina Möntmann, "The Rise and Fall of New Institutionalism Perspectives on a Possible Future," *eipcp:* http://eipcp.net/transversal/0407/moentmann/en.html [accessed 11/19/2019].

74 Nina Möntmann, "Art Institutions and their Publics: On Relational strategies what is the project of an art institution, and who is its public?", *Placing Art in the Public Realm*, ed. Håkan Nilsson (Huddinge: Södertörn University Press, 2012) p. 98.

number and have become professionalized. This is happening against a backdrop in which government policy has also shifted, settling on a more administrative role and marked by the "retrenchment" of the state (and all other forms of the commons) in recent decades.

Things used to be different. As sociologist Martin Gustavsson has shown, in the 1940s and 1950s the Swedish Art Council functioned not only as a purchaser of art, but also as a controller of the quality of art in general to "counteract inferior art." [75] Until 1953, for example, there was an import ban on "mediocre" art, as part of a drive to ensure authentic goods for the country's population.[76] This, in turn, was intended to strengthen democracy. It is a theme that persists to this day, albeit without the magisterial notion of ensuring quality, but with expectations for other qualities, such as "innovation."

In Sweden and the other Nordic countries, access to the public space and public art have long been guaranteed, funded and defined by the state, region and municipality, that is, by the public. This applies to Sweden's town squares and their role in the democratic process as gathering places and spaces for demonstration. It is also the case that this appeal to the public, where public art has long been seen as a natural part of public spaces, also requires the "public" to take responsibility for identifying and defending what the public space *is*.

This definition of public space (and public art) as more or less dependent on public funds has meant it is largely seen as the counterpart of the private, that is, the private understood as business and their commercial interests. The 1974 cultural policy bill set eight sub-objectives, all of which attempted to define, in more general terms, the level at which cultural policy should operate. The bill sought to adopt general rather than detailed approaches. As evident in the most widely known objective, stipulating that "cultural policy shall counteract the negative effects of commercialism in the field of culture,"[77] it pursued a clear agenda.

In the wording of the cultural policy bill of 1996, the state showed its preference.[78] The same wording remains from the 1996 bill, but it has

---

75 Martin Gustavsson, *Makt och konstsmak: Sociala och politiska motsättningar på den svenska konstmarknaden 1920-1960* [*Power and Taste in Art: Social and political contradictions in the Swedish art market 1920-1960*], doctoral thesis (Stockholm: Stockholm University, 2002) p. 158. Ibid.

76 Ibid., pp. 166ff.

77 Kungl. Maj:ts proposition (governmental bill) 1974:28.

78 Government bill 1996/97:3 p. 15.

been expanded to "promote cultural diversity, artistic renewal and quality."[79] The motivation given for retaining the wording is that the negative effects of commercialization lead to "homogenization, dilution and centralization, but also in growing gaps between different people and groups."[80] However, the objective was removed from the 2009 center-right bill, "Time for Culture", on the grounds that it is not relevant to identify cultural activities carried out on a commercial basis as "primarily harmful or negative and therefore something we need to work against."[81]

The wording of the various cultural policy bills describes different positional shifts in terms of culture and the public sphere as well as in society in general. We saw a shift from a relatively politically radical Social Democratic government in 1974 to a more liberal government in 1996, which culminates with the government of the center-right Alliance.[82] However, the policy change is not only characterized by the changing fortunes of different political parties, but also by a general move toward neo-liberal values, along with Sweden's entry into the EU in 1995. If the 1974 cultural policy bill is characterized by the 'will' of the state, it is also an expression of what Foucault in *Discipline and Punish* called the disciplining of society in which the idea of a 'public'-controlled public space plays an important role.[83] Similarly, the 2009 bill can be seen as a step toward the situation described by Gilles Deleuze in the often-quoted text "Postscript on the Societies of Control." In this work, Deleuze responds to Foucault's theories and argues that the society of discipline is being succeeded by what he calls a society of control, in which human beings are controlled by technologies, rather than by an explicit "will" of the state.[84]

It is thus not entirely clear how we are to understand the political "pull-back" described by Jeff Werner, among others. On the one hand, it can be seen as a lack of political initiative, on the other, as the absence of a political agenda of discipline, which can also be described in

---

79   Ibid., p. 27.

80   Ibid., p. 29.

81   Government bill 2009/10:3 p. 28.

82   For a discussion of the changes in cultural policy since the 1960s, see Bengt Jacobsson, *Kultur-politik: styrning på avstånd [Bengt Jacobsson, Cultural Policy: Arm's length governance]* (Lund: Studentlitteratur, 2014).

83   Michel Foucault, *Övervakning och straff: Fängelsets födelse [Discipline and Punish. The birth of prison]*, trans. C.G. Bjurström (Lund: Arkiv, 2003).

84   Gilles Deleuze, "Postskriptum om kontrollsamhällena" [Postscript on Societies of Control], trans. Sven-Olov Wallenstein, in *Nomadologin* (Stockholm: Raster, 1998).

terms of increased freedom and a greater reliance on the citizens' own preferences. Architectural theorist Sofia Wiberg, for example, notes that there has been a shift in community planning in recent decades, from expert-led to dialogue "with the ideal that planning should be done in dialogue, together with citizens and other actors in the community development sector."[85] And as Joanna Zawieja, curator at Public Art Agency Sweden, says in a conversation to be published in the summary of the project *Art is Happening*: "Just to clarify that it is not the case that the 'Public Art Agency Sweden comes in and enlightens civil society' about what art is. It's a process that happens on many different levels."[86]

Participation: the institution, the audience and listening

As we have already seen, many argue that the artist should have a presence earlier in the process and a presence in the space itself. Another key aspect is how the artwork/artist/curator will engage the viewer, which is in line with the notion that a piece of art should not simply manifest a certain truth and present it to the residents. Here, art scholar Mechtild Widrich sees a shift from the more confrontational practice of traditional, countercultural performance toward what she calls "performative monuments." Her study aims to reveal what this shift looks like: "I will show how the contemporary monument does not 'tell' political facts, but engages the audience in forming new ones."[87] Where Widrich describes the way contemporary performance approaches issues that have previously been associated with monuments, Lena From, project manager for *Art is Happening*, draws conclusions about participatory work and permanence, where Public Art Agency Sweden and its selected artists engaged in many conversations with residents

---

85 Sofia Wiberg, "Att hålla 'både och'" [Keeping both], follow-up report for Public Art Agency Sweden: https://statenskonstrad.se/guides/forskarrapport-konst-hander-att-halla-bade-och/ (2018) [accessed 11/18/2019]

86 Lena From et al., "Konst har hänt: Ett samtal om målsättning, metod och medinflytande" [Art has happened: A Conversation on objectives, methods and participation] in *Konst Händer: Statens produktion av konst inom regeringsuppdraget Äga rum* [*Art is Happening: The state's production of art within the governmental commission Taking Place*], ed. Rebecka Katz Thor & Joanna Zawieja (Stockholm: Public Art Agency Sweden, 2019).

87 Mechtild Widrich, *Performative Monuments: The rematerialisation of public art* (Manchester: Manchester U.P., 2014), p. 9.

and met a greater expectation for permanent works as a result of the dialogue.[88] In other words, the fact that the process is opened up "early" to both artists and users does not mean that the outcome will be a temporary, participatory event. On the contrary, in the best case, it contributes to a de-anonymization of the viewer. According to Annika Wik, it is about "a change in viewing positions that involves a shared physical experience, and ultimately an experience that does not imply the same distance as before but that could be described as closer or from inside the art experience. The focus on the experience of the audience, spectatorship, and reception, also means, as Sobchack and others show, an interesting theoretical shift from an abstract viewer to a specific individual viewer."[89]

However, participatory processes have not always been seen as a necessarily positive feature. In a highly critical and skeptical text, architect Markus Miessen writes that "[p]articipation has become a radical chic, one that is en vogue with politicians who want to make sure that, rather than producing critical content, the tool itself becomes what is supposed to be read as criticality."[90] Miessen is responding to a scenario where the participatory process itself is given neither time nor space to have any significance, where the situation as such becomes a hostage to larger forces.

As we saw earlier, Borén and Craig were able to identify a number of reasons why art needs to be included early in the process. When it comes to the viewer/recipient/participant, the issue is a little different. Sofia Wiberg adopted an approach that attempted to shift the focus from what is said in citizen dialogues and similar contexts to a focus on listening. It is not only *when* someone enters a process that is important, but also *how* they are listened to. In her practice, Wiberg has often found that the citizen dialogues in which she has participated have been deemed "successful" as long as the leaders got the answers they were looking for. Unconsciously, they were not attuned to listening to other voices but were focused on hearing what they themselves thought they would hear.[91]

---

88   From *Konst Händer* [*Art is Happening*] op.cit. , p. 9.

89   Annika Wik, "Vieweing Positions Here *and* There" in *Imagining the Audience*, Malm & Wik eds., op.cit. , p. 39.

90   Markus Miessen, *The Nightmare of Participation: Crossbench practice as a mode of criticality* (New York & Berlin: Sternberg Press, 2010) , p. 44.

91   Sofia Wiberg, *Lyssnandets praktik. Medborgardialog, icke-vetande och förskjutningar* [*The Practice of Listening. Civil dialogue, unknowing and displacement*], doctoral theses, (Stockholm:

The question of the potential utility of public art in an era when it is not defined by a clear "will" or agent is, as we have seen, a complex matter that places high demands on commissioning bodies and practitioners alike. Perhaps the greatest challenge ahead lies precisely in listening – how to listen and what to listen to. Whether we are thinking of "traditional" art objects or not, it is a matter of finding a system that listens to commissioning bodies, recipients and practitioners, but also of finding ways of knowing when the dialogue can or should be limited – such as when artistic integrity is at risk of being compromised.

Royal Institute of Technology, 2018).

The Art of the Million Program in Today's Living Environment.

//Annika Öhrner

Under the framework of the Million Program, a series of artistic initiatives were undertaken in the form of permanent works in new residential areas.[1] The welfare state had a strong belief in the power of art to bring about political change and promote democracy. This faith in the power of art abides; architecture, form and design are considered to be able to counter "the effects of globalization, increasing segregation and ill-health, and the declining attractiveness of many of our cities," as expressed in the governmental investigation *Gestaltad livsmiljö (Designed Living Environment)* (SOU 2015:88). "I believe we can change the world, at least our daily living environment," the investigator writes confidently in the introduction.[2] Today, public art in Sweden has seen a series of publicly-run, often temporary, art projects around the outskirts of large cities, but also in rural areas, as several chapters in this anthology will address. These temporary projects are also interwoven with ideas of promoting democratic processes. By creating encounters with and between inhabitants, such art is considered to have the ability of accomplishing more than any stagnant sculpture and color scheme from previous projects could. This chapter presents a critical discussion of the strong faith in art's ability to change, which tends to obscure the ways in which traces of earlier, parallel initiatives remain in public spaces with a low-intensity impact.[3] The article highlights examples of how the simultaneous presence of art

---

1   The Million Program was a state program for improvement of housing, suggested by the Swedish Social Democratic government in 1964. The program ran from 1965 to 1975, and resulted in high raised building blocks in the outskirts of many Swedish cities, that still prevail. See f.e. Lisbeth Söderqvist, *Att gestalta välfärd. Från idé till byggd miljö, [To Design Welfare. From idea to built environment]* (Formas & Riksantikvarieämbetet, 2008).

2   Christer Larsson, *Gestaltad livsmiljö – en ny politik för arkitektur, form och design [Designed Living Environment – A new policy for architecture, form and design]*, 2015, SOU 2015:88, s. 13.

3   In Stockholm, a long-term project is currently underway that aims to re-activate existing public designs in the city, a project that was initiated by Stefan Hagdahl, Stockholm Konst/Stockholm municipality. Artists work in various sub-projects to create works that become part of a dialogue with existing sculptures. This forward-looking project is expected to generate unique experiences on how public design can be developed while remaining sensitive to its unique temporality.

with different dates of origin can be understood as an alternative to succumbing to a simplistic dichotomy between the old and the new, the enduring and the changing, the outdated and the innovative.

What experiences can arise around the very superimposition of art in a physical place or in a space that activates the consciousness of the viewers or a collective memory? This perspective on public space is unfortunately overlooked in contemporary discussions on public art. In order to capture the encounter between existing art and contemporary practice in a place, I have chosen to use British cultural geographer Doreen Massey's concept of temporality, what she called *space-time*. Massey sees public space as a socially differentiated place where a number of relationships and narratives intersect.[4] She used the concept of space-time in order to describe the disintegration of a linear conception of time in relation to the era of global capitalism. When applied to a Swedish cultural policy context, the concept can serve to provide a view of the contemporary presence of artworks in public space, something that is important to consider in policy, for artists themselves, and those responsible for drawing up public designs. I discuss some of these relationships by looking at two different kinds of sites: first Flemingsberg, an urban environment in Huddinge outside Stockholm established in the context of the Million Program, and second the 'station' as such, as a conceived space for public art. Works by Gert Marcus, Siri Derkert and Goldin+Senneby problematize the notion of public space as an untouched playing field for art intended to benefit democracy.

A neighborhood and a Million Program area.

"Did you know that the county's and perhaps even all of Sweden's largest work of art is a collection of houses?", proclaims a film on the Stockholm County Museum's website about the Grantorp residential area in Västra Flemingsberg.[5] The "work of art," to which the county museum refers, is the eighteen residential buildings produced in 1965-1974 with 2,500 apartments designed by architect Hans Matell and painted in fifteen colors, from green to yellow-red, as well as in shades from white to light grey in the north, by artist Gert Marcus. Västra

---

4   Doreen Massey, "A Global Sense of Place," *Space, Place and Gender* (Minneapolis: University of Minnesota Press, 1994).

5   Rebecka Walan, "I'll paint the whole world...," Stockholm County Museum website, www.stockholmslansmuseum.se [accessed 11/01/2020].

Flemingsberg was built in the middle of what was then a forest and agricultural landscape. Marcus' design is still a dominant feature in the area. The color compositions interact with the people who navigate through the development or between the houses on foot and can also be glimpsed by those walking in the adjacent woodland groves. They are also clearly visible to the traveler passing by on train or by car.

For several decades, the cultural administration in Huddinge municipality has placed public works on streets and squares, often in cooperation with the municipal property company Huge.[6] Institutions such as Södertörn University, Karolinska Huddinge, state archives, Södertörn District Court and others, have gradually moved to Flemingsberg and brought with them even more art. The most extensive art collection is however held by the region through the art collection at Huddinge Hospital, inaugurated in the early 1970s. In addition to Marcus' color scheme, a large number of works find a home in Flemingsberg, like a polyphonic choir and a manifestation of the faith in the power of art to shape a neighborhood.

A first step in understanding the relationship between artworks and place is to investigate where the works are placed and how they physically relate to the surrounding environment. In a master's thesis in art history in 2015, Matilda Sjöblom explored this very matter as a first step of her study. She compiled a list of all publicly owned works placed outdoors in Huddinge, one of the district's two municipalities.[7] She then looked up each of the 108 works, made GPS notations for where they were located, and converted them into a map. Rather than grouping public art by age and date of creation, or by the authority that commissioned the works, as is often done, Sjöblom approached things differently in order to make their spatial relationships and contemporary relevance visible.

In the next step of her analysis, Sjöblom chose also to identify secondary characteristics, like the artist's gender, ethnicity and socio-economic status. These values were then compared with the corresponding values for the population of the various individual districts within Huddinge municipality. Several interesting results emerged during this process. For example, it was found that works by female artists,

---

6   See *Offentlig konst i Flemingsberg [Public Art in Flemingsberg]*, ed. Håkan Bull & Dan Karlholm (Huddinge: Huge Fastigheter, 2007), and *Konsten på Södertörns högskola [Art at Södertörn University]*, ed. Annika Öhrner (Huddinge: Annika Öhrner (Huddinge: Södertörn University, 2016).

7   Matilda Sjöblom, *Männen på fältet – En georeferentiell analys av den offentliga konsten i Huddinge kommun [The Men in the Field: A georeferential analysis of the public art in the municipality of Huddinge]*, master's thesis (Huddinge: Södertörn University, 2016) Full text in Diva.

a strikingly small proportion of the total number, were often placed outside places with female connotations, such as preschools. On the other hand, works created by men were predominantly in areas of the municipality where decisions are made or where academic institutions are located. Sjöblom's study thus shows the consequences of a cultural policy practice superimposed in time. Through an analysis of the decision paths and power relations within the municipality, she also painted a picture of how the producers of public art have shaped the selection of works. In the final discussion, she concluded that "it is fundamentally about a 'general sense' of participation in the common that is lost when public commissions are given to a homogeneous group of Swedish-born men, often with local roots and broad networks."[8] At the time, the art projects had likely been conceived with the good intention of creating a more artistically appealing and democratically designed environment, but Sjöblom's study painted a more complex and problematic picture of the municipality's public art inventory – in map form.

---

8   Sjöblom, *Männen på fältet [The Men in the Field]*, op.cit. , p. 27.

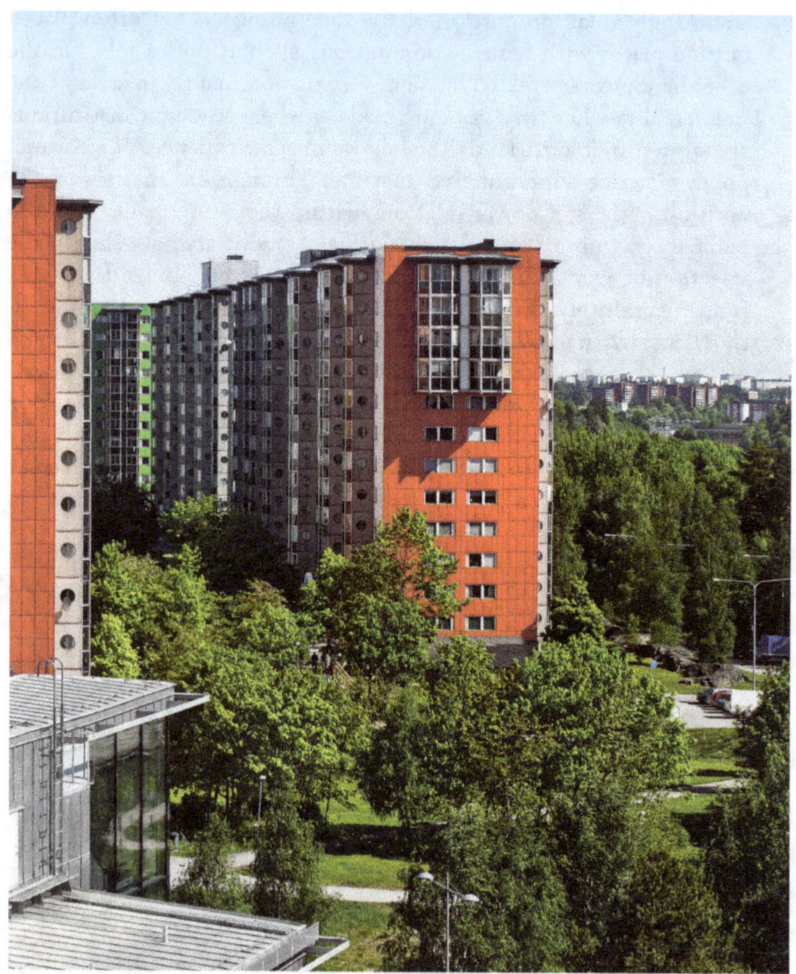

Gert Marcus' Color composition, Västra Flemingsberg.
Photo: Henrik Peel, Södertörns högskola. © Gert Marcus / Bildupphovsrätt 2021

How then did the "apparatuses" surrounding the two giant projects in Flemingsberg function around 1970; that is, the art program for Huddinge Hospital and the design of Västra Flemingsberg? This I think can be related to something the art critic Patricia C. Philips famously highlighted in 1988, namely the idealism of what she called "the public art machine", which she said had developed in New York. Committees and a new decision-making model were established to safeguard both democratic and artistic values. Inherent in these, Phillips argued, was a peculiar blend of idealism and bureaucracy that she said had to do with the temporality of the works themselves, i.e., their permanence. Art that was expected to remain in public spaces created its own parameters for the production process.[9] Do we find traces of such a "public art machine" in a Swedish context?

At the time of its founding in the early 1970s, Huddinge Hospital was the largest hospital in northern Europe. The hospital and its artistic design had a high status and were subject to a careful public planning process. The steering committee, the "Working Group for Physical Environmental Issues" at Huddinge Hospital (AgMiljö), included the hospital's overall project manager, Sune Björklöf, the then leading cultural personality and art gallery director, Eje Högestedt, professor at the Royal Institute of Art, Olle Nyman, and several architects and representatives from civil society. Sune Björklöf describes how the art program was incorporated as part of the overall planning of the hospital's lines of communication, and carried out in dialogue with the contemporary international organizational research community. In addition to the art program, responsibility was taken for selecting colors and the hospital's interior design in a broader sense.[10] Holger Bäckström and Bo Ljungberg's large-scale relief *Hej Patient* (Hello patient), which was then placed on a screen outside the entrance, could be said to be representative of the visual and digital approach. Today, *Hej Patient* has been placed in a new installation on top of the exterior wall, out of view of incoming vehicle traffic but also for the direct interaction of citizens. AgMiljö would not only be responsible for the artistic design; the hospital was perceived as a "self-contained environment" where factors such as sound, textiles, signs, light,

---

9   Patricia C. Philips, "Out of Order: The Public Art Machine," *Artforum* 27:4 (1988).

10 Sune Björklöf, "Konsten i Huddinge sjukhus" [The Art at Huddinge Hospital], in *Huddinge Sjukhus 1972-2002* [*Huddige Hospital 1972-2002*], ed. Anders Persson & Folke Sjöqvist (Huddinge, Karolinska University Hospital, 2010), pp. 31–48.

surfaces, actors and activities had to be considered. There is not enough space here to discuss the project in a way that explores its full scope with different exhibition spaces, larger permanent works, the presentation of artworks such as paintings, drawings, graphic art, as well as architecture and external landscape art. The overarching aim of the artistic design, which was the committee's assignment to fulfill, was to "engage, delight, and comfort." Thus, the Huddinge Hospital project, aggregated a solid trust in the democratic potential of art, paired with an equally robust "machinery" that was set up to secure the outcome.

What was the motivation behind the construction of Västra Flemingsberg? For the municipality, it was about attracting workers to the new hospital by offering access to good housing in the area. However, the artist Gert Marcus distanced himself from that position, pointing out that his role in Grantorp, as the area is called, was purely artistic. It is not entirely clear what he meant by this. While he rejected notions that art should be integrated into a residential area as an idea that emanates from municipal administrations, he also rejected the notion that the role of the artist's commission was to add something to the architecture as a kind of contemporary ornamentation.[11] The qualities that he would like to see added were elaborated in what he considered an objective, albeit artistically based, investigation. If it is an objective line of reasoning, it could also be valid in a later "space–time," and there is therefore reason to examine Marcus' ideas more closely.

In his art, Gert Marcus aimed to inspire the viewer to move around works in which color exhibits both spatial and temporal aspects.[12] He was also interested in the spatial relationship between the viewer and the work. Flemingsberg is characterized by hilly terrain. Matell's eighteen residential buildings vary in height to compensate for differences in the hilly landscape but are the same height in relation to sea level. Minimal excavation work was carried out on the site in order to preserve existing vegetation in line with the ideals of the French architect Le Corbusier. Marcus constructed a color combination of fifteen colors and shades from white to light grey in the north, sprayed in enamel onto the sheet

---

11 Gert Marcus & Hans Matell, "Colors on the Exterior Walls of the Buildings of the Apartment Complex at Västra Flemingsberg, Huddinge, Sweden," *Leonardo*, 12:2 (1979), p. 90.

12 See Håkan Nilsson, *Måleriets rum [The Space(s) of Painting]* (Stockholm: Axl Books, 2009), and his "Gert Marcus: Konstformernas fenomenologi" [Gert Marcus: The Phenomenology of Art Forms] in *Gert Marcus: Distansens förvandling [Gert Marcus: The Transformation of Distance]*, ed. Françoise Ribeyrolles-Marcus (Stockholm: Carlssons förlag, 2013), pp. 87-104.

metal applied to the façades, which rose from the concrete pedestals of the foundation. Beyond the natural surroundings and the constructed contrast – the concrete-grey hospital – the area's space-time was still relatively open and could be recieved visually. Since then, a number of sculptures have been added to the site as well.

Marcus also developed an idea of "color space," which he called *dispositions*. He said he wanted to create a spectrum of colors that would have a spatial impact on the viewer. He explored this idea in a series of sculptures, paintings, and designs for public spaces from the mid-1950s onwards. Marcus' color design for Västra Flemingsberg was conceived in relation to those who walk beside the buildings and those who view the buildings from a distance. To accentuate the buildings' placement and spatial relationships, he created a color scheme that took into account the color dimensions of the intended material, how its colors related to each other, and the opacity versus transparency of the paint. In a 1974 article for the art history journal *Leonardo* (published by MIT Press), Marcus described his quest for more nuanced conceptions of color. He objected to the psychological studies carried out by color scientist Lars Sivik through interviews with test subjects in which terms such as "friendly," "refined," or "vulgar" were associated with different color shades. On the contrary, Marcus believed that an individual's aesthetic sensibility is too limited to be valid as a starting point for modern social construction.[13]

However, in the artist's texts about the objective relationship between color, the building and the viewer, ideas of subjective qualities also emerge. In the *Leonardo* article, Marcus wrote that the residential area, together with the nearby hospital, could be seen as "a self-contained community."[14] He also acknowledged that the color compositions could readily create "positive emotions."[15] Consequently, what Marcus wanted to achieve in Flemingsberg was an objective, color-space design on an architectural scale. This, in turn, was intended to influence the viewer's subjective visual perceptions and movements in relation to the colored surfaces, as well as the interrelationships between those surfaces.

What has the impact of the major projects in Flemingsberg been on the

---

13 Marcus & Matell, "Colors on the exterior walls of the buildings of the apartment complex at Västra Flemingsberg, Huddinge, Sweden," *op.cit.*, p. 89
14 Ibid. , p. 89.
15 Ibid. , p. 90.

time period that the district represents today? The construction of Huddinge Hospital and the works of art that were successively added to the space have generated a significant sediment of art and visual expression. A 2008 inventory of works of art at Huddinge Hospital counted almost 8,000 works by 2,000 artists.[16] Some of the works have been taken down or disappeared, but even more designs are being developed on a large scale by Region Stockholm's cultural department.
A relatively recent work in the hospital is *Färgrum och gränslinjer* (*Color Spaces and Borderlines*) (1997). It is a later work by Gert Marcus in which his theory of color space is translated into a human height sculpture in lacquered iron sheet, and has been placed in the main entrance of the hospital. The colored metal plating suggests a spiral movement and is meant to create a similar cognitive movement in the viewer. The sculpture and its placement in the hospital is an example of how a contemporary curatorial practice can revitalize older public works. Indeed, *Color Spaces and Borderlines* were not created for this site but were moved from another hospital in Stockholm, St. Göran's, by the county council's art producers, Renée Lord and Martin West, around 2005.[17] Several of Marcus' works have been placed in the Flemingsberg area through similar initiatives. In the municipal library in the center of Flemingsberg, there is a sculpture placed on the ceiling that was commissioned by Marcus late in his life, *Tre steg från det obestämda* (*Three Steps from the Undefined*), (2002), consisting of three rods in Plexiglas. The artist's painting *Färglinjer* (*Color Lines*) (1953), from Moderna Museet's collection, has been placed in a conference room at the top of the F building in Södertörn University, next to a window from which one can also look out at the color composition he created for the residential buildings in Västra Flemingsberg.[18] Through these placements, a genealogy is constructed that in some ways dissolves the time of the works and actively allows them to coalesce into a common temporal space. These examples show how the art machinery has continuously given rise to multiple artistic expressions in Flemingsberg, expressions that vie for the public's attention in their everyday lives.

---

16   Björklöf, "Konsten i Huddinge sjukhus" [The Art at Huddinge Hospital] op.cit. , p. 31. The art budget at the time was SEK 6.2 million, which Björklöf recalculates to SEK 52 million in 2010.

17   Information from Martin West, Project Manager, Department of Art, Cultural Administration, Region Stockholm (e-mail to author 11/30/2020).

18   *Konsten på Södertörns högskola [Art at Södertörn University]*, Öhrner ed. op.cit., p. 14.

In the fall of 2020, the Netflix series *Love and Anarchy* became a hit. In this rom-com with a class perspective, a young IT technician who has moved to Stockholm lives in a collective in an apartment in one of Marcus' colorful buildings, here constructed as a counterpoint to the centrally located townhouse where his love interest lives. The juxtaposition of the young, fresh but also poor life in the suburbs and the more rigid, propertied lifestyle in the city is reinforced by the choice of setting, Grantorp, which is presented as both an attractive and exotic place. Marcus' design thus defines a space that reappears in both popular culture and in the day to day lives of real inhabitants. During this period, I also read a litany of instructions from the board of a housing association in Grantorp, about how satellite dishes must not be attached directly to the façade or protrude from the wall. At the end of the more technical arguments for this ban, the artistic origin of the façades is mentioned. Marcus' color scheme thus becomes, as I understand it, an argument for aesthetic discipline and established decorum.

The Station

In this section, I turn my attention to the Station as such, by which I mean a conceived space with a particular capacity to harbor and shape notions of movement and the future, but also the past. In both its physical and imagined versions, the Station recurs in the discourse of public art in post-war Sweden. The background, of course, is that transport systems are publicly funded and are thus, in the best case and often in Sweden, allocated funds for artistic design. One such example is the Västlänken project, the railway tunnel being built under central Gothenburg. Public Art Agency Sweden, in collaboration with the Swedish Transport Administration, has proposed designs at four stations in a project with the thought-provoking name in our context, *Kronotopia* (from the Greek Χρόνος [chrónos] for time and τόπος [tópos] for place). The jury for the commission included representatives from both authorities and from Västtrafik, the Art Unit of Västra Götaland Region, the City of Gothenburg and Göteborg Konst, as well as members with artistic and curatorial expertise, following the same organizational model we have already encountered in this chapter. In the project, as expressed in the invitation to artists, the concept of *Kronotopia* is described as follows:

[it should] inspire an examination of our present, a review of the potential of the past and a potential insight into the future combined with an interest in site-specific exploration. Artists are given the opportunity to highlight the complex web of identities, heritage and the relationship to a globalized world that characterizes the city of Gothenburg and to allow this to be expressed in the city's shared spaces.[19]

The potential client's vision regarding what the artist could achieve aims high, and includes lofty expectations regarding the physical and temporal extent of the work. The winning proposal for one of the stations was *Evig anställning* (*Eternal Employment*) (2017) by the artist duo Goldin+Senneby. This will be examined below as part of the idea of the Station as such as a kind of ideal space for public art.

A design competition is a genre in and of itself, and it is perhaps only natural that a producer, an actor within "the Machine", in this context will present high expectations. Before returning to the *institutional* practices that proliferate in the Station, I would first like to call attention to some perceptions expressed by *users*. The artist and participant observer Monica Sand's report from her 2016-2018 study of *Art is Happening*, a project by Public Art Agency Sweden, is mentioned in several places in this anthology.[20] The report describes, among other things, the wishes expressed through the applications submitted by people from civil society or municipal administrations to receive funding for art projects intended for the Million Program areas. The material offers indications regarding how works created forty or fifty years ago live on, not only in the memories of a bygone era but also, in the wishes for the public spaces of the future. One example is the updating of the playful *Ballongen* [*The Balloon*] (1968) piece in Råby, a Million

---

19 Competition program. Kronotopia: Haga and Korsvägen 2017 Competition 2, Public Art Agency Sweden and Swedish Transport Administration, 04/06/2017, p. 4.

20 Monica Sand, *Tro, hopp och konst. Konst som politiskt verktyg, forskningsrapport om Statens konstråds satsning Konst händer 2016–2018* [*Faith, Hope and Art. Art as a political tool, research report on Public Art Agency Sweden's initiative Art is Happening*] *2016-2018* (Stockholm: Ark-Des, 2019). *Art is Happening* was a response to the government assignment *Dela rum* (*Sharing Space*), to Public Art Agency Sweden and the Swedish Arts Council 2016-2018 and was realized in fifteen locations in the country, in projects where professional artists were invited to collaborate with residents and civil society based on a proposal for a specific location for the artistic intervention.

Program area outside Västerås, in an idea proposal entitled *Ballongen - lek på riktigt* (*The Balloon - play for real*). The legendary exhibition *Modell för ett kvalitativt samhälle* (*Model for a Qualitative Society*, often referred to as "The Model"), which was shown at Moderna Museet in 1968, was then moved to Råby, and the exhibition's curatorial idea – to let children's games serve as a model for a more humane society – had an impact. The new proposal from Råby for *Art is Happening* is to reactivate this. Other applicants draw on memories of their youth, when they were involved in a mural painting project as eighth graders in primary school in 1978. It is proposed as a follow-up to the project, at a time when their neighborhood is being transformed into a cultural center. Another application discusses how works from the time of the Million Program call on the surrounding community to "act for the common good," as "the issues are just as relevant 40 years later."[21] The informant is referring to "Henschen's cave paintings" which speak of siblinghood, peace, and community and "Derkert's metal wall sculpture", which portrays heroes fighting for the environment. The works referred to are probably Helga Henschen's *Min gröna dröm är röd* (*My Green Dream is Red*) (1975), the design of the Tensta subway station, and Siri Derkert's *Sverigeväggen* (*Sweden Wall*) (1967-69), on the façade of the *Sverigehuset* in Stockholm. The station and certain iconic works from the 1960s and 1970s seem to be recreated in the viewer's memory in this way, as good role models. Monica Sand also emphasized in her report how the belief in the democratizing effects of culture and art permeated the *Art is Happening* project. The notion that access to art in public spaces is a democratic right and that the presence of art raises the awareness of residents was echoed both in programs and, as we have seen, by the users themselves.[22]

Some works from the period when the Million Program was first established and local transport was being developed have gained particularly strong, iconic status. The commissioning of Siri Derkert's seven public works from the late 1950s through the 1970s coincides with the institutionalization of public art as a welfare state project. The main significance of Public Art Agency Sweden for public sculpture during this period was its role as a normative and legitimizing body, running parallel with the overall discourse of *Folkhemmet*.[23] The bureaucracy

---

21   Sand, *Tro, hopp och konst* [*Faith, Hope and Art*], op.cit. , p. 55.
22   Ibid.
23   Jessica Sjöholm-Skrubbe, *Skulptur i folkhemmet; den offentliga skulpturens institutionalisering,*

and structure that Public Art Agency Sweden built up in the post-war period for art commissioned by the state became a model for working with public art at other levels as well. This institutional set-up paved the way for progressive and innovative projects to be placed in central locations around the city, where Derkert's *Ristningar i naturbetong* (*Carvings in Concrete*) occupies a special position. Even from the outset, the Station is a powerful space that captures the traveler, and a place characterized by concentrated time and accelerated movement. Siri Derkert's *Carvings in Concrete* was commissioned by Stockholm's *Spårvägar* in 1961-65 and still sit in the Östermalmstorg metro station in Stockholm. Because the platform is 165 meters long, there are four enormous wall surfaces for design, and the waiting traveler is embedded in the work. Through motifs with peace and environmental themes, combined with images from everyday life, several temporal and political positions are established. The rhythm of musical notation is echoed in the composition itself, with drawn images placed along the wall. When Siri Derkert was asked whether in the future, people would recognize the people she had portrayed on the platform, she replied that they would have the opportunity to learn something about these historical figures. One of the clearest markers of time in *Carvings in Concrete*, however, is a drawn hand holding a wrist, entitled: "Women take the pulse of patriarchy. Time is short."

In Siri Derkert's work, there is thus both an eye to the future and an artistic desire to historicize. But the work also contains explicit hopes for political change, hopes that still rest in today's space-time. The motifs that appear in the sandblasted drawings in the concrete recur as references in Derkert's later projects and, as we have seen, in overall discourses on public art and democracy. *Carvings in concrete* came to convey messages of peace, environmental messages and political markers, such as *The Internationale,* the song of the international labor movement that was also the national anthem of the Soviet Union from 1917-1944. The commission was neither something that happened by chance nor was the political content simply 'timely,' as is sometimes claimed when drawing the cultural climate of the 1960s. The artist was established in the art field by virtue of her position in the mass media and in exhibitions. In 1961, her art was shown in what, at the time, was

---

referentialitet och rumsliga situationer [Sculpture in the Swedish welfare state : Institutionalisation, referentiality and spatial situations 1940-1975], doctoral thesis (Gothenburg: Makadam, 2007), pp. 292-293.

the newly established Moderna Museet's first retrospective featuring a Swedish artist, and in 1962, she was Sweden's representative at the Venice Biennale.[24] This strengthened her position and shielded her when the station opened. Her political approach was met with both enthusiasm and criticism. When Stockholms Spårvägar's director Hans von Heland asked Derkert to remove *The Internationale's* notation from the walls of the metro station, she refused and that was the end of the issue. The machinery of public art in this case protected and strengthened the integrity of the work; the motif was preserved for futurity.

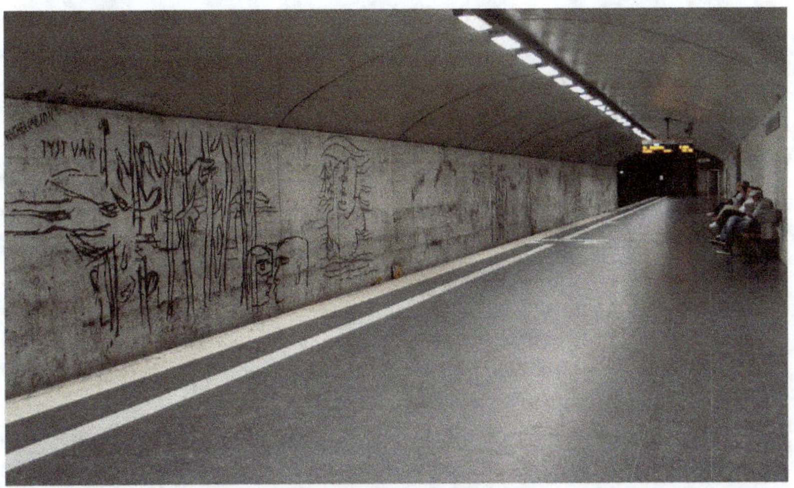

Siri Derkert, Engravings in concrete (1961-65), Östermalms tunnelbanestation,
Photo: Jonas Bergsten, 2005/Wikipedia commons. © Siri Derkert / Bildupphovsrätt 2021

The ambition to give artists access to building processes at an early stage has been a common thread running through public art institutions since the post-war period.[25] The winning concept proposal for the West Link and Korsvägen Station was called *Evig anställning* (*Eternal*

---

24 See, for example, Mats Rohdin, "Konst, politik och klotter. Siri Derkert och Östermalmstorgs tunnelbanestation i mediearkiven" ["Art, Politics and Scribble. Siri Derkert and Östermalmstorg metro station in the media archives"], in *Att alltid göra och tänka det olika. Siri Derkert i 1900-talet* [*To Always Do and Think Differently. Siri Derkert in the 20th Century*] ed. Mats Rohdin & Annika Öhrner (Stockholm: Kungliga biblioteket, 2011), pp. 226-276.

25 Sjöholm Skrubbe *Skulptur i folkhemmet* [*Sculpture in the Swedish Welfare State*], op.cit. , p. 104.

Employment) (2017), designed by the Stockholm-based artist duo Goldin+Senneby. French economist Thomas Piketty's thesis that wages for labor grow much slower than the growth of invested capital was the inspiration behind their idea. It is a conceptual work with a two-part design based on the idea that the project budget should be invested so that any return finances the salary of a person given what the artists call "eternal" employment at the station. Within the position, the employee gets to choose his or her duties, while contractual benefits, such as vacation and pension, are also provided. The duration of the position will be determined by what happens in financial markets, though the artists estimate that it will last around 120 years. The physical design of this station takes its point of departure from the Station as such –that is, as a typical space – while it transfers meanings from a different kind of space, the factory. It recreates the working environment of an industrial worker with a time clock and "factory-like lights above the platforms that turn on a fluorescent light – a work light – when the employee is working." *Eternal Employment* thus relates closely to the historical materialist conception of history and its notion of social criticism, which underlies Derkert's conceptual program for Östermalmstorg. With its long time span, however, *Eternal Employment* is not intended to be a static work, a point that was highlighted as a reason for its selection; this presentation is intended to change with people's understanding of the concept of 'work' as well as with financial markets.

The jury's statement emphasized that Goldin+Senneby's proposal was conceptually magnificent, encompassing the entire main station and having the ability to "travel through its walls," as well as "the potential to become part of Gothenburg's oral history through word of mouth."[26] In a commentary, cultural theorist Josefin Wikström has stated that to ontologically place art speculation on the same level as that of the financial markets is to skew the perspective, thereby ignoring the critical potential of art.[27] I would like to rephrase her thoughts here and suggest that the widely held belief at an institutional level in the ability of art to fill and pass through spaces as if they were immaculate

---

26 *Kronotopia Competition 2. Haga and Korsvägen 2017. The jury's overall statement for the artistic design of the urban transformation project Västlänken (West Link) in Gothenburg.* Public Art Agency Sweden and the Swedish Transport Administration 2018.

27 Josefine Wikström, "Entrepreneurial subjectivity," in *Radical Philosophy*, issue 2.05, Autumn (2019).

and without boundaries is also ontologically suspect. As I see it, this work will be able to survive the entire estimated space–time on one condition: that the art machine persists over the same space–time and is able to protect it.

Historical art was also used as a critical approach in the debate about the winning entry. The critic Frans Josef Petersson argued that by designing the environments in which citizens live their daily lives, public art in Social Democratic post war society was able to preserve "the democratic ideals of equality and justice as living elements in public environments." Twentieth-century public art thus had "a distinct 'futurity,' a view of the future," something that *Eternal Employment* lacks, according to him.[28] The comparison with 20th-century art was made with a broad gesture, while the image painted in one of the articles in which Petersson criticizes Public Art Agency Sweden's initiative was precisely Siri Derkert's *Sverigeväggen (Wall of Sweden)* (1969). In the caption, the work is described as "one of the foremost expressions of socially conscious public art in post-war Sweden." This idealization of the art of the welfare state returns to what Wikström understood as Goldin+Senneby's blurring of the distinction between the speculation of art and the speculation of financial markets. In this line of thought, the very prospect of the future is the capacity of older art to deal with societal problems that have become increasingly evident over time. As democratic values are threatened, these works become increasingly relevant and have greater impact. From this perspective, the relevance of older public art is seen to increase, rather than decrease, over time.

---

28   Frans Josef Petersson, "Statens Konstråd sviker sitt sociala och demokratiska arv" [Public Art Agency of Sweden betrays its social and democratic heritage], *Kunstkritikk.se*, [accessed 11/17/2017].

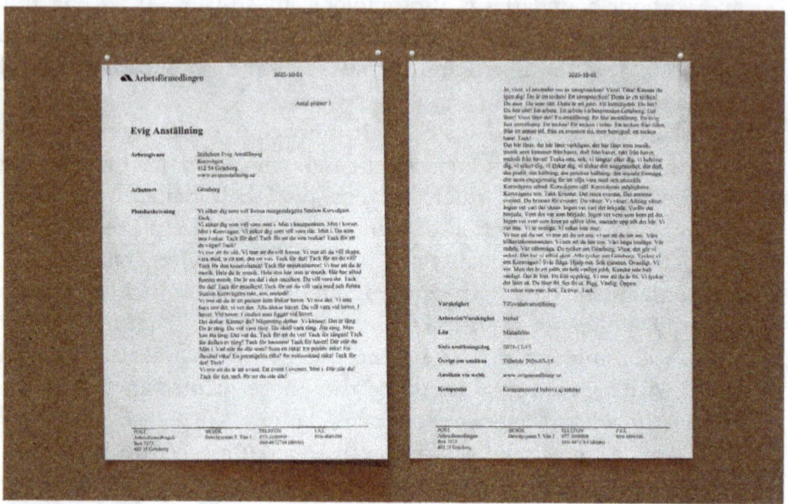

Sketch for *Eternal Employment* by Simon Goldin and Jakob Senneby
© Simon Goldin and Jakob Senneby / Bildupphovsrätt 2022

However, when one goes back to the start of that project, to the competition program where the commissioning body draws visions of what should be achieved, a clear artistic boundary is also established. The program stipulates that a winning proposal should not be "typical public art, or typical station art [sic], or the like."[29] Exactly what this means is hard to interpret except for the obvious, namely that the Station remains especially bound by space-time, though the organizers of the competition seem to hold out hope that successful proposals, contrary to the art-critical stance, will be innovative precisely by breaking free from the history of public art. It should be art that is placed in a station but not look like art in a station, it should occupy a space based on ideas of both history and the future, but at the same time carefully avoid artistic, historical references. This seems contradictory for a project that in many respects rests on an artistic and institutional platform established decades ago, a platform that we have seen in various ways lingering in the space–time the new design occupies.

---

29   Kronotopia competition program, p. 5.

A broader concept of public design

The problem of how to preserve the public art of the era of the Million Program, is a pressing issue today and is the subject of state investigations.[30] In the government's bill on *Kulturarvspolitik* (Cultural policy for the heritage sector) (prop.2016/17:116), it was concluded that, after a few years of inventorying the physical vulnerability of public art of that period, the conditions for preserving building-related art from the 20th century should be enhanced. In the Heritage Conservation Act (1988:950), for the first time, the concept of cultural heritage included works of art in the public environment. It argued that while cultural heritage had previously been used to refer to objects, works of art and buildings, it needed to include intangible cultural heritage, such as customs and exchanged knowledge. Another essential dimension, according to the bill, is that cultural heritage should be defined for things that are of concern to all. This concern needs to be rooted in the place in question; the bill states that "in a general sense, cultural heritage can be understood as traces and expressions of the past that are attributed value and are used in the present."[31] With this understanding, it becomes less important to draw a line between an object and its use, which is a perspective that I also advocate.[32] If cultural heritage policy is opened up in this way, the question of permanence or temporality need not structure public art or determine which works are relevant.

At the policy level, there is thus an indirect readiness to consider public art other than art that can be linked to physical artefacts or objects of a respectable age, as part of the cultural heritage. This opens the door to the consideration of a number of different aspects of art's effects in space. The study *Byggnadsanknuten offentlig konst Kunskapshöjande insatser för förvaltning av den offentliga konsten som del av kulturmiljön* (Building-related Public Art. Knowledge enhancement for the management of public art as part of the cultural environment) articulates the tremendous need for changes in regulations around supervision practices and conservation as a whole, but also in terms of knowledge enhancement. An interesting passage discusses conflicts

---

30 See, e.g., the report Karin Hermerén and Henrik Orrje, *Offentlig konst – ett kulturarv. Tillsyn och förvaltning av byggnadsanknuten konst [Public Art - A Cultural Heritage. Supervision and management of building-related art]* (Stockholm: Public Art Agency Sweden, 2014).
31 Cultural heritage policy bill (prop. 3016/17:116), p. 58.
32 Cultural heritage policy bill (prop.2016/17:116), pp. 57-58.

that can arise in the valuation of cultural heritage, aesthetic, social, environmental and economic aspects. The same phenomenon can be interpreted differently by different "areas of interest, such as artistic interests, art history or cultural heritage" with their perspectives. The space–time concept of public art as I have established, which would also include institutional practices and considerations for how art and cultural policy practices from different times interact, could serve as a useful tool in this change.

This chapter has presented some examples to highlight an inherent contradiction between, on the one hand, a strong belief in the art of creating solutions to problems that fall within the political sphere and, on the other, an insufficient ability to see how previous initiatives can linger and operate in a low-intensity fashion over time. Public sculpture is an articulation of social power relations rooted in institutionalizing practices.[33] The main focus of this chapter has been art that coalesces in space, creating dynamic and sedimented layers – not only in relation to artistic practices but also institutional practices. When art is to be placed in public spaces based on a strong democratic and cultural-political vision, a tension arises between two distinct fields: on the one hand, the art world, where we find art with different aesthetic expressions and artists with individual preferences; on the other hand, we have the commissioning bodies, the machine, where political processes and authorities interact. Analyses that arrive at highlighting the complex space–times in which public art is placed, are called for, as well as explorations of the ideas of political and artistic trust in the agency of art, on which public art seems to depend.

---

33 Important studies in this area include Catharina Gabrielsson, *Att göra skillnad. Det offentliga rummet som medium för konst, arkitektur och politiska föreställningar* [*To Make a Difference: Public Space as a Medium for Art, Architecture and Concepts of the Political*], doctoral thesis, (Stockholm: Royal Institute of Technology, 2006). and Jessica Sjöholm *Skulptur i folkhemmet* [*Sculpture in the Swedish Welfare State*], op.cit.

Art Work in Public Time:
a study of Forest Calling, Ställbergs Gruva and Eternal Employment

// Dan Karlholm

In the allocation of public funds, a distinction is made between what used to be called project grants and operations support, which, regardless of their content and quality, are defined primarily in terms of time – as short-term and long-term activities respectively.[1] In other words, there are temporary, short-term, fleeting, occasional or even ephemeral elements (intended to disappear) and long-term, ongoing (indefinite), permanent or even perpetual events (intended to endure). The former can be occasionally supported, the latter need more continuous backing.[2] In both cases, we are talking about investments in the unknown, the future. The fact that artists have been working on projects for quite some time (with no set end dates) has certainly become a cliché, much like the fact that they do research (whatever it is they do), which affects how we understand the notion of *artwork* today. However, the oft-cited notion that the development of the art field has moved from unique works or products to undefined projects or processes needs to be problematized. Here, I will discuss the issue of art, time and projects based on three recent public artworks with theoretical support from art theorist Boris Groys.

The three works mentioned in the title all relate to what could almost be called *longue durée* (Braudel), in terms of the extended time perspectives involved. They can all be said to challenge the accelerating fluidity and adaptive flexibility of late modernity. They are also at odds with all notions of marketization and commodification, as well as the modern need for instant gratification. The first example is Malin Arnell and Åsa Elzén's *Skogen kallar – Ett oändligt kontaminerat samarbete eller Dansandet är en form av skogskunskap* (*Forest Calling – A Never-ending Contaminated Collaboration or Dancing is a Form of Forest Knowledge*)

---

1 Today, we speak of greater limits to grant funds and increased or decreased funds for ongoing management. However, these categories do not necessarily correlate with support for temporary or more permanent art projects.

2 However, this is a theoretical division. In practice, the permanent is understood as more than five years - perhaps even 20 years - as discussed in Håkan Nilsson's contribution Temporary Liaisons and Far-reaching Convergences" in this anthology.

(2018-20), which although relatively short-term has the idea of infinity inscribed in the forest. In short, the work is about seeking legal protection for 3.7 hectares of Sörmland forest in order to take it out of production and protect it permanently. The Fogelstad group (1925-54), pioneers of both the women's movement and organic farming, are also brought to the fore here. The second work is the collective *Ställbergs Gruva (Ställberg's Mine)*, led by Carl-Oscar Sjögren and Eric Sjögren, which is based on a disused mining site in Västmanland on 9 hectares of land and a number of buildings, which they acquired in 2015. The work explores the living conditions in a depopulated corner of the world through various artistic and cultural activities, which also involve the local population. The third artwork, *Evig anställning (Eternal Employment)* by Goldin+Senneby (Simon Goldin and Jakob Senneby), was the winning proposal in 2017 for Korsvägen station in the *West Link: Kronotopia* competition in Gothenburg. The work – essentially a job position without a job description – was intended to be inaugurated alongside the station in 2026, but in 2022 Trafikverket decided to abort the project, due to financial difficulties. The position was expected to last for around 120 years. It deals with, among other things, wage labor, capitalism and the meaning of life.

All three works deal with long timeframes, while these time perspectives also constitute the works' conditions of existence. They are very much about extended periods of time (a piece of forest in Södermanland, a depopulated mining community in Västmanland and a permanent job in Gothenburg) but are thus themselves extended in time, which is not a necessary condition for their existence as works, only a possibility resulting from a concept of art favorable to open-ended processes. The roots of this concept of art lie far in the past, in the transformation of the 1950s and 1960s, of an increasingly closed and pure form of modernism that had reached its apogee at the same time as it was becoming an object of historiographical interpretation.[3] This applies in particular to the process art of the 1960s, as an extension of conceptual art in which the physical work was subordinate (though not eliminated, since a work must take some kind of form, if only

---

3   A testimony to this period of change in Sweden is Leif Nylén, *Den öppna konsten. Happenings, instrumental teater, konkret poesi och andra gränsöverskridningar i det svenska 60-talet* [*Open Art: Happenings, Instrumental Theatre, Concrete Poetry and Other Border Crossings in the Swedish 60s*] (Stockholm: SAK, publication 107, 1998). See also Hans Hayden, *Modernism as Institution. On the Establishment of an Aesthetic and Historiographic Paradigm* (Stockholm & Stehag: Brutus Östlings bokförlag Symposion, 2006).

through words, in order to exist). Relational aesthetics represented a kind of continuation, which from the 1990s onwards became one of the most influential tracks in global contemporary art. The fact that a government agency started commissioning public artworks of an explicitly short-lived or "temporary" nature can be tied to this history, albeit with a previously unknown emphasis on the end part of processes.[4] It is thus the temporary works that are delimited and closed, while permanent works are open and undefined.

Time, projects and art projects

Now, if we look more closely at the temporality of these works, are they all examples of what is often described as an evolution in the global art field from work to process or project? I will question this in what follows and instead suggest that they are works as process and processes as works. It is only if we understand works as identical with a physical form or material entity that the above description can be justified. But works must first be understood as shorthand for artworks, and there can be little doubt that these three examples of public art also exemplify this abstract category. Secondly, all works of art must be understood as both material and immaterial, contemporary and deeply rooted in history, in that they all, briefly put, materialize an idea.

The projectification of society, and in particular its organization of work, is a phenomenon that has taken hold globally in recent decades.[5] In his text "The Loneliness of the Project," Boris Groys discusses how project applications have come to proliferate in the arts as much as in academia.[6] It is about securing a period of "socially sanctioned solitude" or freedom to make something of one's own, which also means mortgaging the future.[7] Given that only a minority of all project applications in all fields and in all sectors are approved, it also

---

4   Works that are explicitly temporary were given space within the activities of Public Art Agency Sweden starting in 2012, at the same time that Magdalena Malm began her stint as director of the council, a position she held until 2019. The temporary work is reminiscent of the classical drama's emphasis on "beginning, middle and end." https://statenskonstrad.se/arbeta-med-konst-i-offentliga-miljoer/arbetsprocesser-inom-offentlig-konst/arbetsprocess-for-tillfallig-offentlig-konst/ [accessed 10/08/2020].

5   For example, Anders Jensen, Christian Thuesen & Joana Geraldi, "The Projectification of Everything: Projects as a Human Condition," in *Project Management Journal*, June/July 2016, pp. 21-34.

6   Boris Groys, "The Loneliness of the Project," in *Going Public* (Berlin: Sternberg Press, 2010), pp. 70-83.

7   Groys, "The Loneliness of the Project," op.cit.

means that the future that will actually emerge is one that bears the stamp of the predictable and the feasible, a future that the assessors of the applications understand, recognize and confirm. All results should be expected, and nothing strictly speaking should come as a surprise. The diverse array of rejected projects represents as many possible or rather impossible futures. Projects in both science and public art also usually have their own project duration, typically three to five years, after which they must be finalized and some kind of concrete result demonstrated.[8]

Groys certainly discusses other types of projects, orchestrated by sects or religious practices, but sees projects in particular as something typically modern. He cites the various "projects" of the artistic avant-garde as an example, but the question is whether the project, more than anything else, reflects the culture and public sector of our time, fundamentally imbued with new public management. NPM can be said to revolve around the idea of evaluating short-term projects in two stages: before (conditions, objectives and expected returns) and after (results, outcomes, impacts). Documentation (and evaluation) has a central role here, which Groys builds on, as we shall see shortly.

In all three of the works discussed in this text, the outer limit of the artwork lies several decades in the future, which means that these works must be left to themselves before their effects or degree of fulfilment can be verified.[9] The planned, conceptually extended time, which thus runs into the unknown future, makes these works impossible to definitively evaluate. They can, of course, be documented

---

8   For example, The Swedish Art Grants Committee specifies the following: "Project grants may be applied for by individual artists for a limited experiment or development work. The project must have a clearly formulated goal, be limited in time and have a budget." In addition: "the results of the project must be publicly demonstrated in some way" https://www.konstnarsnamnden.se/projektbidrag_bild_form [accessed 10/25/2020]

9   Henrik Orrje, Administrative Director of Public Art Agency Sweden, describes the art project process as follows: "Completed temporary projects are given final approval by the responsible curator at Public Art Agency Sweden, or a partner such as a municipality, but the artists participating in temporary projects do not create a final report. In government commissions that Public Art Agency Sweden has taken on in recent years, the production of artworks (permanent and temporary) has been combined with other cultural policy objectives concerning knowledge development, such as interdisciplinary collaboration, development of the concept of design, the participation of civil society, self-organized art practitioners and common meeting places for the people. In these assignments, artists have played an important role in strengthening knowledge development and have actively participated in the dissemination of lessons and experiences, i.e., mainly qualitative aspects, through texts, films, conferences, seminars, etc. Artists have also participated in program activities and other dissemination activities after the commissions have ended." (email correspondence with author 11/27/2020)

and evaluated *to some extent*, but never completely, which may actually add to their attractiveness.

Groys stresses that projects are always about (future) time:

> Each project is above all the declaration of another, new future that is thought to come about once the project has been executed. But in order to build such a new future, one first has to take a leave of absence, a time in which the project shifts its agent into a parallel state of heterogeneous time. This other timeframe, in turn, disconnects from time as society experiences it – it is de-synchronized. Society's life carries on regardless – the usual run of things remains unaffected. But somewhere beyond this general flow of time, someone has begun working on a project – writing a book, preparing an exhibition, or plotting a spectacular assassination – in the hopes that the completed project will alter the general run of things and all mankind will be bequeathed a different future: the very future, in fact, anticipated and aspired to in this project. In other words, every project thrives solely on the hope of being resynchronized with the social environment.[10]

First, the project is described as a new future, then as the time it takes to imagine this future. A time frame in the form of a new future and one in the form of "another time frame," which constitutes the conditions of the first time frame. The project thus requires a project to come into being (money = time and necessary resources). The project is both the path and the goal, both the condition and the result, which makes it extremely difficult to even think outside this project box. Are we even witnessing a translation of art into projects? No, it is not a question of one replacing or being able to stand in for the other, but of a two-component combination – art projects.

Each project, according to Groys, represents a proposal for a new future, which is generated by the project. It is perhaps a slight exaggeration but aptly put. When it comes to the project period, which includes working on the project, as a researcher I certainly know the feeling. Every draft and idea worked out in the artistic field can also be described in project terms, even if art projects are a different kind of time-based

---

10   Groys, "The Loneliness of the Project," op.cit., pp. 76-77.

project where the important thing is the "result" that develops over time, neither its preliminary work nor its definitive final report. What is important is what unfolds along the project's own time axis, what is in progress, the activity rather than the finished work. Or – the work is the activity. The work of art is the art activity (the artwork).

The conceptualization period of the work and its production period (for which project grants can be applied for) precede the result, which is also called a project (and is listed as such, i.e., in its finished or historical form on websites and in archives).[11] In academia (including artistic research), projects end with the delivery of something: one or more texts or an exhibition, for example. In the art world, a project ends with – a project.[12] Despite this difference, Groys' ideas about an alternative temporality for the project are relevant here, for even the completed project (which in turn extends into the future) can, after all, be likened to a heterogeneous temporality in relation to ordinary time, a parallel time that is thus desynchronized from ordinary time: the time of the clock, the almanac, and the seasons of the year. The aim, Groys then writes, is to reconcile or re-synchronize the time removed from this flow with ordinary, social time. This does not mean that it will disappear or become invisible, but that it will be integrated with and add to, influence or change this temporality (the extent of which is unclear). What artists are applying for is time outside the ongoing everyday social flow in order to contribute something back to this flow and to some extent change its course.

In a continuation on Groys' insightful essay on the loneliness and particularity of the project, he becomes an exponent of the clichéd notion that the development of art has moved from the work to process or project. After all, what is described in the quote above is that each project aims to realize a new future, that is, as I understand it, an ever-so-small shift in what is to come, what comes next. But for this to happen, project time itself - understood as the time taken to conceive and flesh out a future project - establishes a parallel "heterogeneous" time, a time separate from ordinary time. Project time can be likened to a pocket of time or alternative time, which aims to make its mark on the dominant, more or less homogeneous, normal or 'ordinary' time to which project time is an alternative. Thus, two aspects of

---

11   On Public Art Agency Sweden's website, in 2020, works of art are listed under the tab "Our art projects."

12   This name, of course, can conceal all kinds of physical manifestations.

projects emerge as a result and as a time for the realization of this. But the category is even more flexible, and Groys discusses unfinished projects, and even contends a little later that projects "cannot" be finished, even though he exemplifies the project results with books and exhibitions: "...even if the heterogeneous project time cannot be finished, it [...] can be documented." But since it was the heterogeneous time that was desynchronized from standard time with a view toward resynchronization of the two, this must reasonably imply that it is also completed as such, not only touching or overlapping but integrated with the standard time it has also influenced in some way.

Groys continues, "One could even argue that art is nothing more than the documentation and representation of such project-based heterogeneous times."[13] This argument has also been presented in an earlier essay of his and is reused here, I speculate, without the author being in full control of the implications for the project discussion.[14] Of course, that art "is nothing other than" the documentation/representation of art-as-project not only sounds barren and meaningless, it also empties the concept of art of substance – reducing it to a conduit or mirror while also emptying the concept of project of substance by removing its life-giving connection to art. After all, the whole value behind the idea of art projects is that they are a new type of artwork. When he claims that "art is no longer understood as the production of works of art but as documentation of life-in-the-project - regardless of the outcome," he misunderstands both what art and projects are about here. Further: "...art is no longer manifested as another, new object, for contemplation that has been produced by the artist but as another heterogeneous time frame of the art project, which is documented as such." The conclusion is that "art documentation is, by definition, not art."[15]

By simultaneously adopting the term art project, Groys' entire argument as presented above seems to nullify itself. Such a project obviously involves, or is itself art, or alternatively – the art in question manifests itself here in the form of a project. What at first appears to be a posthumous documentation is in fact the finished manifestation, a presentation of the completed art project, whose content – actions, events and forms

---

13   Groys, "The Loneliness of the Project," op.cit. p. 77.
14   Boris Groys, "Art in the Age of Biopolitics: From Artwork to Art Documentation," *Art Power* (Cambridge, Massachusetts & London: MIT Press, 2008), pp. 53-65.
15   Groys, "The Loneliness of the Project," op.cit., pp. 78-79.

– has been largely consumed and dissipated over the years. The only thing that is never consumed or dissipated is the idea of the artwork/ art project. It is not the documentation but the presentation of this idea in its most mature form that a viewer ultimately encounters when the work is exposed. This stage does not mean that the work becomes historic or ceases to exist, as its very survival may well be inscribed as a mode of artistic existence in the project. The work may have been programmed as "definitively unfinished" to paraphrase Marcel Duchamp.[16]

In all these cases, art presents itself as an art project (with a time frame that is heterogeneous in relation to everyday, normal time). According to Groys, an art project is a project in two senses of the word: from the draft or planning to the result via the journey between these two points (which also lends itself to the name project). In sum, there are rather three meanings of project contained in the word art project: 1) someone puts together a project, a document describing the intentions and expected consequences, 2) then (in the best case) implements this project (as conceived or with a number of deviations) during a certain stipulated time and finally 3) presents the project as a result. The idea is of course present throughout the process, but it is only realized during the development of the project and in all its aspects (accumulated as sediments) only at the very last stage.

Now, what is the role of project and temporality in the three works *Forest Calling*, *Ställbergs Gruva* and *Eternal Employment*?

---

16   Cf. *The Definitely Unfinished Marcel Duchamp*, ed. Thierry de Duve (Cambridge, Mass. & London: MIT Press, 1991).

Forest Calling

In the work *Forest Calling* (*Skogen kallar*), with the English subtitle, *A Never-ending Contaminated Collaboration or Dancing is a Form of Forest Knowledge*, the word project is removed in favor of "collaboration," referring of course to the collective work of the artists Malin Anrell and Åsa Elzén, but certainly also to the activities that are organized and take place in this forest (including dance in the form of raves).[17] The main action, as presented by the artists at a public presentation of the work, is "to take a piece of forest out of production," which I interpret as a symbolic act of protest against the highly efficient industrial forest industry that defines a young forest such as this, which is no more than 70 years old, as a "production forest": a forest only there to be harvested and sold (more like a plantation than a forest and, significantly, with little biodiversity).[18] The land covers 3.7 hectares and is located in Julita, Katrineholm municipality in Södermanland. This anything but pristine piece of cultivated nature is owned by Fogelstad estate, whose origins as a mill date back to the 17th century. In 1925, Elisabeth Tamm founded the *Kvinnliga medborgarskolan* vid *Fogelstad* (Fogelstad Citizen School for Women), a veritable home for the Fogelstad Group, which was formed in 1921 by, among others, Elin Wägner, and became one of the Swedish women's movement's most important centers.[19] What the artists today seek to realize through this work is a lease agreement (*Skogsavtal*) for a maximum of 50 years for this patch of forest, which cuts like a rectilinear wedge into a much larger forest area, thus resembling a piece of a large cake.[20] The forest is not classified as worthy of protection today, mainly because of its young age, but in another 50 years, it may well be. The plan is therefore to spare this area from the ravages of extraction and exploitation, so that the forest can both regain its natural agency and age without direct external influence and be classified as a protected old-growth forest in half a century, with the intention of achieving legally protected status in perpetuity.

---

17 "This is one of twelve local art projects that were part of Public Art Agency Sweden's government commission Knowledge Hub Public Art (2018-2020). The projects aimed to explore the concept of art and what art can be." https://statenskonstrad.se/konst/skogen-kallar/ [accessed 10/02/2020].

18 Conversation on "Temporality and Public Art," Public Art Agency Sweden, 04/12/2019: https://www.youtube.com/watch?v=OeqAbQ5gb78 [accessed 10/10/2010].

19 https://statenskonstrad.se/konst/skogen-kallar/ [accessed 10/02/2020].

20 At the time this text is due to be published, I am informed that such an agreement has been signed.

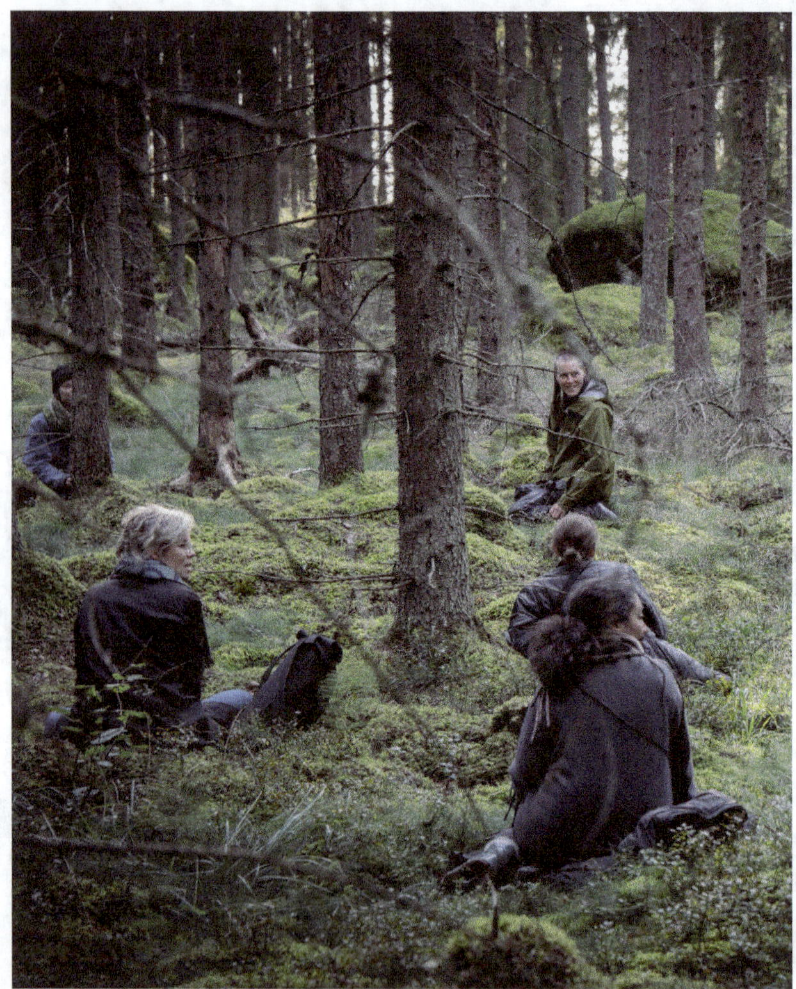

Malin Arnell & Åsa Elzén *Forest Calling – A Never-ending Contaminated Collaboration or Dancing is a Form of Forest Knowledge* 2019, Photo: Ricard Estay/Statens konstråd

Forests are a collective singularity, as evidenced by the expression "can't see the forest for the trees." The dialectic between the component trees and the forest as a whole is intricate, and if too small an area of 'forest' had been clipped off, the very definition of forest could have been compromised. A certain degree of distribution and diversity thus seems necessary, but this narrow sliver of land is now bordered by neighboring trees with extensive roots and continuous vegetation that are sacrificed, biotopes are split, animal trails cut... Is it not a problematic act of violence to carve out a segment of the forest from the forest? How do we delineate and maintain these boundaries? Will the carved-out forest become an unnatural, cultural entity as well? A question that brings to mind the philosopher Jean Baudrillard's reflections on the small tribe discovered in the Philippine jungle in 1971, where they had lived for centuries without contact with the outside world, but who were nonetheless transformed by the artificial act of leaving them alone in their "primitive" virginity.[21] Transformed, or even "contaminated."[22] There is an ethical dilemma here that could be explored further. *Forest Calling* also has points of contact with artist Henrik Håkansson's *The Reserve* (2009-12), a 2500 square meter area at Wanås Castle in Skåne that was enclosed with fencing to allow a piece of terrain to "develop without human intervention and contrast with the surrounding nature."[23]

I cannot help but connect the idea of a separate era of seclusion or "solitude" for this forest with Groys' basic idea of projects. The forest here becomes de-synchronized from the normal and normative flow of time and develops in a time outside this hegemonic time with its cyclical demands to produce. A heterogenic, or rather heterochronic, parallel temporality emerges here, which aims to let the forest be itself and which, through this artistic intervention in an economic

---

21   Jean Baudrillard, "The Precession of Simulacra," *Simulacra and Simulation*, trans. Sheila Faria Glaser (Ann Arbor: The University Of Michigan Press, 1994), pp. 7-8.

22   The title revives the negatively charged term contamination, which may refer to a linguistic confusion of expressions but otherwise means something stained, polluted, soiled... *Svenska Akademiens ordböcker* [*Swedish Academy Dictionary*]: https://svenska.se/tre/?sok=kontamination&pz=1 [accessed 11/01/2010]. However, the term is reclaimed today, e.g. Anna Lowenthal Tsing, *The Mushroom at the End of the World: On the Possibility of Life in Capitalist Ruins* (Princeton & Oxford: Princeton U.P., 2015), 27-34.

23   Even without large mammalians, there can be an impact on the environment, which helps not only to lock in a space for sustainable development but also to influence and partially redirect the immediate environment from an animal perspective. http://www.wanas.se/svenska/Konst/Konstn%C3%A4rer/Konstn%C3%A4r.aspx?fid=67 [accessed 10/08/2020].

system, offers a critique of the system as such.[24] A number of more evocative and metaphorical associations are also attached to the work, expressed as "3.7 hectares of symbioses, histories, temporalities and relationships," not least through the concept of "desire," both to lesbian love and to "a larger space–time and a different future," which fits well with Groys' analysis.[25]

Furthermore, the forest becomes, according to the artists, an "assemblage with its own temporalities," but also a "monument." Its monumentality sounds somewhat more static and definitive. However, unlike most monuments, what is emphasized is continuous change: "The forest becomes a monument - an on-going, transformative, performative public artwork."[26] It is also "a public artwork, a forest and a habitat for endless and endless dead or alive vibrant matter," which indirectly refers to the work of the New Materialist theorist, Jane Bennett.[27] But if it becomes a changing, transformative monument, one might also say that such a monument becomes inseparable from its own documentation – how else are we to make transformation visible (and of what?). This actualizes and problematizes Groys' argument in an interesting way. For Groys, the starting point seems to be a sentiment of disappointment that an increasing number of art exhibitions are content to showcase what has already been done elsewhere (the dullest aspect of documentation), rather than creating a presentation that becomes one with itself and the artwork that 'happens' each time it is activated by a viewer/visitor/audience. This is also, of course, a case of the continuous response to the calling of the forest in the form of excursions, walks, conversations, dance and interaction with the forest itself.[28]

---

24 On heterochrony see, e.g., Keith Moxey, *Visual Time: The Image in History* (Durham & London: Duke U.P., 2013); Dan Karlholm, *Kontemporalism. Om samtidskonstens historia och framtid* [*Contemporalism. On the History and Future of Contemporary Art*]. (Stockholm: (Stockholm: Axl Books, 2014), pp. 276-286.

25 The artists have a close relationship with the organization *Naturens Rättigheter (Rights of Nature)*, which is modelled on the Declaration of Human Rights and led in Sweden by the activist Pella Thiel.

26 Presentation of *Forest Calling - A Never-ending Contaminated Collaboration or Dancing is a Form of Forest Knowledge* by Malin Arnell and Åsa Elzén: https://statenskonstrad.se/events/programdag-in-forests-call [accessed 10/10/2020].

27 Ibid, Jane Bennett, *Vibrant Matter: A Political Ecology of Things* (Durham: Duke University Press, 2010).

28 These activities are in turn a contemporary echo of the activities of the Fogelstad Group, which was a group of (newly enfranchised) women who met in a sheltered context and learned to act as political subjects.

Interestingly, something performative also happens in the mere classification of the forest as "public art": "When the forest is understood as a public artwork, it is lifted out of its predetermined context and becomes a kind of resistance to the Western teleological concept of time."[29] The lease would lift the forest from immediate logging, but the public art classification also lifts the forest out of the Western concept of time. Or is it more accurate to say it is lifted from the economic system? That this concept of time would find symbiosis with capitalism and the forest industry complicates the artists' reliance on the same concept of time in their negotiation of a fifty-year lease.

A more serious ethical problem ultimately presents itself: "What is our obligation to the forest? Our responsibility? Who should we listen to? Something whispers that it is completely impossible to own 'nature', to own land. Making a profit on the commons, the land, is a loss of our future."[30] But in the meantime, would not responsibility be exercised toward the forest through what is called forest management? And what to do about the potential ravages of the spruce bark beetle (it is mentioned but in more poetic than alarmist terms), which could jeopardize the future protection classification it hopes to achieve? How do we protect against increasingly frequent forest fires during the Anthropocene? After all, sometimes nature does consume itself, which is really only a transformation of the energy it holds. In a very sympathetic way, this work seeks to counter the harmful effects of capitalism embodied in the successive felling of forests, in favor of the forest's own agency and its own rights. This certainly comes at the cost of an anthropogenic divestment in which the carved-out forest risks becoming an unhappy singularity that may in a few years miss its symbiotic environment, though in return emerge as a protest against and a monument to the documented greed of modern humans.

---

29 See note 153.

30 See note 153. The concept that the earth cannot be owned is a central theme. An important source of inspiration for this project was Elin Wägner's and Elisabeth Tamm's *Fred med jorden* [*Peace with the Earth*] (Stockholm: Bonniers, 1940). The book was also included in Åsa Elzén's exhibition "Träda - Fogelstadgruppen och jord" [Notes on a Fallow – The Fogelstad group and earth] at Sörmlands museum 05/30/2020 – 01/26/2021.

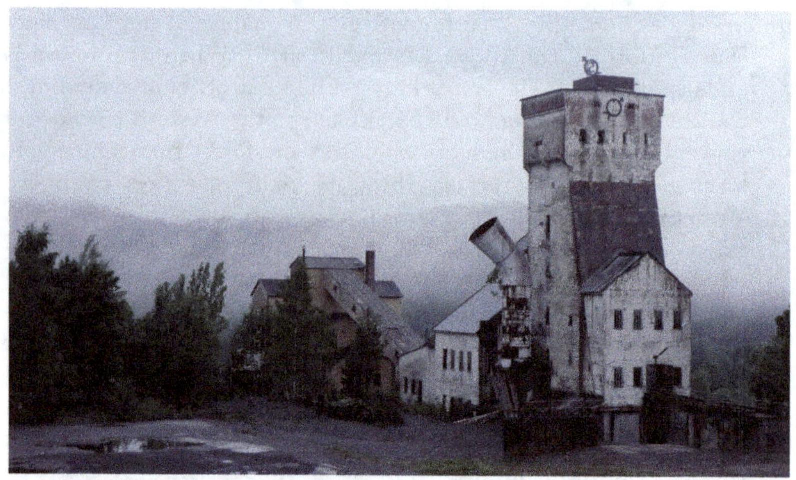

The Non Existent Center, Ställbergs gruva, 2018,
Photo: The Non Existent Center

Ställbergs Gruva (Ställbergs Mine)

The work *Ställbergs Gruva* is described by the artists as follows:

> Ställbergs Gruva aims to be a place where the big issues become more personal – and the personal part of the big issues. A place for learning, doubt and living. Collectively and individually. Existential and political. A place where space and the market live side by side with the roots of the field pea and the sound of an engine room. Ställbergs' mine is run by the economic association The Non-Existent Center [sic!] and spans nine hectares of land and 1000 square meters of buildings in Ställberg's decommissioned iron ore mine in the municipality of Ljusnarsberg.[31]

---

31 Ställbergs gruva: https://www.stallbergsgruva.se/ [accessed 10/10/2020]. Unless otherwise stated, quotations in the text are taken from here. This is one of twelve local art projects that were part of Public Art Agency Sweden's government commission Knowledge Hub Public Art (2018-2020). The projects aimed to explore the concept of art and what art can be. The selection team at Public Art Agency Sweden that chose the projects consisted of: Magdalena Malm, former director, Åsa Mårtensson, project manager Knowledge Hub Public art, Elena Jarl, assistant curator, Giorgiana Zachia, coordinator Stärka Konstorganisationer (stronger Art OrganiZations) and Edi Muka, curator." https://statenskonstrad.se/konst/processen/ [accessed 10/10/2020].

Tempus states that this is a vision, something this collective work hopes to be. The text uses classic rhetorical figures of speech, from the opening chiasmus, a few anaphors and contrasts to a breathtaking shift in perspective from "outer space" to "the roots of the field pea." And in the very name of the association – the non-existent center – there is a paradox. Even more intricate is the apparent doubling of the subject in the paragraph: The Ställberg mine emanates from the land and buildings of the Ställberg mine... But as everyone understands, there are two Ställberg mines, yet only one mine.

In the next paragraph, the wording "wants to be" is used by the authors. In light of this phrasing, I consider their text as a vision rather than a program, policy or project description. Here things become more straightforward. The activity has been in operation at this location since 2012, which is also a work (an art space?) with the title (which I italicize for the sake of clarity) *Ställbergs Gruva*, by eleven people with varying backgrounds in arts and handicrafts, in addition to journalism and psychology. As of 2015, the land and buildings are said to be "cultural worker-owned," since "the group's other association, Non Existent Resources, purchased the property." Further: "Ownership is seen as a long-term investment, with a repayment plan extending to 2070." It is one thing for everything to be paid off and the eleven participants to be debt-free in fifty years' time, but the extent of the commitment should also be indicated here and closely linked to the long-term investment in question. This is also roughly the estimated remaining lifetime of the crew.[32] The concept of a project, which can last for many years, but usually connotes something more temporary, is rejected by the authors. This seems to be a question of art in the more open-ended sense of the word. The time perspective is interesting, since nothing here starts from scratch, neither in 2012 nor from the 2015 acquisition. After all, the Ställberg mine has its own history, as does the land, the village, the municipality and this place on earth. Another paragraph on the website describes more about the place in response to the question "Where are we?": "Ställberg's mine is located on manganese and iron-bearing primary rock in the valley of the Hörksälven, just north of Kopparberg in Ljusnarsberg municipality, Örebro county, Västmanland province." A geological link at the bottom leads to a location on the map today. Copper, iron and silver

---

32 Presentation by C-O Sjögren at Temporarity [sic!] and Public Art Symposium 12/12/2019, Public Art Agency Sweden: https://www.youtube.com/watch?v=3h7palzuH4w [accessed 10/15/2020].

were mined here from the Middle Ages to the end of the 20th century. All of the local services that once existed here are gone – not even a grocery store remains. There are no train stops and fewer than 100 people live there today.

In the 1950s, the mine's main shaft is said to have been the deepest in Europe (1072 m). In 1977, everything closed when Jan Stenbeck became the owner of *Ställbergsbolagen*. In stark contrast with the centuries-old mining business, Stenbeck "invested capital in ZTV and Comviq, today's Tele 2, among others." From the industrial age to the information age. Since 2012, TNEC has been conducting "artistic, cultural and social activities based on the mine and its expansive surroundings." From the local to the global, we might be tempted to say, but the correct statement is rather: from the local to the glocal (i.e. the new local is determined by its intertwinement with the global).

The group arranges walks, talks, exhibitions, festivals and more, and also has an international residency (all suspended at the time of writing due to the pandemic). In terms of subject matter, the work revolves around questions about the potential of art and culture to "work through the difficulties today's societies face," not least in relation to climate change. By transforming the site in an energy-efficient and sustainable way, the hope is to facilitate permanent housing in the short term. The activity is further described in terms of "openness to the living, to history and to the common" through "a formative social investigation." Around the corner, it is pointed out, is "the world and its economic, human and ecological conditions," and the question then posed is: "what knowledge is needed in a world where the climate is changing rapidly?" Collective exploration is highlighted, "[an] exploration of known and unknown parts of the self and the world."

The poet Jonas Gren, who was involved in *Ställbergs Gruva*, does not wish to call this kind of art activity a project, which is associated with time: "For me it is important not to call what we do projects but work. It's important for the feeling that you are promising something to yourself. Otherwise, it becomes something to where we go a few times, take something and leave other things behind. That when the project is done, there is still an us and a them. I want to blur the line between the us and them and have that intertwinement persist over time."[33] It is a powerful vision that *Ställbergs Gruva* embodies, both

---

33   Marit Kapla, "Berättelsen om 2070" (The Story of 2070), *Ord & Bild*, 2-3, (2017) pp. 47-52.

as a work and an industrial ruin with networks of invisible tentacles stretching out toward the outside world in a planetary expansion. In 2019, *Ställbergs Gruva* received the Swedish Art Grants' committee structural grant, not to create temporary projects but "permanent places for art and cultural production outside of big cities."[34] One of the goals is to develop residencies of about 40 people per year in this "thought hub" (C-O Sjöberg), where all thoughts are also constantly concretized and translated into action, while depopulation and the dismantling of social services continue all around.

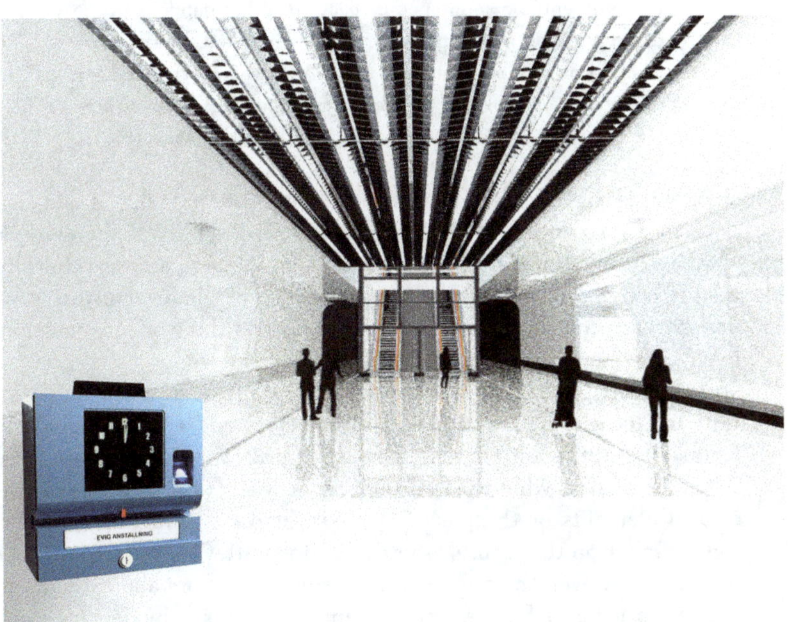

Sketch for Eternal Employment by Simon Goldin and Jakob Senneby
© Simon Goldin and Jakob Senneby / Bildupphovsrätt 2021

---

34   https://www.stallbergsgruva.se/Renovering-2020 [accessed 10/27/2020].

Evig Anställning or Eternal Employment

The artwork *Eternal Employment* by Simon Goldin and Jakob Senneby is presented by Public Art Agency Sweden as:

> an idea-based work in which one person will be employed at Korsvägen station. What the employee chooses to do shapes the content of the work and thus the artwork. In an idea-based artwork, it is the work process itself, the entire creation process, not the realization of a physical object, that is the focus. An idea-based artwork elevates a particular issue and invites debate, comment and spontaneous reaction. What happens in the comments and reactions becomes new material for the work to build on, which continues to evolve based on the changed conditions. The form of the work thus depends entirely on how it is received, and in this way, it is never really finished.[35]

Much of this is true of all art, except for the premise that what is said and done in the reception of the work is absorbed as part of the work, a principle propounded by Lars Vilks and Dan Wolgers, among others. It is an effective defensive strategy that asserts that whatever anyone says or whatever criticism anyone makes regarding the work in question itself contributes to the further "creation" of the work.

At Korsvägen station, which is scheduled to open in 2026 when the West Link in Gothenburg is completed, a time clock and a special light will be installed at the station, as well as a changing room for the employee. "The question of what the future of work will look like is one of the central elements of the piece," it goes on to say, implying that the sights are set on the future, which is in line with Groys' ideas on (art) projects. However, the punch clock seems to be more about the past, as a semiotic figure for the employment conditions of modernity, even a marker reminiscent of the *Folkhemmet* era. The analogue punch clock in the image above transforms the invisible core activity – a job position without a core or pre-defined activity – into a kind of visual theater. The mechanical punch clock with its round dial with Arabic numerals uses paper cards that are slid into the "clock" and are

---

35 https://statenskonstrad.se/konst/evig-anstallning/ [accessed 10/10/2020]. Curator Lotta Mossum, assistant curator Alba Baeza. For the artists' "proposal" in English, see https://statenskonstrad.se/app/uploads/2018/09/3-Eternal_Employment-WrittenDescriptionA4.pdf.

stamped with a date and a precise time.[36] The act makes clear that it is not so much a clock as a control device, manifesting the employer's absolute biopolitical power over the worker, as a monitor that is not concerned with what the worker does, only recording that he or she punches in on time and does not punch out until the end of the shift (although this can be manipulated if the worker has someone else punch in or out). The device becomes not only an agent that controls the worker's movements and work conditions but also a symbol of the power imbalance between the parties. Artists may live precarious lives in scarce, insecure circumstances, but if there is one thing they have, it is the freedom to formulate their work themselves (unless they exclusively perform commissioned work). There is a stark contrast here between the artists and their idea-based artworks imbued with meaning and the meaningless work they have conceived for someone else to undertake.

A further conceptual component of this work relates to the French economist Thomas Piketty's thesis that "today, invested capital increases in value faster than wages increase, which, according to Piketty, leads to increased class divisions."[37] This work of art uses the existing budget and invests it so that the return, according to current projections, is enough to cover one job position for 120 years."[38] To empty the concept of work of all content, all preconceived meaning, to examine what it can be filled with, given the stark formality around a job position, is an interesting thought exercise. What may be perceived as cynical is that this thought experiment involves, indeed requires, a kind of guinea pig in the form of people whose perseverance and willpower are tested in this experiment. Here, then, is an ethical complication that is unusual for conceptual works. How have the artists resolved it? It is of course too early to say, as the work is still only at the first of the three project stages, as discussed above. However, the realization of the artwork has already begun by being presented as a winning competition entry and documented as such. After all, when the art critic Frans Josef Petersson went to great lengths to severely criticize the work in *Kunstkritikk* in 2017, he not only helped to add a dimension to the work, he also managed to get the head of Public Art Agency

---

36 The exact design of the clock has not yet been decided, but the above concepts are based on the image communicated by the artists. Incidentally, many time clocks today are digital.

37 https://statenskonstrad.se/konst/evig-anstallning/ [accessed 10/10/2020].

38 Ibid. See Thomas Piketty, *Capital in the 21st Century*, Lars Ohlsson (Stockholm: Karneval, 2015).

Sweden, which initiated the competition in collaboration with the Swedish Transport Administration, to respond and thus contribute artistically.[39] And now here I am contributing myself... One thing that is corrected in the debate is Petersson's incorrect assumption that the employee must spend his or her time at the station, there "is nowhere in particular that the employee must be at the station,"[40] Malm emphasizes in both her replies. Except twice a day, or nearly 500 times a year, it may be added, as long as the person in question wants to continue receiving a salary!

The question is whether this "idea-based" work could have worked, even done better, as a thought-provoking proposal, draft, project (in the first sense of the word, according to my three-part division above)? Consider the laconism of conceptual artist Lawrence Weiner: "The piece need not be built."[41] Does not the realization of the piece, using actual employees as building blocks for a few years, threaten to lead to elusive, if not insoluble, ethical problems? Many who took note of the winning proposal found the problem to be that no physical "work" would be erected, but for me the problem is, on the contrary, that the piece is to be physically embodied at all costs.[42] In this work, the cliché from-work-to-project seems inverted: an interesting art project, which could have stayed on paper (at the so-called project stage) would thus if it had been realized become manifest in a few years and for over a hundred years using living people as materials.[43]

Comparisons and conclusions

All three works take on something seemingly mundane, something that is just there and that no one really cares about or can grasp. A patch

---

39 In *Kunstkritikk:* Frans Josef Petersson, "Statens konstråd sviker sitt sociala och demokratisk arv" [Public Art Agency Sweden Betrays its Social and Democratic Heritage], 11/17/17; Magdalena Malm, "Statens konstråd försvarar Goldin+Senneby," [Public Art Agency Sweden defends Goldin+Senneby], 11/22/17; F J Petersson, "Ska vi ha arbetsgivarkonst nu?" [Are We to Have Employer Art Now?] 11/22/17; Magdalena Malm, "Med omsorg om arbetstagarens förhållanden" [With Concern for the Worker's Conditions], 12/01/17.

40 Magdalena Malm "Med omsorg om arbetstagarens förhållanden" [With Concern for the Workers' Conditions] 12/01/17. https://kunstkritikk.se/med-omsorg-om-arbetstagarens-forhallanden/ [accessed 10/15/2020].

41 Lucy L. Lippard, *Six Years: The Dematerialization of the Art Object from 1966 to 1972...* (Berkeley: Univiversity of California Press, 1973), s. 73.

42 This is discussed in Per Strandberg, *Monument över Fast anställning [Monument to Permanent Employment]*, bachelor's thesis (Stockholm: Stockholm University, 2018), p. 27.

43 The work reminds me of the deeply controversial art of the Spanish artist Santiago Sierra, where he, among other things, pays people to perform more or less meaningless tasks.

of forest, which cannot even be defined as a unit without a map or a systematic walk through the space it occupies; a disused mine and the more or less deserted community surrounding it, following the conversion and closure of the once thriving mining industry (a fossil activity that made this community possible), and a work in the form of something as bureaucratic and non-visual as an unnecessary job position – without a given task that needs a solution – but more a job as such, for a period of time that transcends an individual's lifespan (and thus challenges the definition of a job), a position that just goes on, even long after the artists/employers have died. I have discussed them in terms of art, projects and time, though not always in that order.

It might sound as if these three public artworks in project form are unusually long in character in that they define themselves temporally in a less common way by way of three specified time spans: 50 years with a view to eternity; 50 years with a view to freedom from debt, or as long as the money lasts; about 120 years according to financial calculations. Paradoxically, however, this makes these works of art relatively short-term. By being absolutely limited in time, like all temporary art, they are exceptions to the rule for art, public and private – works that have an indefinite existence. The latter is not infrequently misunderstood as presumed timelessness. However, timelessness is a projected value and an aesthetic ideal, never a reality, as nothing can take place or exist outside of time. Timelessness is a dream of a long life, survival, beyond the flow of time (Bergson) and "the general run of things" (Groys). In a way, *Forest Calling* is an exception to the temporal, by experimenting with two temporal stages, the first encompassing half a century and the second encompassing eternity. In yet another paradoxical twist, however, it is temporally limited works like these that are able to articulate, concretize, and portray the notoriously elusive and potentially infinite phenomenon of time. They can also be said to pose basic ontological questions: what (really) is a forest, a society, a job? And thus: what is (today) a work of art? One work refers to nature (threatened), a second to culture (threatened) and a third to capitalism (unthreatened).

For the first two of these works – within these "projects," according to Public Art Agency Sweden, – it was an important issue to "examine the concept of art and what art can be." An answer to this has already been discussed and seems quite apparent today: art today can be *art projects*, which means that artworks can be project-oriented and can extend into the future, but they also have a limited temporal projection in a way that distinguishes them from common artworks in the form of spatially delimited objects (with unlimited scope). At the same time, I have argued against the notion that development has thus moved "from" works "to" processes and projects because the latter are still (art) works, works that have come to be defined by their projected and prognosticated, immanent and generative processes. It is rather a question of the very concept of art being broadened to include, in parallel and synchronically, works of a project nature. Art today can therefore be art-as-project and projects can, under certain circumstances, be art.

The work that is most clearly art, for me, is *Eternal Employment*, which presents an elaborate idea in a clever and evocative way (but where the impending realization of the idea can be seen as an accompanying complication). It is a conceptual work of art that threatens to become absurdist theater. *Forest Calling* is a multi-level collaboration, interspersed with performative elements and activities, and with a clear goal in mind. That everything that happens in and with the forest from now on is art follows from the art project paradigm. As for the relationship between *Ställbergs Gruva* and the concept of art, things become more diffuse. Does it even matter to the artists and academics involved that this is art (other than the fact that the classification opens up certain pockets of funding)? At the risk of repeating Groys' view on projects, I still have to wonder whether a production and residence site for art and culture can really also, as such, be counted as art? Is every studio and exhibition space also art (work)? Public Art Agency Sweden has answered yes to this question in the most emphatic way possible, by allocating funds to the "project," but somewhere along the way the line becomes so blurred between the conditions for the production of art and culture in general and what is generated from such production – ideas, physical forms and art projects – that the categories risk becoming obscure. In a text about this particular work, obtained during the final stages of writing this text, the subject behind *Ställbergs Gruva* slips between an it and a they. *Ställbergs Gruva*, unlike the mine itself, is alternately an activity, a project, a collective and an "artist-driven place." It is also meta-art: a public artwork that aims to "promote careful thinking about public art."[44]

---

44 Unsigned, "Processen" [The Process], in *Vi förändrar varandra. Kunskapsnav offentlig konst [We Transform Each Other. Knowledge Hub Public Art]* (Stockholm: Public Art Agency Sweden,

All these works problematize the established definition of *public art*. The forest is hardly a public arena; it is more or less removed from the public sphere (despite the right of public access), and the mining community as a place is a mixture of public and private, but without labeling what is art in this project in a way that we are used to when it comes to public art. In the final work, this link – (public) art – is absent or largely invisible despite being public art in the most obvious sense by being delineated as a kind of addition to (hardly an embellishment of) a municipally funded train station.

Public art has been strongly tied to ideas of space and place,[45] but what has been touched on above points more toward what I call public time.[46] And the moment this is uttered, everyone realizes that it must be about public *space-time* and always has been. Time is extremely confined to a station in the third work, albeit within the context of the whole of Gothenburg; it unfolds in a small, depopulated settlement in the second work, albeit globally linked to the world and the planet; it is a virtually "detached" patch of forest in the first work, albeit linked to the imaginary and queer space that Fogelstad denotes, with extensions and symbiotic links to other socialities, human and non-human, and the dream of a literally eternal space–time. The conversation about public art today would benefit from a reflection on the temporalities and temporal spaces accompanying it. The latter word is an Einsteinian composition of the main coordinates of human and non-human existence, but the very concept of time contains two different dimensions. Time as space or scope must be related to time as speed, rate, rhythm, velocity. The first dimension of time answers the question "how long?" or "how long does it take?" while the second dimension indicates the speed or frequency at which something happens; it measures or "times" a phenomenon. Length is important in all three works, but also negotiable; it is stated and stipulated though open to change depending on what occurs. Pace is less of a given. In *Forest Calling*, the artists are clear that different tempos and temporalities are intertwined heterogeneously (or

---

2020), pp. 64-65.

45 A Swedish classic is Catharina Gabrielsson's *Att göra skillnad. Det offentliga rummet som medium för konst, arkitektur och politiska föreställningar* [*To Make a Difference: Public Space as a Medium for Art, Architecture and Concepts of the Political*], doctoral thesis (Stockholm: Royal Institute of Technology, 2007).

46 The term is unusual but is discussed, for example, in a more narratological sense by Paul Ricoeur in "Narrative Time," *Critical Inquiry*, 7:1 (1980), pp. 169-190.

heterochronously) in a broader and more diverse sense than Groys' use of the word. *Ställbergs Gruva* also overlaps a range of activities at different speeds, from slow-paced restoration projects to short events, from poetic glimpses of eternity to the anticipated cancelation of debt by those responsible for systematic exploitation during decades gone by. In *Eternal Employment*, there is no eternity, despite the title, but rather a long and monotonous embodiment of the social and capitalist standard time, controlled by the clock, the calendar and the annual work hours that mechanically accumulate year after year.[47]

Forest Calling and *Eternal Employment* are both similar in that they have an almost avant-garde experimental character (also a project quality according to the Arts Council) and both engage in a kind of investigation. They are also both abstract in that they abstract – "deselect, separate, remove"[48] – a sliver from the exploited forest in the first case – and in that they enact what Marx called "abstract labor" in the second case.[49] Thus, as it were, these drafts or projects also remain a form without content. However, even now *Forest Calling* fills its form with content of various kinds (walks, dance, performance, etc), but these activities can hardly affect the big question of the exploitation of natural resources. Rather, they burden the forest that is to be protected. In *Eternal Employment*, a basic idea is to let form constitute or rather completely replace content. The work becomes abstract by exposing pure work time, pure labor power, without regard to results, meaning or utility value. Rather, it becomes a celebration of speculation in capital growth as a supreme principle. Both of these works can also be described as unrealistic in relation to the real or actual and are thus both utopian and symbolic. *Forest Calling* stages an important action on sound ethical and ecological grounds, but can hardly contribute other than symbolically (3.7 hectares) to a better world. *Eternal Employment* stages the utopia in the present though without substance, in a specific place where nothing or anything can happen, and also becomes symbolic by taking a thought-provoking experiment to its

---

47 Eternal is in the title of the work, but that is not what it is about; it is about the temporal "indefinite," as it says alternately in the artists' proposal for *Eternal Employment:* https:// statenskonstrad.se/app/uploads/2018/09/3-Eternal_Employment-WrittenDescriptionA4.pdf [accessed 10/11/2020].

48 *Svenska Akademiens Ordbok [Swedish Academy Dictionary]* (1893): http://www.saob.se/artikel/?unik=A_0001-0087.Iv3b [accessed 10/26/2020].

49 Karl Marx, *Capital: Critique of Political Economy, Volume 1* (trans. Ben Fowkes, London: Penguin, 1990), p142.

extreme without delivering any clear will or vision of the future. In contrast to these two works, but especially the latter, *Ställbergs Gruva* appears to be free of abstraction, utopianism and symbolism. In an extremely concrete, yet both visionary and poetic way, the work here is really about creating a place for creative activity, thus saving and recreating a piece of society. That this work is art is a little odd, but no worse than that.

All three works, in the end, are interesting, ambitious, transgressive and problematic. All of them have (at least) one foot in the past in order to activate new futures. The artists behind *Eternal Employment* do not work themselves; they only ask the question "What is work?", now and in the future, but delegate to the future the search for an answer. *Forest Calling* is a collaborative work, with the aim of moving toward "a different future," one better than the ecological devastation we face unless urgent preventative measures are put in place, while *Ställbergs Gruva* does the slogging, collective work in the here and now based on the idea, I suppose, that the future is already here; there is nothing to do but roll up your sleeves and get to work.

Listen!

A Sculpture in the Square and a #MeToo Monument

//Anna Rådström

Camilla Akraka's sculpture *Listen!* stands in a corner of Rådhustorget in central Umeå.[1] Three and a half meters above the ground, on a shiny stainless-steel plate, supported by five steel tubes, sits a meter-tall feline. The polyester composite body is painted with glossy car paint: Mazda's Soul Red Crystal. The jaw is cast in Nordic gold bronze alloy.[2] The steel base is meant to resemble a cage, meaning that the animal has broken out and is now enjoying its freedom on top of its cage.[3] It flexes its muscles and throws the weight of its body forward. The throat is elongated, the ears are swept back, and the eyes are half-closed. The golden jaw is wide open: *Listen!* This permanent sculpture, a municipal monument to the #MeToo movement, firmly anchors the exclamation mark that is part of its title.

When, in this anthology, Håkan Nilsson describes the changing playing field within public art, he concludes that today it is more rare for this category of art to consist of "sculptures in the square." He also notes that "no more statues in the square" has become a mantra that characterizes the changing view of the permanent in recent decades.[4] Unsurprisingly, this changing view, which emphasizes the temporary and the changeable, also includes the monument. For example, art scholar Jeff Werner notes that one of the trends in contemporary public art practice and discourse "is a movement away from the monument and the autonomous artwork toward temporary art and

---

1   The artist includes an exclamation mark in the title of the piece. I also use it here because it is an exhortation. However, in most of the sources referred to in this article, this exclamation mark does not appear. For Akraka's inclusion of the exclamation mark see: Umeå Municipality, "Listen, metoo-monument" [Listen, metoo Monument] https://www.umea.se/umeakommun/kulturochfritid/kultur/konst/listenmetoomonument.4.2126f616dccfdd9431577b.html (accessed 02/09/2020). Updated 11/19/2020.

2   Umeå Municipality, "Listen, metoo-monument"; Sara Meidell, "Camilla Akraka skulpterade ett vrål" [Camilla Akraka Sculpted a Roar] *Västerbottens-Kuriren* (VK), 10/19/2019.

3   Umeå Municipality, "Listen, metoo-monument"; Umeå Municipality, "Klart med metoo-monument på Rådhustorget" [Green Light for metoo-monument in Rådhustorget] https://via.tt.se/pressmeddelande/klart-med-metoo-monument-pa-radhustorget?publisherId=1422393&released=3252651 (accessed 05/22/2020).

4   Håkan Nilsson, p. 43 and p. 181 in this anthology.

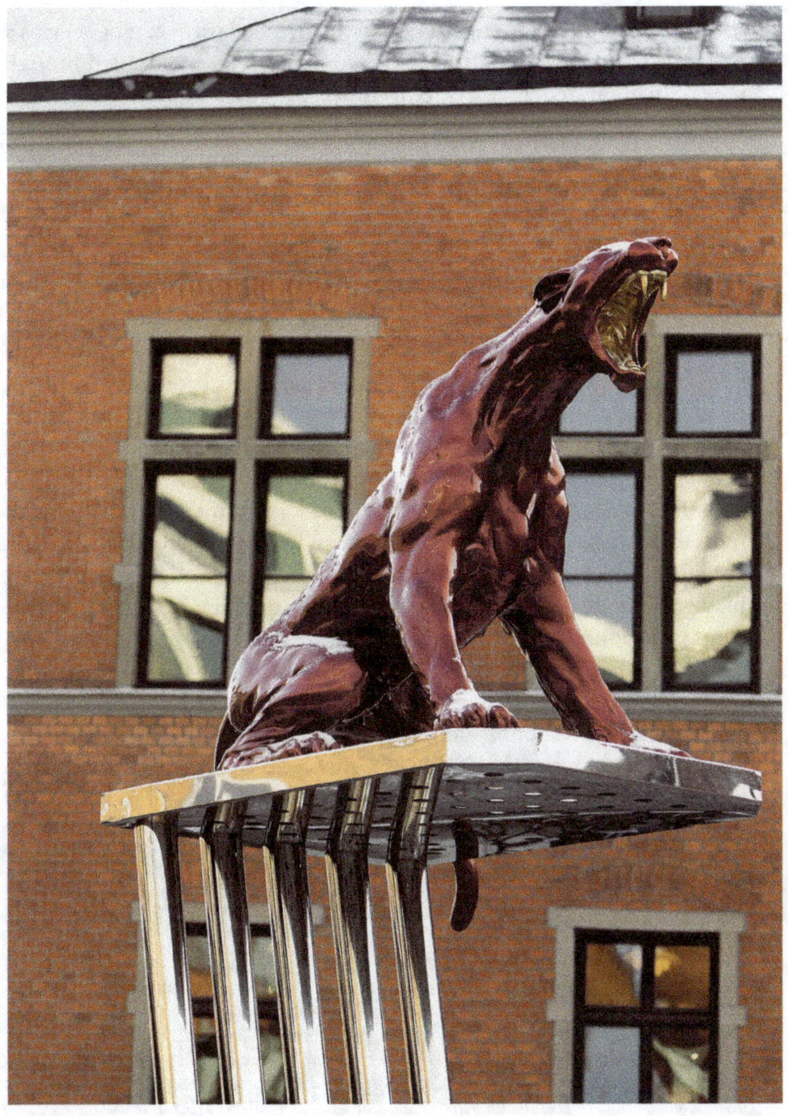

Camilla Akraka, Listen! Rådshustorget Umeå 2019. Photo: Fredrik Larsson
© Camilla Akraka / Bildupphovsrätt 2021

social art."[5] Based on these kinds of assessments, *Listen!* can be seen as a work that does not quite fit into the contemporary mold, even though it was inaugurated in early November 2019 and addresses a highly topical issue. Through its dual function as a monument and a sculpture in the square, the work can be seen as an example of the less attractive contemporary component of the "temporary/permanent" dichotomy. In this chapter, however, I want to address the critical potential that the permanent can possess by drawing attention to how a work like *Listen!* can provoke focus of thought and the production of ideas.[6]

The aim of the chapter is to examine the meaning-making and place-making processes that occur when Umeå municipality, against the backdrop of the feminist #MeToo movement, positions itself against sexual harassment through Akraka's work.[7] I am interested in what *Listen!* does, that is, what meaning the work helps to create. I am primarily interested in the meanings it contributes in its capacity as an animal sculpture in the square and as a monument to the #MeToo movement. I look at how the animal subtly contributes to thinking about contemporary #MeToo manifestations but also about feminist history, practice and analysis. A significant part of my argument centers around what happens when the feline, which has also been categorized as a cougar, is made a symbol of a movement that predominantly includes women. The association with the feline, with the cougar, creates ambivalence. In conclusion, I note that *Listen!* has become a landmark for the city of Umeå, and that the work is used to position the Umeå municipality as a progressive cultural municipality that actively takes a stand on gender equality.[8]

---

5   Jeff Werner, *Postdemokratisk kultur [Postdemocratic Culture]* (Halmstad: Gidlunds förlag, 2018), p. 96.

6   See also Håkan Nilsson's discussion of the critical potential of permanent art and its potential function as a space for reflection in a neoliberal age in which the changeable, ephemeral and flexible constitute a cornerstone, (p.14-15 in this anthology). See also Annika Öhrner's discussion of simplistic dichotomies in the chapter "The Art of the Million Program in Today's Living Environment."

7   The emphasis on the meaning making and place making processes situates the chapter in the vicinity of Jessica Sjöholm Skrubbe, in her *Skulptur i folkhemmet: Den offentliga skulpturens institutionalisering, referentialitet och rumsliga situationer 1940-1975 [Sculpture in the Swedish Welfare State: Institutionalisation, referentiality and spatial situations 1940-1975]*, doctoral thesis (Gothenburg & Stockholm: Makadam, 2007) and Beatrice Oroug, *Skulpturförflyttningar i det offentliga rummet: En analys av temporära konstprojekts effekter på det offentliga rummet och skulpturers betydelsebildningar [Moving Sculptures in the Public Space: An analysis of temporary art projects effects and significance on the public space and its sculptures]*, master's thesis (Huddinge: Södertörn University, 2019).

8   The investigation that follows is based on in situ studies of *Listen!* and the square setting. The

A monument is made: a brief background

Akraka's work was inaugurated in 2019, two years after what has come to be known as the #MeToo autumn. It was claimed at the time to be Sweden's, and perhaps the world's, first #MeToo monument.[9] The Umeå municipality erected it as a symbol of the fight against sexual harassment and it was dedicated to those who together broke the silence in connection with the metoo movement."[10] The idea behind the monument was conceived by public art curator Moa Krestesen. In an interview a few days before the inauguration, she explained that the idea was an expression of the frustration that she, like others, felt "when metoo picked up steam." She also said: "It's part of my job to take the initiative and see where there might be opportunities for art. Once I took a spot on the board, it was a unanimous decision that was carried out in a lengthy process."[11] So the emotional response could be used within the scope of the work description and the preparation of a municipal case began. Krestesen describes the process as lengthy, but in relation to the installation of a permanent public monument to a historical event, it appears to have proceeded rather quickly. In April 2018, the Cultural Committee decided to initiate a public design procurement, and in March 2019, Akraka was awarded the contract.[12] The Cultural Committee was in agreement, but the

---

literature spans a register that includes art history research, critical essays and classic feminist texts. Contemporary sources for facts and opinions on Akraka's work include news reports on SVT and SR, as well as articles, columns and letters to the editor, published mainly in daily newspapers. Information is also taken from the Umeå municipality website.

9   Filippa Armstrong & Fanny Vedin, "Första #metoo-monumentet i världen" [First #metoo Monument in the World], Sveriges Radio, P4 Västerbotten, 3/22/2019, https://sverigesradio.se/artikel/7181932 [accessed 02/09/20], "De bygger en rytande puma - som monument över metoo," [They Are Building a Roaring Cougar - as a monument to metoo] *Aftonbladet* 22/3 2019, Yvonne Rittvall, "Metoo-puma väcker känslor i Umeå," [Metoo-cougar stirs emotions in Umeå] *Dagens Nyheter* (DN) 1/11/2019.

10   Umeå municipality, "Listen, metoo-monument."

11   Alexzandra Granath, "Kommunen om metoo-puman: 'Konst måste få kosta'" [The Municipality on the metoo Cougar: 'Art must cost'] SVT Nyheter, Västerbotten, 10/29/2019, https://www.svt.se/nyheter/lokalt/vasterbotten/kommunen-om-metoo-puman-konst-maste-fa-kosta [accessed 08/17/2020].

12   For information on the decision date, see Umeå Municipality, "Klart med metoo-monument på Rådhustorget" [Green Light for metoo-monument in Rådhustorget]. The municipality's call for monument proposals was aimed at active professional artists with at least 5 years of university education or equivalent. The procurement process was carried out in three stages: application; selection for the award of the sketch assignment; decision on the commission. See Umeå Municipality, "Gestaltningsupphandlingar, Uppdrag #metoo-monument på Rådshustorget i Umeå," [Design Procurements, Commission #metoo-monument on Rådshustorget in Umeå] https://www.umea.se/umeakommun/kulturochfritid/kultur/konst/foryr...stnarer/gestaltningsup-

process was also fraught with conflict. Representatives of the Sweden Democrats questioned the cost of the work, and the media described the monument as a "watershed moment among citizens."[13]

However, more than half of the cost was covered by funds from a 1970s donation from *Sparbanken* to the municipality to be used for art in Rådhustorget.[14] The fact that it was placed in the newly rebuilt square was thus largely due to funding. Added to this was the municipality's awareness of the impact of the location. "The square," the municipality writes in the assignment description, "is an important democratic meeting place all year round," and by placing the work "in the center of town, it symbolizes an active stance of zero tolerance for sexual harassment and abuse – locally, nationally and globally."[15] The municipality thus shows an awareness of the symbolic value of public art, which is also reflected in the final assessment of Akraka's work.

In making the selection from among the proposals submitted, the evaluation team considered the following four aspects: "aesthetic and artistic value of the material presented"; "artistic originality"; "artistic expression in relation to the purpose of the work"; and "the artist's brief description of how they intend to approach the assignment."[16] The reasoning for the decision was published in the press release accompanying the award decision. It stated that Akraka's proposal corresponds well with the municipality's stance against sexual harassment; that class, gender, ethnicity and age are themes consistently

---

phandlingar.4.20c92392148f96bd89f18adc.html [accessed 08/01/20]. The page is now removed. It is documented by the author.

13 Regarding the debate in the municipal council where the cost of the #MeToo monument was questioned by the Sweden Democrats, see: Kerstin Erikson, "Het debatt om Metoo-puman i fullmäktige" [Heated Debate about Metoo-cougar in Council] *Västerbottens-Kuriren* (VK) 10/29/2019; Anne Pettersson, "Puman direkt in i hetluften" [Cougar Immediately Raises Temperatures], *Folkbladet* 10/29/2019. On the Metoo monument as a watershed moment, see: Granath, "Kommunen om metoo-puman: 'Konst måste få kosta'" [The Municipality on the metoo Cougar: 'Art must cost'].

14 Umeå Municipality, "Listen, metoo-monument." The budget for the artwork was SEK 500,000 plus approx. SEK 100,000 for the three artists who were awarded the sketch assignment. The donation from *Sparbanken* covered approximately SEK 350,000 while the rest was taken from the culture committee's budget for the purchase of art.

15 Umeå Municipality, "Gestaltningsupphandlingar, Uppdrag #metoo-monument på Rådshustorget i Umeå." op.cit.

16 Ibid. The evaluators included Moa Krestesen, art curator and project manager for procurement, Helena Wikström, artist representative and artistic director of Vita kuben [The White Cube], Åsa Adolfsson, art educator and Anja Boman, curator. Among the invited representatives was Jennie Forsberg, art historian and development manager for the Women's History Museum, Umeå Municipality.

covered in her artistic practice, and that her work often challenges entrenched positions in the same way as those who broke the silence during the #MeToo movement. The reasoning concludes: "The strong visual expression of her work combined with the meaningful symbolic elements form a multi-faceted design that brings a new aesthetic approach to Umeå's public space."[17] While the evaluators' justification reflects the selection aspects without going into further description of the work, the press release states that the symbolic elements consist of "male-coded materials and symbols of power, such as steel, car paint and muscle mass."[18]

The press release also contains wording relevant to my study, since it relates to the central categorization of the red-lacquered feline. It reads: "The artwork is called 'Listen' and depicts a cougar [...]."[19] Another key phrase appears in an article published shortly thereafter. Krestesen is reported here as saying: "It [the cougar] is tall and I think it can also be a landmark. 'See you at the cougar,' one can both stand under, behind or next to it [...]."[20] The cougar theme is further reinforced when an accident occurred in early summer 2020. A skylift backed into *Listen!* during the renovation of the façade of city architect Fredrik Olaus Lindström's brick-red town hall from the early 1890s (now a restaurant). Commenting on the incident, Lars Sahlin, the municipality's deputy head of culture, said: "It was an accident. It can happen in the best of families."[21] The statement was probably warranted due to the fact that the restoration work was carried out by a contractor hired by the municipality, but it can also be interpreted as an expression of a desire to emphasize that the damage was not intentional. Following the damage assessment, the municipality's website stated that *Listen!* – which was now called not only "the cougar" but also "the metoo cougar" – would be moved for repair and then returned to the square.[22]

---

17 Umeå Municipality, "Klart med metoo-monument på Rådhustorget" [Green Light for metoo-monument in Rådhustorget]

18 Ibid.

19 Ibid.

20 Anne Pettersson, "Metoo-monument ska sättas på upp på Rådhustorget: 'Har en uppkäftighet'," [Metoo Monument to be Put up on Rådhustorget: 'Causes a stir'] *Folkbladet* 3/22/2019.

21 Anders Wynne, "Metoo-puman skadad – tar lång tid att återställa i ursprungligt skick" [Metoo Cougar Damaged – Will take a long time to restore to its original condition], *Västerbottens kuriren* (VK) 6/2/2020.

22 Umeå Municipality, "Me too-puman är skadad och flyttas för att lagas" [Me too Cougar is Damaged and is Being Moved for Repairs]. https://www.umea.se/umeakommun/kulturochfritid/kultur/konst/arkivpumanarskadadochflyttasforattlagas.5.2adf2b2d1724e9f24668ee0.html

The examples above communicate something different from what is simultaneously explained via a municipal website that aims to educate the public on *Listen!*. When asked why the municipality has chosen a cougar, the answer is: "The artist has not identified the species of animal; it could be a cougar and has become so in popular speech. It could also be another type of feline." [23] It is not clear what this other animal is, but according to Akraka, it could be a panther.[24]

Design and location play a clear role in the process of creating meaning and space. Equally important are the words used in connection with the design and how this relates to the tasks assigned to it. The word "cougar," which categorizes the sculpture, has crept into municipal documents; it has found its way into "popular speech" and spread through the media, as many of the titles in the article's notations testify. The impact of categorization on meaning making cannot be ignored. A cougar is a large feline, but it is also a slang word. Regarding the latter, the word is defined in letters to the editor and columns discussing *Listen!*. It is defined in different ways: a cougar can be an attractive woman.[25] Alternatively: a cougar can be a sexually attractive woman.[26] Or: a cougar is "a mature woman who is sexually attracted to and attracts younger men."[27] Whatever definition is assumed, they participate in the production of meaning in which the cougar is thought to be female and therefore a (sexualized) woman.

[accessed 08/01/2020]. The page was published on 06/05/20 and has since been removed. It is documented by the author. The main part of this chapter was written before *Listen!* was returned to its place in the square and partly exists in an interstice. In this interstice, there is no reason to shift focus from presence to absence – my attention is fully directed toward the enthroned animal.

23 Umeå municipality, "Listen, metoo-monument."

24 Meidell, "Camilla Akraka skulpterade ett vrål" [Camilla Akraka Sculpted a Roar], op.cit.

25 Daniel Persson, "Ryt till mot politisk konst" [Roar Against Political Art] 11/26/2019, https://timbro.se/smedjan/ryt-till-mot-politisk-konst/ [accessed 05/22/22].

26 Kjerstin, "Obegripligt och tankelöst med röd puma" [Incomprehensible and thoughtless with red cougar] Ordet fritt [The Word is Free], Västerbottens-Kuriren (VK) 5/7/2019.

27 Johanna Lindqvist, Friday column, "Fortsätt lyssna på hennes vrål" [Keep Listening to Her Roar], *Folkbladet* 11/1/2019.

The cougar, the feline and #MeToo

Based on the above, "cougar," or the "#MeToo cougar," manifests as a meaning-making guide for the general public.[28] If the feline had been defined as a panther, the interpretive guide would not have been the same.[29] But irrespective of the species chosen, one essential thing would remain – the traditional association between the woman and the animal. Accordingly, as this study delves into meaning-making in relation to #MeToo, women's history and feminist thought, the "cougar" will be discussed alongside the non-species specific feline.

#MeToo can be traced back to 2006 in the US, when women's rights activist Tarana Burke drew attention to sexual violence against racialized black women by consistently emphasizing the importance of adding a "me too" to every story of abuse. Eleven years later, in 2017, actor Alyssa Milano added a hashtag to "metoo," emphasizing the use of social media. Today, #MeToo is a global movement highlighting the critical importance of speaking up and sharing individual experiences. The manifestations cast a spotlight on "a patriarchal social structure that allows the perpetrator, usually a man, to abuse his position of power by committing sexually motivated acts that vary in their degree of criminality."[30] The translated description above was formulated by political scientist Maud Eduards for the *Nationalencyklopedin* and does not convey anything particularly new. Rather, it is – to paraphrase the subtitle of one of Rebecca Solnit's books – a description of an old conflict to which a new chapter has been added. Yet, according to Solnit, the watershed moment created by #MeToo did bring something new. What was new, she notes, was not that women spoke out, but that people listened.[31]

---

28   Here, I borrow Dan Karlholm's line of thinking. In his discussion of what a monument can be, he argues that some form of verbal anchorage on, or in proximity to, an the monument, is one crucial aspect. Such an anchor is an inscription that serves not as title but an "interpretive guide and motive." See "Det tomma monumentet" [The Empty Monument], in *Vad betyder verket?: konstvetenskapliga studier kring måleri, skulptur, stadsplanering och arkitektur* [*What Does the Artwork Mean?: Art historical studies around painting, sculpture, urban planning and architecture*], ed. Thomas Hall, Ewa Kron & Lempi Borgwik (Stockholm: Department of Art History, Stockholm University, 2001), p. 45.

29   The impact this may have on meaning making is discussed later in the chapter.

30   Maud Eduards, "me too-rörelsen," [The me too Movement] in *Nationalencyklopedin* [NE], https://www-ne-se.till.biblextern.sh.se/uppslagsverk/encyklopedi/l%C3%A5ng/me-too-r%C3%B6relsen (accessed 7/30/2020).

31   Rebecca Solnit, *Whose Story is This: Old Conflicts; New Chapters* (London: Granata Publications, 2019), p. 7.

Where does *Listen!* fit into all of this, apart from the fact that the sculpture/ monument has also been said to have created a watershed moment? Is it not only a textbook example of biologism but also an example of anthropomorphism? Are women's accounts of abuse expressed through the jaws of the cougar? Are their experiences projected onto the feline's body? I contend the answer is no; it is not a textbook example of either, though it is an example that generates ambivalence. This is not necessarily negative, however. Ambivalence is a highly active ingredient in meaning-making processes and is central to feminist thought. The writer, philosopher and literary scholar Hélène Cixous, for example, argues for "Thinking of/on both sides."[32] While Peggy Phelan, a leading scholar in performance studies, argues that feminism "makes ambivalence a necessary worldview. In these days of hideous fundamentalism, the capacity to acknowledge ambivalence is revolutionary."[33] So, while I raise the red flag for biologism and anthropomorphism, I also see that the cougar/feline in the square - the public space *par excellence* - is anchoring a call to action: *Listen!* The call harkens back to #MeToo, as well as other inseparable chapters of feminist struggle. The meaning making that unfolds is harrowing but can also be empowering.

Thoughtprints

The concept "thoughtprints" signals the imprint of the cougar/feline on thinking while indicating that the activity of thinking itself also leaves traces.[34] Thinking, argues cultural theorist Mieke Bal, is neither individual, particular nor bound to the time in which ideas are articulated. The life of thoughts is similar to the life of images: they are both enduring but also changeable and are maintained

32 Hélène Cixous & Mireille Calle-Gruber, *Hélène Cixous: Rootprints: Memory and Life Writing* (London & New York: Routledge, 1997), p. 25.

33 Peggy Phelan, "Feminism Makes Ambivalence a Necessary Worldview," *ArtForum*, 2 (2003) p. 149. I have drawn on both Cixous' and Phelan's ideas about ambivalence in an earlier text. See "Ambivalens och ett 'emellan': Reflektioner genom och runtomkring ett av Annika von Hausswolffs fotografier" [Ambivalence and an 'In Between': Reflections through and around one of Annika von Hausswolff's photographs], in *Att känna sig fram: Känslor i humanistisk genusforskning*, [*To Feel One's Way: Feelings in gender studies within the humanities*] ed. Annelie Bränström Öhman, Maria Jönsson & Ingeborg Svensson (Umeå: h:ström-Text och kultur, 2011), pp. 168–189.

34 The concept appears in critical animal studies based on Jacques Derrida. See Anne E Berger & Martha Segarra's "Thoughtprints," *Critical Studies*, 35 (2011), pp. 3-22.

collectively. They are subject to debate and thus provoke thinking that is not primarily *about* the world but takes place *with*, *through* and *in* the world, including its visual manifestations. We do not "read" the thoughts conveyed in an image but create it and interact with it.[35] Bal's performatively rooted reasoning is significant for the thinking that occurs here, even though *Listen!* is not an image but a public sculpture that also serves as a monument.

In her analysis of the work on the redesign of Stortorget in Kalmar in the early 2000s, architect Catharina Gabrielsson highlights the following: "The geometric pattern on the surface of the manhole cover is reminiscent of a large paw print, as if a monster has wandered over the site; monster derives from (Latin) *monere* to show, urge or recall, the etymological roots of the monument."[36] Based on this observation and linguistic derivation, the cougar in Rådhustorget in Umeå can be likened to a monster. It does not leave indexical paw prints on the stone pavement, but its red, muscular and big jawed appearance creates a presence that envelops the space. From its elevated, distant position in a corner of the square, it can also be said to be reminiscent of something else.

When I discuss *Listen!* in the context of the cougar and the feline, it inevitably highlights the part of Western women's history that has struggled for centuries with associations to the animal, to the female. The struggle can be traced in the classic and indispensable writing of the author and philosopher Mary Wollstonecraft, *A Vindication of the Rights of Woman* (1792). When clarifying her own position in relation to men, she feels compelled to emphasize that she is a woman, doing so while referring to the "government of the physical world", where "it is observable that the female in point of strength is, in general, inferior to the male. This is the law of nature; and it does not appear to be suspended or abrogated in favour of woman."[37]

The struggle takes center stage almost 160 years later when the philosopher

---

35   Mike Bal, "Thinking in Film," in *Thinking in the World*, ed. Jill Bennet & Mary Zournazi (London & New York: Bloomsbury Academic 2020), p. 173.

36   Catharina Gabrielsson, *Att göra skillnad: Det offentliga rummet som medium för konst, arkitektur och politiska föreställningar* [*To Make a Difference: Public Space as a medium for art, architecture and concepts of the political*] doctoral thesis (Stockholm: Royal Institute of Technology, 2007), p. 398.

37   Mary Wollstonecraft, "A Vindication of the Rights of Woman: With Strictures on Political and Moral Subjects", in *The Works of Mary Wollstonecraft*, ed. Janet Todd & Marilyn Butler volume 5 , (London: William Pickering 1989), p. 74.

Simone de Beauvoir writes her seminal analysis in *The Second Sex* (1949). Like Wollstonecraft, she proclaims her biological sex and addresses the female-male dichotomy. Though, in her case the tone is different. The study is divided into two books. The first book, *Facts and Myths* begins with a discussion of "Destiny". The first chapter of this part is called "The Data of Biology" and begins with a definitional question:

> Woman? Very simple, say the fanciers of simple formulas; she is a womb, an ovary; she is female – this word is sufficient to define her. In the mouth of a man the epithet female has the sound of an insult, yet he is not ashamed of his animal nature; on the contrary, he is proud if someone says of him: 'He is a male!' The term 'female' is derogatory not because it emphasizes woman's animality, but because it imprisons her in her sex [...].38

Beauvoir then proceeds at a brisk pace and in colorful language with a litany of clichéd descriptions of the behavior of different species of females to show the man's distaste and fear of castration, but also his imaginative powers of sexual conquest and domination. As for the latter, she writes: "[...] the most superb wild beasts – the tigress, the lioness, the panther – bed down slavishly under the imperial embrace of the male."39 The analysis does not explicitly include the cougar, but it does point to reasons why the idea production surrounding "the female" causes friction. There are elements not only of biologism but also of sexism – even the strongest female is subordinated to the male.

Biology as a woman's destiny did not end after Beauvoir had dissected it, but where she had used the female feline to paint a linguistic picture of submission, seven decades later Camilla Akraka brings out a sculptural feline that signals the radical opposite and thus disrupts the "law of nature" described above. When Akraka designed the proposal for *Listen!*, she was already working with a feline theme. An example of this can be found in her solo exhibition *Colonial Rooms* at *Passagen* in Linköping (2014). This included three panthers (*Sisters*) and a bull. The constellation was described by one critic as follows:

---

38   Simone de Beauvoir, *The Second Sex* (London: Vintage, 1997), p. 35. The second book of the study is "Woman's Life Today".

39   Ibid.

Three female panthers walking in a circle (the feminine) and
a toppled bull (obviously the masculine) create a dramatic scene. The patterns of fixed structures, in the encounter with the
three-dimensional animals, subtly here become a metaphor for
movement and change of - perhaps position and power?40

The gender choreography staged here differs from the scene of submission
in the chapter "The Data of Biology". Here it is the regal male bull, one
of the symbols of male potency, that is in a vulnerable position.

The exhibition in Linköping reveals that her work deals with colonial
spaces, which means working with both history and the present, and
with issues of identity and power.[41] The work with these spaces can
be linked to the artist's own experiences. Akraka, who was born in
London in 1968 and grew up in Stockholm, where she studied at the
Royal College of Art, explains in an interview with cultural editor
Sara Meidell how the experience of being black and growing up in
Sweden in the 1970s contributed to her decision to apply for the Umeå
municipality's monument assignment. She says: "Being considered less
worthy because of who you were born as, is what the metoo movement
is fundamentally protesting against."[42]

In the interview, Meidell raises the issue of the word "cougar." She
obviously has the slang word in mind and seems to find it problematic.
Meidell asks Akraka how she sees "an objectifying concept about
women" coming to symbolize what #MeToo stands for. To this, the
artist replies that it can be argued that the term is being reclaimed.
But at the same time, she says, it is interesting that the feline has been
interpreted as a cougar and not a panther, which was also an option.

---

40   Lotta Ekfeldt, "Med fokus på det koloniala" [With Focus on the Colonial], *Om konst: konstnärer skriver om konst [On Art: Artists write about art]*, 09/01/2019, https://omkonst.se/14-akra-ka-camilla.shtml [accessed 05/22/20].

41   Two years after *Colonial Rooms, Sisters* was exhibited at Vallentuna Kulturhus. According to the title of one of the exhibition's press items, the three panther females now represented "the clash between the colonial era and the present and the encounter between African and Scandinavian nature." See Anna Wilson, "Pantersystrar till Konstkuben," [Panther Sisters to Konstkuben] *Mitt i Kungsholmen* 08/16/2016, https://www.mitti.se/nyheter/pantersystrar-till-konstkuben/lmphp!394407/ (accessed 07/27/2020). Akraka has also carried out *Shades of the Tiger* (2019), a public sculpture commission for the Agora activity center in Skäggetorp, Linköping, which is funded by the municipal real estate company Lejonfastigheter. See Susanne Hasselqvist, "Tiger till Skäggetorp" [Tiger to Skäggetorp] in *Corren* 02/17/2017, https://corren.se/nyheter/linkop-ing/tiger-till-skaggetorp-om4508708.aspx (accessed 11/20/28).

42   Meidell, "Camilla Akraka skulpterade ett vrål" [Camilla Akraka Sculpted a Roar], op.cit.

The intention of the proposal, she says, was to "broaden the idea of the feline – a panther can also be a black jaguar or a leopard, it's just a matter of pigmentation."[43] Here, she is presumably referring to the fact that an excess of the color pigment melanin can cause leopards and jaguars, for example, to turn black instead of spotted.[44] This means we cannot base our categorizations of felines on their pigmentation. But there is uncertainty surrounding how to interpret the "just pigment" statement in the context surrounding *Listen!*. The #MeToo movement began through Burke's efforts to make visible sexual violence against racialized black women but has broadened to include others. Is Akraka's statement alluding to this and emphasizing the universality of her work beyond issues of race (and gender)?[45] In other words, is she saying that #MeToo affects and concerns everyone?

When a work is introduced to its audience, the artist's intentions are not decisive for the viewers' production of meaning, and Akraka's intention to "broaden the concept of the feline" seems to have gone unnoticed. Instead, a gender-specific slang word gets stuck in the minds of the viewers, which must be reclaimed for use in the context of #MeToo. Reclaiming a term that, after all, may never have been one's own, is neither straightforward nor without its perils. Words matter and they tend to carry baggage, or as filmmaker and writer Trinh T. Minh-ha puts it: "Words empty out with age. Die and rise again, accordingly invested with new meanings, and always equipped with a secondhand memory." [46] *Listen!* has given rise to a process to reclaim the word "cougar." This can be considered as a form of "empowerment in action."

In the spring of 2019, shortly after the assessment panel announced its choice of Akraka's work, art historian Katrin Steen wrote a column contrasting the cougar with the lion – the ubiquitous symbol of power in history and in the public sphere. The lion is described both as a male with a thick mane and as a female member of the pride, but no gender

---

43   Ibid.

44   Roland Johansson, "Kattdjur – evolutionens mästerverk" ["Felines - Evolution's masterpiece,"] *WWF Magasin*, 1 (2020), p. 19.

45   Akraka's statement about the black panther can also be associated with the Black Panther Party, which was formed in the United States in the mid-1960s. When viewed in relation to this party and to the recent Black Lives Matter movement, it is not a question of "just pigment."

46   Trinh T. Minh-ha, "Difference: A Special Third World Women Issue," *Feminist Review*, 25:2 (1987), p. 5. The power of words became well known through the work of philosopher J.L. Austin. See *How to Do Things with Words* (Oxford: Oxford University Press, 1962).

definitions are made for the cougar. This does not mean, however, that it necessarily remains genderless. If the reader has the slang word "cougar" in her or his vocabulary, the association with the female easily comes to mind. The cougar is said to sneak into the game but once in the square it attracts attention. Steen describes how it roars, flexes its muscles and gets ready to attack while reminding us of #MeToo and the ongoing struggle. However, the cougar's roar is said to be possibly drowned out by delighted cheers.[47]

Steen's short and popular chronicle stimulates thoughts about the square as a stage where performative actions take place. They play out physically in reality or imaginatively inside the head of the person standing or moving across the square. A square is, as Umeå municipality and many others point out, an important democratic meeting place, but it is also "the arena of power *per se*."[48] Power can take many forms, including gendered power structures. In feminist practice and theory, this form of power is of course something that is analyzed and challenged. Two important tools in this work are the voice and the gaze. These tools are used both practically and analytically.

Listen! is placed in the south-east corner of Rådhustorget. In the north-west corner one finds Sean Henry's sculpture *Standing Man*. Henry's silent, solitary male figure arrived temporarily in the square via Andersson Sandström gallery in 2007 and immediately aroused photographic fervor and nurturing feelings. Over the years, the lone man has been fitted with a hat and scarf as protection against the often cold weather. The sculpture was then purchased by Umeå municipality in 2008 and has since found a permanent home in its corner, apart from a period in 2016-2017 when the square was being rebuilt. A contributor, whose real concern is to call for nameplates for the two works, notes the eye-catching constellation that has been staged. He refers to *Listen!* as "cougar," and wonders if there is a pedagogical motivation behind the lack of information, describing the scene as follows: "Two distinctive poles of male and female talking to, or possibly past, each other across the square."[49] The question of pedagogy is highly relevant, and

---

47   Katrin Steen, "En puma tar plats bland lejonen" [A Cougar is Taking Place Among the Lions], Folkbladet 04/02/2019. For a broader and deeper discussion of the lion's role in public space, see Oscar Svanelid's chapter "Safety Art: On art as a security/safety measure for public spaces" in this anthology.

48   Jeff Werner, *Postdemokratisk kultur [Postdemocratic Culture]*, op.cit., p. 38.

49   Anders (Verner) Kristoffersson, Ordet fritt: "Varför anonyma konstverk på Rådhustorget?" [The Word is Free: "Why anonymous works of art on Rådhustorget?"], *Västerbottens kuriren* (VK)

not just in terms of nameplates. It seems unlikely that the diagonal across Rådshustorget, which both connects and distances, was not taken into account in the installation of *Listen!* My interpretation is that the mute, solitary man, by being clearly addressed by the feline, is forced into a relationship. As I stand beneath the cougar, I trace an imaginary roar that is flung diagonally across the square. The roar hits one side of *Standing man's* face. Here a connection arises with the other tool mentioned above: the gaze. The scene created and the imaginary diagonal roar evokes an interesting association with artist Barbara Kruger's iconic photomontage *Untitled (Your gaze hits the side of my face)* (1981). But where Kruger's work addresses the problem of the ubiquitous male gaze, here it raises questions about the roar of the female cougar and its reception. Does the roar enter the ear of the closed male figure?

A golden jaw

On the aforementioned municipal website dedicated to *Listen!* the question is asked: "Why does it roar, cougars can't roar?" The municipality answers: "But art can roar, art is free to be shaped and to express itself in a different way than reality."[50] Despite the municipality's ode to the freedom of art, it becomes clear here how a categorization ("cougar") can limit a voice, a roar.

The author and art critic John Berger is one of many who have discussed the relationship between the human and non-human animals. In this discussion the question of language is fundamental. He writes that the animal's "lack of common language, its silence, guarantees its distance, its distinctness, its exclusion, from and of man."[51] Berger here uses "man" as a stand-in for the "human being". If his formulation were to be slightly reworked and placed in relation to the scene in Rådhustorget, the following could be suggested: the language of the

---

03/18/2020.

50 Umeå Municipality, "Listen, metoo-monument." Here it would be possible to debate the municipality's ambition to educate its citizens, and to insert Hanno Rauterberg's assertion that the emancipatory effect of the #MeToo movement lies in the fact that it does not have to wait for the help of institutions. But such a discussion is not within the scope of this chapter. See Hanno Rauterberg, *Hur fri är konsten? Den nya kulturstriden och liberalismens kris [How Free is Art? The New Cultural Clash and the Crisis of Liberalism]* (Gothenburg: Daidalos, 2019), p. 91.

51 John Berger, *About Looking [Electronic resource]* (Knopf Doubleday Publishing Group, 2011) pp. 11-12.

female human exists, she is not silent, nevertheless there is a distance, a distinction, her exclusion from and of man (in reference to biology). To this can be added a short passage from Jacques Rancière's *Ten Theses on Politics*. In the eighth thesis, Rancière explains an effective ruling technique, a sure way to deny another political animal (i.e., a human being) agency. If there is someone you do not want to acknowledge as a political being, you should start by not acknowledging them as the bearer of politicalness, you should not seek to understand what is being said, nor should you hear the utterance made.[52] Such a technique throws the speaker out of balance unless they are in a position to directly resist by demanding that their thoughts be heard. This domination technique can be used in different situations, including when sexual abuse and harassment have been reported during the age of #MeToo.

As early as the 1970s, social psychologist Berit Ås analyzed techniques of domination, including invisibilization. In the early 2000s, the *Empowerment Network at Stockholm University* (ENSU) took on the task of challenging these techniques and developed both counterstrategies and what they called affirmation techniques. Consequently, the domination technique of invisibility was countered by the counterstrategy of claiming space, and this strategy was reinforced by an affirmation technique aimed at visibility.[53] Similar strategies become relevant when voice and listening are emphasized.

A cougar can thus, according to Umeå municipality's website, not roar. No, but it has a call. A special issue of *WWF Magasin* takes a closer look at all the world's cats. They are described as evolution's masterpieces and are said to be famous for their calls. The lion, the leopard and the jaguar roar. And while the tiger does not roar, it has a mighty call. The cougar, on the other hand, "has a famous scream that sounds a bit like a woman in distress."[54] The description does not specify whether this applies to females as well as males, but it fits poorly with the roar supposed to emanate from the golden jaw. I suggest, however, the sound can be linked on a metaphorical level to the #MeToo monument's task of memorializing. It recalls what Rebecca Solnit points out, namely that feminism, like other human rights movements, has consisted of a

---

52   Jacques Rancière, "Ten Theses on Politics," *Theory and Event*, 5:2 (2001), p. 10.

53   Louise Andersson & Anna Lena Lindgren, "Feministiska perspektiv på konstpedagogik" [Feminist Perspectives on Art Education], in *Konstfeminism: Strategier och effekter i Sverige från 1970-talet till idag* [*Art Feminism: Strategies and Consequences in Sweden from the 1970s to the present*], ed. Anna Nyström, Louise Andersson et.al. (Stockholm: Atlas, 2005), p. 169.

54   Johansson, "Kattdjur – evolutionens mästerverk" ["Felines - Evolution's masterpiece,"] op.sit. p.17

process whereby voices have been amplified until they have carried the weight by themselves; through solidarity, weaker voices come together so that they are powerful enough to stand up to those whom Solnit calls dictators.[55] This process of the gathering force of the dominated, which I argue is made possible by the technique of affirmation, is a prerequisite for the kind of impact that #MeToo has had and continues to have.

The process of empowerment is a fundamental part of feminism's work to ensure that women are ready, willing and able to make their voices heard.[56] *Listen!* gives a reminder of the process of sharing experiences but also of how those who do not have experiences to share react when they learn about those of others. The reminder makes clear that there were those who listened even before #MeToo. The Swedish translation (*Våldtäkt*) of Susan Brownmiller's seismic and eye-opening study on rape was published in 1977, three years after it was first published in the US under the longer title *Against Our Will. Men, Women and Rape*. The study begins with "A Personal Statement." The first lines read: "The question most often asked of me while I was writing this book was short, direct and irritating. 'Have you ever been raped?' My answer was equally direct: 'No'."[57] Brownmiller describes how listening to those who had these experiences fundamentally changed her perception of what rape is and motivated her to write the book, which in turn changed many other people's views.

Another description is given by Maria-Pia Boëthius in *Skylla sig själv: En bok om våldtäkt (Blaming yourself. A book about rape)*. Here, traumatic experiences are described while the *Sexualbrottsutredningens* (Sexual Offences Inquiry's) proposal for a new legal wording on rape is opposed. The first chapter begins with a description of Sweden's first so-called sensitivity training course for women at the Tylösand beach resort in January 1975. Boëthius, who was one of the participants, recalls how they talked, compared stories and rejoiced in the discovery that they were not "crazy."[58] Other women had the same experiences; they were not alone. Thus, this was, *avant la lettre*, a clear moment of "me too". The first edition of the book was published in 1976 and the

---

55 Solnit, *Whose Story is This*, op.cit., p. 36.

56 I am referring to the song "Befrielsen är nära" [Liberation is near] in Margareta Garpe and Suzanne Osten's 1974 play *Jösses flickor [Jeez Girls!]*.

57 Susan Browmiller, *Against Our Will. Men, Women and Rape* (New York: Fawcett Books, 1975), p. 7.

58 Maria Pia Boëthius, *Skylla sig själv: En bok om våldtäkt [Blaming Oneself. A book about rape]*, 2nd edition. (Stockholm: Liber Förlag, 1981), pp. 7-8.

second edition came out in 1981. In the new preface to the otherwise unedited text, Boëthius writes: "Today I understand that it is already a piece of the puzzle in Swedish women's history. Time moves fast. What happened barely five years ago is already 'history'."[59]

In the assignment description that follows the design procurement for the #MeToo monument on Rådhustorget, Umeå municipality writes that there is a before and an after #MeToo. The future monument is described as a "contemporary document" and a brief contemporary historical background is given with references to Tarana Burke and the #MeToo autumn of 2017.[60] When historian Kerstin Nordlander receives a quick question from a journalist about the #MeToo monument, she expresses criticism of the idea and argues that Umeå municipality is acting too soon. #MeToo is an important movement, but it is not yet possible to know whether it will lead to change, she says. In order to bring about change, she believes that it is new legislation that is needed. And she continues, "[t]he risk is that in five years, no one will know what the metoo cougar stands for. Then the monument will just be a cat sitting in the square [...]."[61]

Presently, it is not possible to speak fully of a "post-MeToo"; the movement is still creating ripples and facing a backlash. But just because it is not yet possible to talk about an after does not mean that it is impossible to talk about #MeToo. It is also possible, as journalist Alexandra Pascalidou does, to adopt the perspective of a different moment in time. When the anthology *Me too: så går vi vidare – Röster, redskap och råd* [*Me Too: Moving Forward – Voices, tools and advice*] was published in 2017, she was asked whether it was too soon to publish the book. Was there not a risk that important stories would be excluded? Pascalidou replied: "It's not too early. It's too late."[62]

Debating whether it is too early or too late to recognize, or document, an ongoing event is beyond the scope of this chapter. What is important

---

59 Ibid., p. 5.

60 Umeå Municipality, "Gestaltningsupphandlingar, Uppdrag #metoo-monument på Rådhustorget i Umeå" [Design procurement, Commission #metoo monument in Rådhustorget in Umeå]. As Sjöholm Skrubbe points out, it is not possible to make a general distinction between a memorial and a monument. The word monument comes from the Latin *monumentum* meaning memorial (see Sjöholm Skrubbe 2007, footnote 44, p. 326).

61 Rittvall, "Metoo-puma väcker känslor i Umeå" [Metoo Cougar Stirs Emotions in Umeå], op.cit.

62 Johanna Palm, "Pascalidou om nya boken: Årtusenden av tystnad och tabun bryts äntligen" [Pascalidou on the New Book: Millennia of silence and taboo finally broken], SVT Nyheter 11/3/2017, https://www.svt.se/kultur/metoo-sa-gar-vi-vidare-alexandra-pascalidou (accessed 11/29/20).

here is the meaning-making of which *Listen!* is a part and the history that accompanies it. A monument that ceases to memorialize is no longer a monument in the strictest sense of the term, and it matters little whether the feline is called a cougar or a panther. It is impossible to know what future meaning-making processes the monument will be a part of, but that meaning-making will continue is fairly certain. *Listen!* is therefore built to stand the test of time. The work has its sights set on permanence and continuous relevance.

The exclamation mark on the square

In her comprehensive study of public sculptures in the Swedish public domain from 1940-1975, art scholar Jessica Sjöholm Skrubbe highlights depictions of animals as a common motif. Animals native to Sweden dominate: bears, deer and sometimes lynx. The sculptures, often depicting cubs playing or females with cubs, are found on school grounds, in public parks and residential areas. This, writes Sjöholm Skrubbe, "means that it is easy to see these sculptures as a kind of fable – that is, that the themes in the sculptures can be transferred to a large extent to the human condition."[63] For example, in residential areas, the relationship between female/mother and kid/child is a common theme, leading to the metaphorical reference to stereotypical notions of the woman as mother and the home as her domain.[64] Sjöholm Skrubbe thus shows how a sculptural choreography of gender, under the guise of the animal, is played out in the era of *Folkhemmet* (the golden age of the welfare state).

Today, *Folkhemmet* has more or less been dismantled, but the animal has not disappeared. In November 2019, it arrives at Rådhustorget in the heart of Umeå. The feline, a stranger to Sweden, has been equipped to withstand the cold climate of the Västerbotten region in the north of the country. The animal sculpture firmly anchors the exclamation mark in its title: *Listen!*. As a monument, the work recalls something that has occurred, but something that also remains active in the present. A feminist and politically charged choreography unfolds around the cougar in the square, which differs from the more low-key gender choreography described by Sjöholm Skrubbe.

---

63 Sjöholm Skrubbe, *Skulptur i folkhemmet* [*Sculpture in the Swedish Welfare State*] op.cit. , p. 185.
64 Ibid., p. 186.

When *Listen!* was inaugurated, hundreds of people were in attendance. The chair of the Culture Committee, Helena Smith (Social democrat politician), Camilla Akraka and Ida Östensson from Make Equal and co-founder of the consent movement, Fatta, gave speeches. According to an article in the daily press, Östensson called *Listen!* "a contemporary document dedicated to us who broke the silence." She also informed the audience that "there are a hundred rapes a day. This means that at some point during my speech, a girl or woman will probably be raped."[65] During the inauguration, the group Mäkt performed and included *Listen!* (called cougar) in one of their songs.[66] There was also a performance entitled *Kort kjol (Short Skirt)*.[67] The performance was the result of artist Gunilla Samberg's art education work. In connection with her exhibition *Som kropp - till Marie och Marlene (Like a body - for Marie and Marlene)* at the municipal art gallery in Umeå, workshops were held for young women (16-18 years).[68] On the opening day of *Listen!, the* young women took over the square. In doing so, they joined previous actions in feminist art. For example, in the early 2000s, the artist group High Heel Sisters invited women to walk with them for an hour across Sergels torg in Stockholm. "Feel like you own the place," was the invitation.[69] A cumulative effect continues almost twenty years later at Rådhustorget.

Epilogue

Listen! is used today. An active user is Umeå municipality, the commissioning body for the #MeToo monument. The same year that *Listen!* was inaugurated, the municipality of Umeå was said to invest the most in culture per inhabitant in Sweden.[70] Gender equality work

---

65 Sigrid Törnqvist, "Hundratals slöt upp för Metoo-pumans invigning" [Hundreds Turned up for the Metoo Cougar's Inauguration] *Folkbladet*, 11/4/2019, Sigrid Törnqvist, *Västerbottens-Kuriren* (VK) 11/4/2019.

66 Ibid.

67 See Cultural Secretary Anja Boman's answers to Håkan Nilsson's questions about Umeå municipality's investments in temporary art in the chapter "Temporary Liaisons and Far-reaching Convergences: Public art under municipal auspices" in this anthology.

68 "kort kjol" (short skirt) https://gunillasamberg.com/2019/11/05/kortkjol/ (accessed 09/08/21).

69 Eva Hallin, "Med motstånd mot förändring": Samtal med Sapphos Döttrar, High Heel Sisters, Johanna Gustafsson och Fia-Stina Sandlund" [With Resistance to Change: Conversations with Sappho's Daughters, High Heel Sisters, Johanna Gustafsson and Fia-Stina Sandlund], in *Konstfeminism* [Art Feminism], p. 159.

70 *Nyistan: En tidning för alla nya i Umeå kommun*, [*NewInTown: A magazine for everyone who is new in Umeå Municipality*], 2019, p. 6.

through culture has been part of the municipality's profiling efforts for a number of years. During its stint as the Capital of Culture 2014, the Museum of Women's History was inaugurated and presented as "a new and unique museum in Sweden."[71] The museum, which is run by the municipality, is located in the cultural building Väven on the Ume River not far from Rådhustorget and *Listen!*. Much like the municipal #MeToo monument, the museum is also said to be a call "for action."[72] There is an "empowerment ambition." But the ambition does not only cover the "gender equality issue" but also the attractiveness and potential for growth of the city of Umeå in general. In this, *Listen!* plays a prominent role. The sculpture/monument (the new aesthetic element in Umeå's public space) is the face of the tourist industry via *Visit Umeå*. Here *Listen!* serves both as a marker of the municipality's stance against sexual harassment and as a cover image for a brochure for an art tour in Umeå's city center.[73] In another context, Akraka's work is used to promote Umeå as "the city that speaks out for gender equality." With an eye on population growth (200,000 inhabitants by 2050), the municipality emphasizes gender equality as a "natural part of sustainable urban development."[74] Here, *Listen!* is not only tasked with memorializing the #MeToo movement, it is also expected to attract people to the city.[75]

Listen! has become a landmark and as such seems to be involved in identity building, with elements of empowerment even reaching beyond the auspices of the municipality. The #MeToo cougar is tattooed on the arm of a well-known Umeå resident, and a columnist with roots in the punk scene exclaims that she is proud to live in Umeå because of the cougar. Another columnist writes: "So beat your chests, residents of Västerbotten. Whether you hate the red #metoo cougar or not. Disruptive art is the best thing we can have because it is evidence that we live in a society where you and your children and grandchildren are

---

71 *Nyistan: En tidning för alla nya i Umeå kommun*, [*NewInTown: A magazine for everyones who is new in Umeå Municipality*], 2014, p. 3.

72 Ibid.

73 Umeå Municipality, Visit Umeå, "Metoo-monumentet", https://visitumea.se/sv/metoo-monumentet-listen (accessed 07/06/2020), Umeå kommun, "Konstrunda i Umeå centrum" [Art Tour in Umeå center].

74 Umeå Municipality, "Staden som ryter för jämställdhet" [The City that roars for Gender Equality], https://www.umea.se/platswebbar/flyttatillumea/arkiv/nyhetsarkiv/nyheter/stadensomryterforjamstalldhet.5.5d9221f0174f9921146e4c.html (accessed 12/01/2020).

75 Compare, e.g., with Håkan Nilsson's discussion of public art, cities and suburbs in the chapter "Public Art: An attempt to navigate" in this anthology.

allowed [...]."[76] But *Listen!* also comes up in crisis contexts. The feline has appeared in cartoon form on a banner during a demonstration against cuts in Region Västerbotten's ASTA clinic in Umeå. In a short article (in which *Listen!* is called both "cougar" and "Metoo cougar"), one of the participants in the demonstration is quoted saying: "Given all the experience we now have of violence and abuse against women, it actually feels a bit absurd to have to do this sort of thing [...]."[77] The banner with the familiar red feline serves as a reminder that there is a struggle going on beyond Rådshustorget in the center of the city. *Listen!*[78]

76 Anna Sundelin, "Umeåprofil har #Metoo-puman på sin arm - 'Jag bär den med stolthet'" [Notable Umeå Resident Has the #MeToo-cougar on Her Arm – 'I wear it with pride'] Affärsliv 24 [Business Life 24], in *Västerbottens-Kuriren* (VK) 4/5/2019; Erica Sjöström, "Punkiga puman passar perfekt" [Punk Cougar a Perfect Fit], *Västerbottens-Kuriren* (VK) 11/8/2019, Jonas Danielsson, "Se till att akta er för mjäkig kultur" [Beware of Soft Culture], *Folkbladet* 12/6/2019.
77 Niclas Holmlund, "Umeåbor i manifestation för hotad Asta-mottagning" [Umeå Residents in Demonstration for Threatened Asta Clinic], *Västerbottens-Kuriren* (VK) 06/02/2019.
78 *Listen!* has been back on Rådhustorget since December 2020. It is now accompanied by a plate which explains the monument's purpose. The exclamation mark is included in the title.

The Place of Play in an Anthropocene Public Sphere.
On Vril Båt Sten/Fijfere Vanás Geađgi
(Burl Boat Stone) by Joar Nango and Anders Rimpi
//Charlotte Bydler

We are at the Giella preschool in Jokkmokk, or Jåhkåmåhkke, as it is locally known in Lule Sámi. Here, at this place, we find the public artwork *Vril Båt Sten/Fijfere Vanás Geađgi* or *Burl Boat Stone*, created by Joar Nango and Anders Rimpi. A couple of children are climbing around and cling to a stone, they then turn around, carefully sneaking in and out from under a boat. It is sitting upside down over a group of rocks, propped up against a cluster of birch trunks cut to form a sloping shape. And the children are listening to something inside: a voice speaking Lule Sámi to the sound of lapping water.[1] Then they carefully climb a stepladder – a log with carved steps and handrails – that leads to a *njalla's* doorway. The *njalla* is a wooden Sámi storehouse where people store hides, clothing, food and other valuables they want to prevent animals from destroying. Hence its location on a smooth tree trunk, which makes it difficult to access. Inside the *njalla*, a so-called burl is screwed to the floor. A burl is a natural deformity found on trees, a knotty growth formed by twigs whose fibers grow in all directions, rhizomatically, without beginning or end.

In this text, I will explore the public artwork *Vril Båt Sten/Fijfere Vanás Geađgi (Burl Boat Stone)*. It is both a public artwork and a play installation by the two Sámi multi-artists Joar Nango and Anders Rimpi. The aim is to discuss the work using Sámi history as a starting point, as well as an understanding of temporality during the Anthropocene. The work was commissioned in 2017 by Public Art Agency Sweden as a "permanent" work and was ready for the children to play in the following year. The fact that Public Art Agency Sweden commissioned the work raises historical and contemporary issues

---

1   I would like to thank Moa Höglund, Håkan Nilsson, Dan Karlholm and above all, Oscar Svanelid, for their invaluable help with this text. From now on, I will use the Northern Sámi, *Sámigiella*, when writing Sámi terms. This is partly for reasons of convenience, but also because it is still the most widely spoken language among the Sámi who still speak a Sámi language at all.

surrounding the relationship between the majority Swedish-speaking population and the Sámi, who are Europe's only recognized indigenous people. On January 23, 2020, the Girja Sámi village won a case in the Supreme Court stipulating that they have the right to all hunting and fishing rights on their lands.[2] Since the installation was conceived as a site-specific work for Giella preschool in Jåhkåmåhkke/Jokkmokk as part of their pedagogical work surrounding Sámi languages, it might be interpreted that the Swedish state makes a concerted effort to invest in Sámi languages. But, in reality, what are we to make of public art commissioned by a nation state that does not recognize the rights of the indigenous Sámi people to the land, even though they can show without question that they have been legitimately living there since time immemorial?[3] Is it too much to ask in return that Sweden guarantees a similar time span at least for public art, i.e. "ancient times", but directed towards the future instead? And last but not least, did the work allude to the long list of injustices to which Sweden has historically subjected the Sámi – and continues to subject them? Of course, and I will show that in the following.

Giella means "language" in the local Lule Sámi and Northern Sámi, and the diversity of languages became an important tool in the preschool's pedagogical activities to strengthen the children's Sámi identity. At the *Giella* preschool, children learn Southern Saemie, Lule Sámi and Northern Sámi, among other languages.[4] Mikael Pirak, who at the time was the head of the Sámi School Board, contacted Public Art Agency Sweden because he needed an artistic spatial design, or possibly a collection of wall-hung framed pieces for the newly opened preschool:

---

2   Supreme Court, Courts of Sweden, judicial decision published January 23, 2020, https://www.domstol.se/en/nyheter/2020/01/girjas-sameby--men-inte-staten--har-ratt-att-upplata-smav-iltsjakt-och-fiske-pa-samebyns-byomrade-ovanfor-odlingsgransen/ [accessed 09/08/2021]

3   "*Time/s immemorial*", "a time antedating a period legally fixed as the basis for a custom or a right," "time immemorial," *Merriam-Webster Dictionary*, https://merriam-webster.com/dictionary/time immemorial [accessed 11/20/2020].

4   Southern Saemie has about 500 speakers from northern Dalarna County, Sweden, at the latitude of Røros and Trondheim in Norway. The Central Sámi languages include Lule Sámi, Ume Sámi, Pite Sámi and Northern Sámi, which are bounded by the Ume, Pite, Lule and Torne Rivers. Northern Sámi is used by four times as many speakers (about 40,000 or 85%) as other languages. Above the Torne River, Enare Sámi takes over, according to the website of the journal *Samer* [*Sámi*], http://www.samer.se/nordsamiska [accessed 11/19/2020]. However, the language mix continues with the Eastern Sámi languages: Enare Sámi, Skolt Sámi and Ter Sámi on the Finnish and Russian sides of Sápmi.

> We first thought along the lines of permanent installations, artworks on the walls, borrowed images. Now things will be even better - an artistic process where the children are involved and become part of the finished work. It's definitely innovative for this kind of building and location, but very much in line with the Sámi tradition of knowledge transfer through participation in everyday work – the unspoken knowledge, based on the Sámi inherited knowledge - *árbediehtu* - that is passed down through the generations.[5]

For this assignment, curator Anders Olofsson and Henrik Orrje, then head of operations at Public Art Agency Sweden, contacted Åsa Bergdahl, who at the time was an art consultant at Public Art Agency Sweden. Bergdahl grew up among Sámi people, which was probably one of the reasons she was considered suitable for the assignment. She in turn contacted Joar Nango, who has worked extensively with issues concerning Sámi spaces, which in his artistry are located as much in his choice of tools as in the surrounding space and landscapes. When Nango, who is a Sámi from the Norwegian side, suggested that Anders Rimpi should be asked if he wanted to be involved in the work to create a public art piece, he chose another person with roots in the Swedish area of Sápmi.[6] Although Rimpi has mainly worked on the west coast in the area around Gothenburg, he still considers the environments of Jåhkemåhkke to be his Sámi homeland. Rimpi's work includes musical scores for theater and opera productions, but he is also training to become an opera singer himself.

---

5   Mikael Pirak, "Statens konstråd engagerar välrenommerade multikonstnärerna Joar Nango och Anders Rimpi för unikt konstnärligt arbete på Giella" [Public Art Agency Sweden Engages Renowned Multi-Artists Joar Nango and Anders Rimpi for Unique Artistic Work at Giella] *JOKKMOKK*, https://jokkmokk.se/Nyheter-och-Event/Nyheter/Kommun-och-samhalle/statens-konstrad-engagerar-valrenommerade-multikonstnarerna-joar-nango-och-anders-rimpi-for-ett-unikt-konstnarligt-arbete-pa-giella/ [accessed 11/22/2020]. The entire block quote is italicized in the original.
6   Åsa Bergdahl, telephone interview and email correspondence with the author, 11/16/2020.

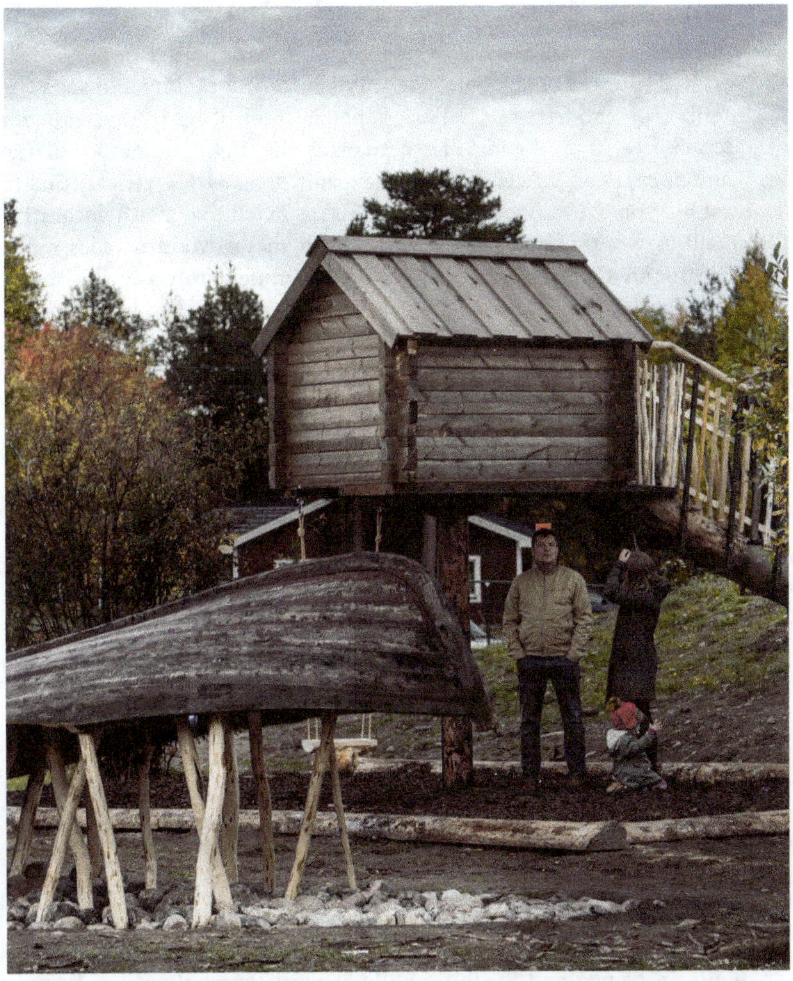

Ill. 1. Vril Boat Sten/Fijfere Vanás Geađgi (Burl Boat Stone) toward the installation. Photo: Ricard Estay. In collaboration with Håvard Arnhoff (spatial solutions), Britt Inger Bær (educator at Giella preschool), Patricia Fjellgren (voice of the burl), Lisa Lyngman-Gælok (dúodji detail on the stone), Anders Sunna (stencil graffiti on the speakers and pole), Sigbjørn Skåden (author of all texts), Per Tjikkom & Petter Tjikkom (carpentry and assistance in the assemblage of the njalla), and others.

The language issue is raised straight away in Bergdahl's project description, where she writes: "Separated or integrated/assimilated into Swedish society? Interest in the Sámi identity is growing rapidly and so is the number of children at Giella."[7] What is interesting is that *Vril Båt Sten/Fijfere Vanás Geađgi* also actualizes the linguistic nature of the Sámi craft, *dúodji*. According to the tradition, *dúodji* is strictly tied to usability, but in Nango's work it has just as much to do with decorative qualities, whether it is a craft made of horn, metal, wood, textiles, roots, hides, or anything else that happens to be immediately available to the artist. Nango's work can seem to break the rules of *dúodji* at times, as in the example of the *guótha* (an immobile home covered with turf), which in his work often appears in its bare, bent frame-skeletal form. Nango's designs also replace the traditional lacing of rattan threads or reindeer sinew with, for example, nylon straps, or some other synthetic material.

In the sketch of the work, Nango writes that they, in "good Sámi tradition", wanted to reuse what already existed on the site, which happened to be a pair of fully functional tool sheds outside the old preschool.[8] To fully understand the work's meaning, the artists say it is necessary to provide a linguistic background for its title: *fijfere* is Southern Saemie for "burl", *vanás* means "boat" in Lule Sámi, while *geađgi* stands for "stone" in Northern Sámi. The words evoke the multilingual pedagogy of the preschool. The children who will play in and around the work come from different families, even linguistically speaking, two different language families (Southern Saemie and Central Sámi). Instead of being separated by age, the children are divided into groups based on the language they speak. This is one reason why we can describe the work as site-specific, as it clearly interacts with the language pedagogics at *Giella* preschool.

As I understand Rimpi, the birch burl, the outgrowth placed inside the *njalla* in Nango and Rimpi's public artwork, symbolizes the future.[9] Originally, the burl was intended to be turned into a swing, but the artists realized that its weight risked injuring the children. So, it was screwed to the floor of the *njalla* instead. The burl is a beautiful piece

---

7   Åsa Bergdahl, *Project Description (Short description of the project)*. E-mail to the author, 11/16/2020.

8   Joar Nango, *Jietna aittit*, project sketch signed and dated November 2017, sent to the author by Åsa Bergdahl in an email correspondence, 11/16/2020.

9   Anders Rimpi, telephone interview with the author, 09/06/2019.

of wood, and speaks here, in the voice of actor Patricia Fjellgren, of its future in South Saemie: "Maybe I'll be this or that, this kind of vessel or something else...?" The children at the preschool can hear it deliberating with itself about what it might become. To understand this, it is important to note that the burl is a highly valued piece of wood that is suitable as a raw material for all kinds of wooden *dúodji*. Since the burl is a central material in Sámi craftsmanship, it is highly sought after, and you select it long before you harvest it. It is usually collected in the summer or autumn when the sap is unlikely to damage the wood, otherwise it makes the burl change color or even rot. This is exactly what the two artists did. An assistant took down the burl with a chainsaw and transported the heavy block of wood to Jåhkåmåhkke/ Jokkmokk in Nango's red van, which reads "FFB," otherwise associated with transport in connection with temporary architecture by FFB (*Felleskapsprosjektet for å Fortette Byen*, an architectural collective of which Nango is a co-founder).

According to Rimpi, the wooden boat, *vanás*, into which children can sneak, signifies a complex relationship with the present. The boat once belonged to Rimpi's father but is now too old to be used. As the children climb under the protection of the boat's keel, they can hear a text by Norwegian author Sigbjørn Skåden read in Lule Sámi against the backdrop of lapping water. It is a sound reminiscent of the water gently stroking along the sides of the boat, carrying it along the waterways when it was in use. In this way, the boat can be said to signify the fleeting present, and the moments that, like the water under the boat, disappear during the journey. Or does this element of Nango and Rimpi's work rather symbolize the great dams that dried up the waterfalls and flooded pastures and entire villages in Sápmi in order to bring electricity to Sweden? This state-initiated disaster took place at the terminus of the electric grids, far from the major cities in Sweden that, in seemingly good conscience, exploited the "clean" energy of the Sámi lands with damaging hydropower. But the children are playing with the boat, perhaps blissfully unaware of this event. The references are there, however, when they are ready to take them to their hearts.

The last significant element in *Fijfere Vanás Geaðgi* is the stone, *geaðgi*. The two artists had a craftsman drill several holes in the stone with the same drilling dimensions used by the multinational mining company Beowulf Mining, Plc. When the artist's stone encounters the preschool children, it speaks Northern Sámi, which is the language spoken by the largest Sámi language community. The stone is heavy, of course, but it also has a certain gravity that declares that it belongs to the land and will likely be part of it for a long time to come. The minerals of which the stone is composed are also specific to the place from where it was taken. Guided by Rimpi's own description, I read this stone as a signifier and as a concretion of a past that will never return, but that is nevertheless embodied by the mineralogical composition of the stone, forever binding it to the place from which it was taken.[10] There is, in other words, a lot that the preschoolers at *Giella* can learn from this artwork. Since the artists had access to a truck offering an easy way for them to move the stone from its place in the woods to the playground, it was decided to transport it that way. One often travels long distances in Sápmi, so going by car tends to be the natural choice.

However, there was a stark contrast between, on the one hand, the transportation of the stone with a truck powered by fossil fuels, and, on the other hand, the artists' attempts to cover the deep marks the stone had left in the ground. In terms of the transport, there is a contrast between the short-sightedness and production requirements of the market-oriented art world and the more traditional Sámi logistics. A hypothetical alternative would have been to wait for the snow to fall and drag the heavy stone on an *ackja*, a Sámi reindeer sledge, all the way to Giella preschool. However, this would have been difficult to implement in today's art world where time frames are tight and rarely allow artists to put any special effort into the logistics, unless it is specifically mentioned as a conceptual part of the artwork.

At the Norwegian Office of Contemporary Art (OCA), Nango says he works with site-specific installations and self-made publications,

> that explore and challenge the boundaries between architecture, design and visual art. Thematically, his works relate to issues of indigenous identity, often by exploring contradictions in contemporary architecture. He [Nango] has worked on the theme *The Modern Sámi Space*, among others. [11]

---

10 Rimpi, telephone interview.

11 Joar Nango, website of the Office of Contemporary Art, Norway, http://www.oca.no/oca-pop-up/oca-pop-up-20181122-1330, (author's italics) [accessed 11/17/2020].

The choice between muscle power and the combustion engine is undeniably an ethical dilemma, and it would not be unreasonable to expect that the two artists – one of whom claims to have worked and thought about "the modern Sámi spatiality" – would consider the issue of transportation as an aspect of this spatiality.

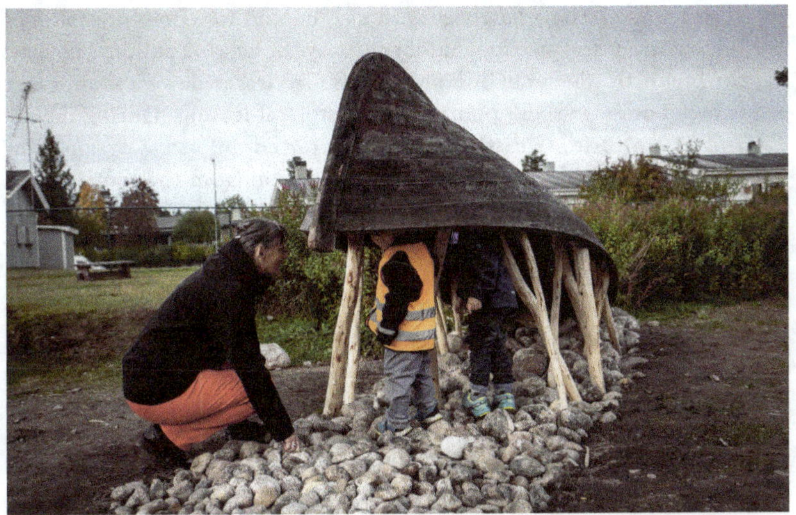

Joar Nango and Anders Rimpi , Fijfere Vanás Geaðgi/Vril Båt Sten.
Photo: Ricard Estay. /Statens konstråd

Language and learning

In my analyses, I have shown how Sámi material and linguistic history is an important part of Nango's and Rimpi's installation at Giella preschool. When read against the backdrop of the Sámi's constant struggle against colonialism, burl, boat and stone – the three essential elements of Nango and Rimpi's public artwork – can be interpreted metonymically as symbols of an Anthropocene exploitation of forests, water and minerals in the form of mining. Learning through specific pedagogical examples is (or is perhaps once again becoming) an important feature of many Sámi communities. There, the validity of a current case can be revealed and whether this case has any limitations of a social nature.[12] From this perspective, histories form complex

---

12   Rimpi, telephone interview.

relationships, the multiplicity of which can be understood as a ball of yarn with tight and repeated knots, which can furthermore be said to relate to the stories that ring out from the burl where it lies in the *njalla*, stories the boat and the stone tell as well.

Thus, in *Fijfere Vanás Geađgi (Burl Boat Stone)*, three Sámi languages are represented with the help of these three words. On a more abstract level, these languages can also be said to represent modes of imagination, and an equal number of ways of looking at life. The need for linguistic elements in *Fijfere Vanás Geađgi's* pedagogical approach is based on both socio-political and historical reasons. During the 17th and 18th centuries, Christian missions were a common way of depriving Sámi of their culture. When the colonization from the south began, during the 17th century at the latest, exploitation of natural resources and other forms of taxation to fund the current regent's wars were common, later with racial biological claims.[13] It is also the case that the Southern Sámi language, Saemie, encountered the Swedish language earlier than the Central Sámi languages. The ban on Sámi languages in schools from the 1920s to the 1960s is another reason, not to mention *Renbeteskonventione*n (The Reindeer Grazing Convention) between Norway and Sweden, which was signed in 1919 and came into force in 1923. The latter has been seen as the last nail in the coffin for the Sámi who were relocated by force from the north into Southern Saemie territory, losing their language as a result.[14] This certainly puts Nango and Rimpi's artistic intervention at a preschool in a historical light.

It is also possible to imagine *Fijfere Vanás Geađgi* as the starting point for a critique in which the preschool teachers use the work to teach children about the Sámi struggle against the Swedish nation-state. A gateway to this critical pedagogy could be the holes that the artists had craftsmen drill in the stone, in their playground installation. As I mentioned before, these are of the same dimensions as those used by the mining company Beowulf Mining Inc. When the highly relevant question about what local people say about the company's large-scale mining operations was put to the company's Executive Chairman, Clive Sinclair-Poulton, he replied "What local people?" To support

---

13 Marte Spangen, "Without a Trace? The Sámi in the Swedish History Museum," *Nordisk museologi/The Journal Nordic Museology*, 2 (2015), p. 20.

14 Elin Anna Labba, *Herrarna satte oss hit. Om tvångsförflyttningarna i Sverige [The Masters Put Us Here: About the Forced Relocations in Sweden]* (Stockholm: Norstedts förlag, 2020), pp. 10 and 31.

his claim, he showed photographs of a landscape from Gállok/Kallak, seemingly devoid of people.[15] This could serve to remind the children of how the global mining industry disregards Sámi traditions and their rightful claim to their own lands.

What does permanent and temporary mean in one of all Sámi perspectives?

Fijfere Vanás Geađgi/Burl Boat Stone is a permanent work. The term "permanent" as used by Public Art Agency Sweden is understood as the opposite of "temporary." What interests me in this article, however, is what these terms mean in the Sámi perspective portrayed by Nango and Rimpi. I have suggested that permanence in this work should be understood first of all politically, in a long-term historical perspective, which at the same time takes into account the injustices of the past and directs itself toward ecological sustainability. At the same time, permanence must be understood as a relative and multifaceted concept. Rather than promising that the artwork will endure in perpetuity, it comes down to its physical endurance, about its ability to withstand the elements and being durable enough not to be worn down by the children's daily play. Since the work, in its current shape, includes electronic elements (Rimpi's recorded voices and background sounds), it could be considered less "permanent." The *njalla* may hold up, but the electronics will not. Perhaps not even according to Public Art Agency Sweden's more pragmatic definition of "permanent" – that it should exist for a decade, or a half of it.

More interesting, however, is the permanence that Nango and Rimpi draw attention to through their focus on the Sámi languages and their view of the natural environment. It is in this context that the work can be said to possess a critical agency as a pedagogical and political tool during the sixth mass extinction, the Anthropocene epoch in which nature itself is threatened, as well as insects, animals and humans. But it is not only physical humans that are in peril, their cultural heritages and languages are in danger of dying out as well. The total number of people who speak Lule Sámi today can be counted in the hundreds. When a language becomes extinct, its world view is also endangered.

---

15   Sofia Persson et al, "'What Local People?' Examining the Gállok Mining Conflict and the Rights of the Sámi Population in Terms of Justice and Power," *Geoforum*, 86 (2017), pp. 20-29.

In this case, a specific view of history and the environments that have made their imprint on the ethnic groups' language are also threatened. In other words, a kind of linguistic tragedy occurs when a language disappears, and with it all the words that through generations have been used to denote their worlds. That children are not able to share their experiences with older generations has serious consequences for the Sámi's sense of identity and history, as this has been passed down through stories.[16] It is when *Fijfere Vanás Geađgi* is read in relation to this risk that the political dimension of the work emerges.

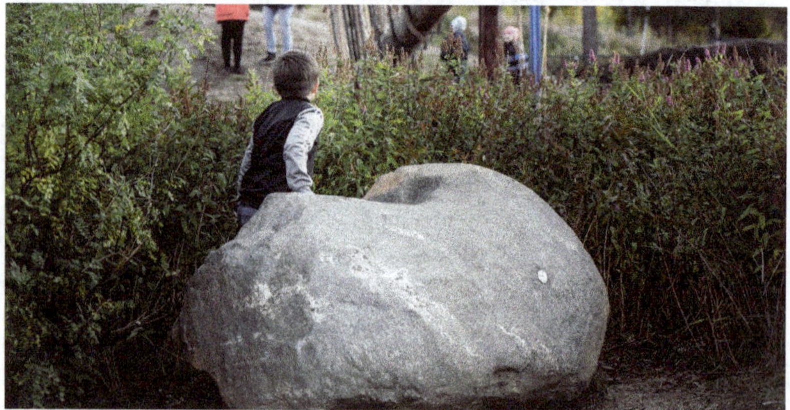

Joar Nango & Anders Rimpi, Vril Båt Sten/Fijfere Vanás Geadgi, 2018. The rock has an inbuilt speaker, which is telling a story. Photo: Ricard Estay/Statens konstråd

Anthropocene

I do, however, have one more thing I wish to emphasize. The stories, both linguistic and material, that I have uncovered in my analysis of Nango and Rimpi's public artworks also aim to make children care about, re-enchant, or perhaps re-sanctify their view of nature.[17] This practice highlights what is hopefully part of a paradigm shift, which breaks the Swedish hegemony whereby Sámi artifacts have been collected in historical and ethnographic museums. Today, social and cultural development has led to the verge of an existence where Sámi

16 Rimpi, telephone interview.
17 Labba 2020, p. 10.

people participate on their own terms. Demands for repatriation have been raised and reburials of Sámi human remains held by Swedish museums has also been initiated. The remains of the Saemie "shadow man" have been returned to Deárna/Tärnaby, where he was buried in 2002 after a long time spent in the basement of the Swedish History Museum in Stockholm. It is disheartening to think that Ernst Manker, a well-known Swedish ethnologist who should have known better, "borrowed" his skeletal remains and brought them to Stockholm in 1954 for further research.[18] This is also a shift within the arts, where indigenous people have received more attention in the last decade, not least at *documenta 14* (2017) where Nango and Rimpi contributed with an artwork. Public Art Agency Sweden can be said to be following this trend through its investment in *Fijfere Vanás Geađgi (Burl, Boat Stone)*, which Åsa Bergdahl describes as "the first project Public Art Agency Sweden is doing on Sámi terms."[19]

In Giella's playground, Nango and Rimpi, with the support of the pedagogues and the recorded voices, want to teach the children (and others who visit the work) to care for the earth, as well as to revitalize the vision of the Sámi in which the land, the rivers and the forest appear as enchanted. By ascribing nature its own voice and agency, a different view of the Sámi territories currently being exploited by transnational corporations, such as Beowulf Mining and the Swedish state-owned *Bergsstaten*, emerges. On this point, the artwork makes a statement in the debate on the Anthropocene.

As sustainability researcher Gail Whiteman and geographer Katy Mamen have shown, indigenous populations are hardest hit by the climate crisis and exploitation that characterize the Anthropocene. They are critical of global mineral extraction, which mostly takes place on indigenous lands and whose decisions are made in forums where indigenous people are rarely represented.[20] This can subject already hard-hit groups to further marginalization and oppression. Geographer Kathryn Yusoff further emphasizes that the exploitation of the earth's resources is historically and in a contemporary perspective closely linked to

---

18 For more information on the reburial of the shadow man in Tärnaby in 2002 and the skull in Lycksele in 2011, see *Sameradion* and *SVT-Sápmi*, https://sverigesradio.se/artikel/7276136 [accessed 11/30/2020].

19 Bergdahl, interviewed by email and telephone by the author.

20 Gail Whiteman & Katy Mamen, "Examining Justice and Conflict Between Mining Companies and Indigenous People: Cerro Colorado and the Ngäbe-Buglé in Panama", *Journal of Business Management*, 8:3 (2005), p. 13.

ongoing colonialism, with its continuous destruction of indigenous life-worlds. Her own experiences at conferences on the Anthropocene, which often have only white attendees, shaped her view that there was no place for the thoughts of racialized people.[21]

Here, then, she contrasts with the likes of environmental economist Clive Hamilton, who advocates a radically increased anthropocentrism in which humans, rather than nature, become the focus because of their agency.[22] In *The Future of Hegel* (2005), philosopher Catherine Malabou argues that the nature of agency is based on "the anticipatory structure operating within subjectivity itself," which makes it possible to conceive that something will happen, without knowing exactly *how* it will happen.[23] We can infer that, unlike Hamilton, she does not subscribe to the Western view of science that requires everything to be measurable. Hamilton's assumption is problematized by the works of Nango and Rimpi, whose critical potential is more about highlighting a Sámi approach (of several), and linguisticity, where nature is re-enchanted and given agency. Rather than Anthropocentrism, they show the necessity of imagining nature and humans as in a peaceful, harmonious relationship (in the sense of the Martinican philosopher, poet and playwright Édouard Glissant).[24] They demonstrated this, for example, in their careful treatment of the nature which was damaged when they removed the stone, and their reuse of materials such as the small storage sheds on the grounds of the preschool.

Finally, their installation shows how the work to shape alternative views of the Earth, a necessity in the Anthropocene, can begin in preschool, through a practice of learning that is at once playful and critically informed. Moreover, the Swedish state's forced relocation of Sámi people, which is behind the language confusion – and thus the need for the Giella preschool – has resulted in a decrease in the number of Sámi individuals, since only people who can make it likely that Sámi were spoken in their home can be included on the list for the Sámi

---

21 Kathryn Yusoff, *A Billion Black Anthropocenes or None* (Minneapolis: The University of Minnesota Press, 2018), p. xiii.

22 Clive Hamilton, *Defiant Earth: The Fate of Humans in the Anthropocene* (Cambridge, UK: Polity Press, 2017), pp. 27-35.

23 Catherine Malabou, *The Future of Hegel: Plasticity, Temporality and Dialectic*, trans. Lisabeth During (London, UK: Routledge, 2005), p. 13.

24 Édouard Glissant, *Poetics of Relation. Poétique III* (Paris: Gallimard, 1990). Unfortunately, Glissant's "relationship" is not necessarily peaceful, his thought presents no guarantees to rule out the possibility of the Anthropocene occurring.

Parliament, and thus counted among the Sámi people.[25] In the states' population registers, too, the language revitalization project at the Giella preschool will help to increase the number of the Sámi people. The same thing happened to Sámi in Norway, where the Sámi were relocated by force with the willing help of the Norwegian state. So, the nation states of Norway and Sweden made it a common cause, as Sámi languages cross the border between Norway and Sweden along the rivers. The traditional migration of Sámi reindeer herders across the border to Sweden caused major headaches for Norway's border administrators in the first decades of the last century. It is therefore not surprising that Åsa Bergdahl, for Public Art Agency Sweden, chose a Norwegian Sámi, Joar Nango, and a Swedish Sámi, Anders Rimpi. As the quote from Inga Idivuoma in Elin Anna Labba's book *Herrarna satte oss hit (The Masters Put Us Here)* seems to predict:

> We thanked Norway and the high mountain peaks there, the
> sea, the boats, the people. [...] Norway's rocks will echo our
> joiks, echo our thanks to the generations to come.26
> Defá Biette Ingá (Inga Idivuoma)

We can only hope that the children growing up in the north will, with the help of Giella, hold on to their languages, so that they can pass them on to their own children.

---

25 *SFS (Sami Law) 1992:1433 through SFS 2019:881* By Sami is meant, for the purposes of this law, a person who considers himself or herself to be a Sami and 1. can demonstrate a probability that he or she has or has had Sami as a language in the home, or 2. can demonstrate a probability that one of his or her parents or grandparents has or has had Sami as a language in the home, or 3. has a parent who is or has been registered in the electoral register of the Sami Parliament.
26 Labba 2020, p. 183.

Safety Art:
On Art as a Security/Safety Measure for Public Spaces
//Oscar Svanelid

A recurring idea about publicly funded art is that it should contribute to creating more attractive urban environments. Such initiatives assume that art has an instrumental value, which justifies its utility as a measure to create safety/security. In recent decades, research on public art in the Nordic countries has analyzed the critical role of art and its ability to promote social integration and community.[1] There have also been studies on how public art can play a role in urban development and "placemaking," which has been understood as a contributing factor in gentrification and increased segregation.[2] However, a survey of current research shows that the contemporary phenomenon of using public art as a political instrument precisely to enhance safety and security in society has fallen by the wayside.[3]

This article critically reflects on how public art has been used as a political tool to create safe/secure public environments in Swedish cities. The political use of art for this purpose emerged in the early 2000s but has become increasingly widespread in the last decade. This can reflect the increased insecurity among the country's population, especially among young and older women, as identified by the Swedish National

---

1   Sabine Dahl Nielsen, *Kunst i storbyens offentlige rum: konflikt og forhandling som kritiske politiske praksisser [Art in Public Spaces: Conflict and Negotiations as Critical Political Practices]* doctoral thesis (Copenhagen: University of Copenhagen, 2015); Line Marie Bruun Jespersen, "Velkommen udenfor! Kunst som mødesteder i byens rum" [Welcome Outside! Public Art and the Staging of Meeting Places in the City] *Periscope*, 17, (2017), pp. 116-132; Siv Mie Buhl and Werner Hansen, "Home Is to Be Understood: The role of contemporary art museums facing current immigration challenges" in *Flucht und Heimat: Sondierungen der pädagogische Anthropologie* [*Flight and Homeland: Probing of an educational anthropology*], eds. Jörg Althans et al. (Weinheim Basel: Juventa Verlag, 2018).

2   Louise Fabian & Kristine Samson, "Claiming Participation – a Comparative Analysis of DIY Urbanism in Denmark", *Journal of Urbanism: International Research on Placemaking and Urban Sustainability*, 9 (2016), pp. 166-188; Hjørdis Brandrup Kortbek, "Contradictions in Participatory Public Art: Placemaking as an Instrument of Urban Cultural Policy" *The Journal of Arts Management Law and Society*, 49:1 (2018), pp. 1-15.

3   Kjell Caminha, Håkan Nilsson, Oscar S and Mick Wilson, *The Public Art Research Report: A Report on the Current State of Research on Public Art in the Nordic Countries, and in a Wider International Context* (2018). Available at https://statenskonstrad.se/app/uploads/2019/03/Public_Art_Research_Report_2018.pdf [accessed 11/26/2020].

Council for Crime Prevention in its annual safety surveys.[4] What interests me is that safety has also been framed as an artistic problem, and my study contributes to understanding how safety is shaped and formed by public artworks. I shall also look into the works' contexts, such as the municipal reports in which the commission is formulated and evaluated. Yet another critical part of what is understood in this article as the "publicness" of art concerns the reception of the works, how they are made the subject of political debate, and other kinds of interactions. This is part of what I, informed by a concept coined by anthropologist Arjun Appadurai, call the "social life" of public art, whereby the public works to be looked into here are best understood as shaped by the encounters and relationships created over time.[5]

The article is divided into two case studies. The first is based on *Stockholmslejon (Stockholm Lions)* by artist Anders Årfelt, the first version of which was exhibited on Drottninggatan in Stockholm in 1995. The works are traffic barriers, designed in the form of lions, that constitute concrete examples of how public art is used to prevent access and create safer, more secure streets. This study will also discuss what happened to *Stockholm Lions* during and after the terrorist attack on Drottninggatan in 2017, when their security function was severely put to the test. *Stockholm Lions* did not fall under the supervision of the Cultural Administration but was created on behalf of the transport department in Stockholm, demonstrating that the artistic design, in this case, came about under the supervision of another administrative body. The second case study analyzes the City of Gothenburg's significant investment in light art in tunnels under the project *Safe, Beautiful City* (2005-2018). The project resulted in around ten light works, which local artists created in collaboration with lighting designers. The aim was to beautify and create safety, mainly in the city's vulnerable areas. Through these chosen cases, my aim is to highlight a few examples of public art, which were created with the specific purpose of contributing to urban safety/security. They will allow me to capture certain norms within this kind of public art, in which light art and street barriers often are used as standard solutions.

---

4   Sofie Lifvin et al., *Nationella trygghetsundersökningen 2020: om utsatthet, otrygghet och förtroende [National Safety Survey 2020: On vulnerability, insecurity and trust]* (Stockholm: Swedish National Council for Crime Prevention, 2020), pp. 10–11.

5   Arjun Appadurai, *The Social Life of Things: Commodities in Cultural Perspective*, ed. Arjun Appadurai (Cambridge: Cambridge Univ. Press, 1986).

With these cases, I intend to show a diversity in the security/safety task itself. While Åstrand's lions in central Stockholm were related to terrorism, the light art in Gothenburg was aimed at residents in the city's suburban areas.

The safe/secure city

An increased interest in the potential of public art to contribute to safety can be understood in the context of the global project to design safe cities. Notions of the safe, secure city can be found in policies where crime control and prevention strategies are part of more general measures to promote the well-being of the urban population.[6] The concept is associated with democratic participation, social cohesion, ecological sustainability, safety, and security. This notion is in line with the recent *smart city* trend, where digitalization and new technologies are combined with other forms of data collection, such as citizen dialogue, and are considered tools that can help optimize the quality of life of city residents.[7] The smart city has been seen as a democratic tool for urban development. Still, it has also been criticized as part of the neoliberal agenda, according to which social problems are addressed by way of technological rather than socio-political solutions.[8]

The contemporary construction of the smart, safe city is closely linked to the multidisciplinary approach known as "Crime Prevention through Environmental Design" (CPTED). The concept was coined in the 1970s by criminologist C. Ray Jeffery and further developed by architect and urban planner Oscar Newman, among others. The guiding principle behind this approach is that crime can be prevented through the built environment, which can be summed up by the motto "the opportunity makes the thief".[9] Crime prevention through architectural design, which is seen as a form of situational crime prevention, continues to be promoted as an effective measure for creating safer urban

---

6   Carina Listerborn, "Feminist Struggle Over Urban Safety and the Politics of Space," *The European Journal of Women's Studies*, 23:3, 2016, pp. 251-264; Carina Listerborn, *Trygg stad: diskurser om kvinnors rädsla i forskning, policyutveckling och lokal praktik, [Safe City: Discourses on Women's Fear in Research, Policy Development and Local Practices]*, doctoral thesis (Gothenburg: Chalmers University of Technology, 2002).

7   Devi Mega Risdiana & Tony Dwi Susanto, "The Safe City: Conceptual Model Development - A Systematic Literature Review," *Procedia computer science*, 161 (2019), pp. 291-299.

8   Shannon Mattern, *A City Is Not a Computer: Other Urban Intelligences* (New Jersey: Princeton University Press, 2021).

9   Oscar Newman, *Defensible Space: Crime Prevention Through Urban Design* (New York: MacMillan, 1972)

environments. However, many now advocate what has come to be called the second generation CPTED. This approach is a response to a common criticism of Newman, namely that he underestimated the importance of social factors in crime. His methods have also been criticized for creating disciplined and dehumanized urban spaces as well as for contributing to gentrification.[10] Second generation CPTED has generally incorporated these criticisms, for example, by grounding situational crime prevention in democratic processes that seek to engage the local community.[11] When situational crime prevention was widely introduced in Sweden in the 2000s, it was often combined with social measures, attributed to the features of the Swedish welfare state.[12] However, urban theorist Carina Listerborn, who has researched safety issues in Swedish cities, has argued that contemporary notions of the safe city are usually based on the interests of the white middle class. This, she argues, undermines already marginalized social groups, such as racialized women and their experiences of racist and sexist violence in public spaces.[13] The safe city is often underpinned by a post-critical discourse based on a universal definition of quality of life and well-being. Still, my investigation shows that it is crucial to understand that feelings of safety are formed in a politicized field. Therefore, in relation to contemporary safety art, it is necessary to discuss which groups have interpretive prerogatives and to highlight the adverse effects of such projects, which in my analysis, are linked to issues of racism and gender.

Although the study of the safe/secure city is an established and

---

10 Sarah Schindler, "Architectural Exclusion: Discrimination and Segregation Through Physical Design of the Built Environment," *The Yale Law Journal*, 124 (2015), pp. 1934-2024; Chiara Certomà, "Expanding the 'Dark Side of Planning': Governmentality and Biopolitics in Urban Garden Planning," *Planning theory*, 14:1 (2015), pp. 23-43; Paul Cozens & Terence Love, "The Dark Side of Crime Prevention Through Environmental Design (CPTED)," *Oxford Research Encyclopedia of Criminology*, (2017), https://oxfordre.com/criminology/view/10.1093/acrefore/9780190264079.001.0001/acrefore-9780190264079-e-2 [accessed 11/26/2020].

11 For discussion of this see Walter S. Dekeseredy, Joseph F. Donnermeyer and Martin D. Schwartz, "Toward a Gendered Second Generation CPTED for Preventing Woman Abuse in Rural Communities," *Security Journal*, 22:3 (2009) p. 178; Cozens & Love "The Dark Side of Crime Prevention Through Environmental Design (CPTED)," op.cit.

12 Kerstin Johansson, "Crime prevention cooperation in Sweden: A regional case study," *Journal of Scandinavian Studies in Criminology and Crime Prevention*, 15, 2014, pp. 143-158; Asifa Iqbal and Vainia Ceccato, "Is CPTED Useful to Guide the Inventory of Safety in Parks? A Study Case in Stockholm, Sweden," *International Criminal Justice Review*, 26:2 (2016), pp. 150-168.

13 Listerborn, "Feminist Struggle Over Urban Safety and the Politics of Space", op.cit., pp. 251–264; Carina Listerborn, "Geographies of the Veil: Violent Encounters in Urban Public Spaces in Malmö, Sweden," *Social & Cultural Geography*, 16:1 (2015), pp. 95-115.

multifaceted field of research, the role of public art in this context is less explored. However, there is an overlap with research that discusses how public art is used within urban development and gentrification. Cultural theorist Josephine Berry has analyzed how public art in the UK in the 21st century has been assimilated by neoliberal urban development, creating environments optimized for clickstreams, differentiated marketing, and financial gain. She argues that modern art's democratization of the Duchampian "creative act," echoed in the participatory and new genre public art of the 1990s, culminated in the public art of the neoliberal city. Berry also highlights how public art is used as a symbol of an inclusive social community, but which at the same time is undermined by privatization and the suppression of socio-political mobilization.[14] Although safety/security-creating art may seem compatible with strategies for urban development in which undesirable individuals and behaviors are no longer acceptable in urban spaces, it would be misleading to think of the use of art for this function solely as an outcome of neoliberalism. More nuanced studies are needed in order to isolate the role of public art in creating contemporary safe/secure cities. This is where the present article seeks to contribute.

Although security art has not been manifested the same way in the past, it builds on an idea of socially instrumentalized art. Art historian Jessica Sjöholm Skrubbe has described how the Swedish cultural debate of the 1960s and 1970s was characterized by a view of public art as a socio-political tool. The bourgeois idea of art as a form of education was re-actualized in the context of the Social Democratic project to educate citizens in the welfare state. She argues that public art aimed to contribute to the creation of "positive foundations for public life [...],"[15] as well as "a sense of community that characterized a Gemeinschaft *within the framework* of a Gesellschaft." [16] In this perspective, contemporary safety art is seen as a bearer of the legacy of the welfare state and its notion of the vital role of public art in building a functioning society. However, this is performed on a

---

14 Josephine Berry, "Everyone is Not an Artist: Autonomous Art Meets the Neoliberal City," *New Formations*, 84/85 (2015), pp. 20-22 and 38.

15 Jessica Sjöholm Skrubbe, *Skulptur i folkhemmet: den offentliga skulpturens institutionalisering, referentialitet och rumsliga situationer 1940-1975 [Sculpture in the Swedish Welfare State. Institutionalisation, referentiality and spatial situations 1940-1975]*, doctoral thesis (Göteborg: Makadam, 2007), p. 290.

16 Sjöholm Skrubbe, *Skulptur i folkhemmet [Sculpture in the Swedish Welfare State]*, op. cit p. 289.

different premise than in the 1960s and 1970s, since currently public art is used to manage security and safety issues. Rather than creating a communal safety for all based on the representation of the welfare society's imaginary world, the examples examined in this article use public art as a targeted measure to increase safety/security in places.

Stockholmslejon (Stockholm Lions)

Anders Årfelt's *Stockholmslejon (Stockholm Lions)* have stood guard at Drottninggatan in Stockholm since 1995. The works were created before visions of safety/security began to feature more frequently in municipal public art policy documents, making them veritable pioneers in the field this article addresses. The lions are strategically placed at street intersections and act as roadblocks to keep pedestrians safe on this busy pedestrian street in central Stockholm. Sculpted from fully cast concrete with a polished surface and undulating manes, these male lions also contribute to the artistic decoration of the road. *Stockholm Lions* have been part of Stockholm's public space for 25 years and have found their way into many homes with miniature replicas having been sold. However, the artist behind these works is less well known. Årfelt began his career by showing charcoal pencil drawings of everyday objects, such as buns and fig trees, at the Nationalmuseum's *Unga Tecknare (Young Draughtsmen)* exhibition in 1959. In the 1960s, he was a student at the Royal Institute of Art in Stockholm and then studied to become an art teacher at Konstfack – University of Arts, Crafts, and Design. His first public artwork, *Boll med skruv (Ball with a Curve)* (1986), stands outside a sports hall in Visby and consists of an eight-meter-high concrete sculpture depicting the dynamic movement of a tennis ball through space. In the 1990s, Årfelt began working with traffic barriers as an art form, first with *Gutebaggar (Gute-Wethers)* on Gotland and afterward with *Stockholm Lions*. In the 2010s, the artist created *Säfstaholmsäpplen (Säfstaholm Apples)* in Vingåker, which serve the same function.

Årfelt's *Stockholm Lions* are physically anchored to the site and have firm connections to the symbolism of the city ward. The work engages in dialogue with the lion in the Swedish Coat of Arms and the 18th-century French artist Bernard Foucquet's lion sculptures below Stockholm Castle. Lions are a common symbol of royal power but they function as a religious motif as well. The Old Testament is full of lions, and the predator often appears in icons and ornaments in Romanesque and medieval churches, even in the Nordic countries. Art historian Morten Stige describes how the Christian lion is characterized by kindness and a pathos of justice. Christian legends have depicted lions sleeping with their eyes open, thus protecting the congregation from the presumed dark forces of evil. In other words, it is a tame lion that Christianity has metamorphosed into the pastoral shepherd, characterized by its constant vigilance over and protection of the faithful.[17]

Stockholm Lions share features with the pastoral lions of Christianity, where they stand guarding pedestrians on Drottninggatan. But they have neither explicit religious claims nor the aggressive expressions that have been characteristic of royal lions. Unlike the lions in the Coat of Arms of Sweden, *Stockholm Lions* do not bare their teeth and they also lack the protruding, twisting tongues of their counterparts. Nor do these lions turn outwards toward an imagined enemy; their calm and contemplative demeanor instead signals an inner peace. This distinguishes them from the Lion of Saint Mark, whose wings rise above the people and which has historically been used as a fascist symbol.[18] Instead, the *Stockholm Lions* greet the individual as an equal and have a folksy character, as the older lions, whose backs have been polished to a fine sheen after bearing toddlers on their backs, stand testament to. During my visits to Drottninggatan, I noticed that the lions are also used as a collection point for gloves, umbrellas, and other lost items. The lions' association with safety/security thus comes not only from their function as traffic barriers but also from their everyday use.

---

17 Morten Stige, "The Lion in Romanesque Art, Meaning or Decoration?" *Tahiti*, 6:4 (2016), o pag.
18 For an analysis of Italian fascism's use of the Lion of Saint Mark during the interwar period, as well as the anti-fascist "lion hunt" see Kate Ferris, *Everyday Life in Fascist Venice, 1929-40* (Houndmills, Basingstoke, Hampshire: Palgrave Macmillan, 2012), pp. 86-87.

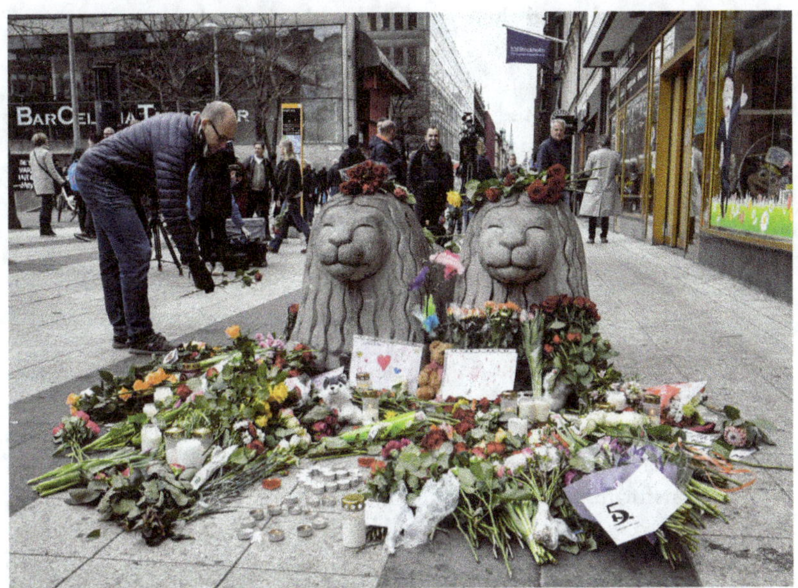

Anders Årfelt, *Stockholm Lions*, 2017, Photo: Jonas Ekströmer / TT

Terror

Årfelt's lions underwent a dramatic transformation in April 2017 when the Islamist Rakhmat Akilov hijacked a truck and drove it at high speed down Drottninggatan. The terrorist attack killed five people and injured many more. The news stream published images showing a lion that had been rammed and dragged several hundred meters in front of the speeding truck. After decades of a quiet and relatively anonymous social life in the public space, *Stockholm Lions* received considerable media attention, both nationally and internationally. The lions were described as heroes on social media and Designtorget's miniatures sold out in just a few days.[19]

People who were on Drottninggatan during the attack told the media how the lion, which became stuck in front of the truck, alerted them to

---

19 "Ny roll för laddad storsäljare hos Designtorget: 'Symbol för att värna staden'" [New Role for an Emotionally Charged Bestseller at Designtorget: 'Symbol to Protect the City'], *Market*, 8/12/2017, https://www.market.se/nyhet/ny-roll-for-laddad-storsaljare-hos-designtorget-symbol-for-att-varna-staden. [accessed 11/26/2020].

the attack and saved their lives. But at the same time, the images of the fallen lion circulating in the media conveyed that these artistic traffic barriers could not fully withstand the terrorist attack. Rather than being interpreted as having failed in their function, the lions drew the public's sympathy. Like a police car parked at the site and the memorial wall created on the shop window of the Åhléns department store, the lions were adorned with flowers, teddy bears, and messages of love. By being swept up in messages of reconciliation and love, their position as the city's kind protectors in the fight against terrorism was reaffirmed.

During the mourning process that followed the terrorist attack, the public related to the notion of safety the lions expressed. *Stockholm Lions* took on the role of a spontaneous memorial, which, according to ethnologist Billy Ehn, is characterized by a kind of collage of objects and messages with an emotional charge. These memorials act as media for transforming inner grief into "something that can be touched and shared with the outside world [...]" and they thus have the dual function of "saving both the one who remembers and the one who is remembered."[20] Like Ehn's description, the lions were transformed after the attack into a kind of public altar, where the public went to find comfort and intimacy. They became surfaces upon which to project a range of emotions and a place to share the traumatic memory of the attack, which helped people process these emotions. With their calm and contemplative demeanor, the flower-covered lions seemed to hover almost in a spiritual realm. This otherworldly transcendence was therapeutic at a time when people were turning to art to heal an open wound. Spontaneous memorials, however, are temporary and the memories and emotions projected onto them are rarely allowed to remain.[21] This was the case with *Stockholm Lions* when, after the Easter weekend, a few weeks after the attack, the municipality of Stockholm decided to clean up the flowers and messages of love placed next to the lions, restoring the place to its original form. However, the memorial wall created at Åhléns after the terrorist attack was dismantled and moved to the Kulturhuset on the other side of Sergels Torg. Today, the

---

20 Billy Ehn, "Hos mig kommer du alltid finnas kvar": Monumentaliseringens uttrycksformer" ["With Me You Will Always Be There": The Expressions of Monumentalisation] in *Minnesmärken: att tolka det förflutna och besvärja framtiden* [*Memorials: To Interpret the Past and Conjure the Future*], ed. Jonas Frykman & Billy Ehn (Stockholm: Carlsson, 2007), pp. 348-350.

21 Ehn, "Hos mig kommer du alltid finnas kvar" ["With Me You Will Always Be There"], op.cit., p. 350.

wall is included in the Stockholm City Museum's collection, and the museum has also set up a website that preserves personal accounts of the attack and other visual documentation.[22]

In parallel with the public glorification of the *Stockholm Lions*, a political debate ensued in the media, discussing the status and function of the works as a security measure. Public art was thus swept up into the mainstream of Swedish debate on terrorism that followed the attack, which was characterized by its focus on the question of future measures to prevent terrorist attacks.[23] Just one day after the attack, Fredrik Jurdell, then deputy mayor of Stockholm, confessed in an interview in *Sydsvenskan* that Drottninggatan lacked terrorist preparedness. Jurdell also notes that the lions had not been designed to withstand this kind of truck attack, which he described as "a pure question of gravity."[24] The emotionalism that characterized the public reception of the lions after the attack thus contrasted with the security-oriented viewpoint in political discourse. Instead of highlighting the qualitative function of the works as a tool to help the mourning process, they were seen as examples of an outdated security calculus where terrorist truck attacks had not been inserted into the equation. This shows how public art's security function is shaped in relation to historical events and physical characteristics, which connects *Stockholm Lions* to the discussion about how the function of public art as a security measure has been affected by terrorism.

Lions XL

The global jihadist network to which Akilov belonged, as well as terrorists from other parts of the political spectrum and their copycats, used vehicles and cars as machines of war in several attacks during this period. Cities worldwide have taken measures to protect themselves against this form of terror, including surveillance cameras, stricter

---

22 Elin Nystrand von Unge, *Samla samtid: insamlingspraktiker och temporalitet på kulturhistoriska museer i Sverige [Collecting Contemporary: Collecting Practices and Temporality at Museums of Cultural History in Sweden]*, doctoral thesis (Stockholm: Stockholm University, 2019), chapter 5.

23 Lars Nord, Karl-Arvid Färm and Lena Jendel, *Fyra terrordåd, fyra mediebilder. En studie av svenska mediers bevakning av attackerna i Paris och Köpenhamn 2015 samt i Stockholm 2017 [Four Terrorist Acts, Four Media Images. A study of Swedish Media Coverage of the Attacks in Paris and Copenhagen in 2015 and in Stockholm in 2017]* (Sundsvall: DEMICOM, Mid Sweden University, 2018) p. 62.

24 "Betonglejon står inte emot en lastbil," [Concrete Lion Can't Stand up to Truck,] *Sydsvenskan*, 04/08/2017.

access control, and closed streets.[25] Terrorism preparedness, as mentioned above, has been criticized for reducing the social life of public spaces and leading to the design of areas that allow people to pass through as quickly as possible. At the same time, there are examples of "softer" measures where signs, flower boxes, and other street designs are used to prevent truck attacks.[26] The City of Stockholm's initiative to continue using public art as a security/safety measure exemplifies this softer approach. The ruling red-green-pink bloc (FI, V, MP, and S) decided to procure new *Stockholm Lions*, which included a couple of innovations. Firstly, the city commissioned new lions. A proportion of these were female lions, which evened out the gender balance; all previously commissioned lions had been male. Secondly, a larger and heavier version of *Stockholm Lions* was procured, known in municipal documents as *Lions XL*. These were males and placed on Drottninggatan alongside a troop of smaller, first edition *Stockholm Lions* to strengthen terrorist preparedness and further contribute to the artistic ornamentation of the street. In addition, the municipality installed heavy flower boxes to further enhance the area's terrorist preparedness.

The effect of the terrorist attack on the artistic design of the street can thus be summarized quantitatively. Before the terrorist attack, there were 30 lions on Drottninggatan, each weighing 900 kilos. After the terrorist act, 90 lions guarded the same street; 70 of the old format and 20 *Lions XL*, weighing 4 tons each. The terrorist attack thus resulted in a threefold increase in the number of *Stockholm Lions* and a five-fold increase in their total weight. As Fredrik Jurdell pointed out in the quote above, the security function of art was narrowed down to a purely quantitative determination, which did not reflect the elusive qualitative values that emerged in my earlier discussion of the encounter between the lions and the grieving public.[27]

Still, center-right politicians dismissed the red-green-pink investment in additional *Stockholm Lions* and the new *Lions XL* as an empty gesture. In an opinion piece in *Expressen*, Christian Democrat Erik Slottner called for "a much higher level of ambition in terms of physical barriers

---

25   Vincent Miller and Keith Hayward "'I Did My Bit': Terrorism, Tarde and the Vehicle-Ramming Attack as an Imitative Event," *British Journal of Criminology*, 59 (2018) pp.1-23.

26   Cozens & Love, "The Dark Side of Crime Prevention Through Environmental Design (CPTED)," op cit.

27   "Betonglejon står inte emot en lastbil," [Concrete Lion Can't Stand Up to Truck,] *Sydsvenskan*, 4/8/2017.

against terrorist attacks."[28] He suggested that Stockholm should instead use technical solutions to strengthen its terrorist preparedness. As an example, he mentioned the height-adjustable traffic barriers installed at the entrance to Rosenbad in the form of round pillars. In this political debate, what is at stake is the issue of counterterrorism and notions of the (non-)function of public art in creating a safe/secure city. The political discussion of this was based on a consensus that terrorist preparedness must be strengthened. However, there was an apparent conflict between views that this should be addressed through purely technical measures or through art and floral decorations. A common criticism of technological solutions is that they can be counterproductive, since they risk increasing the public's sense of insecurity, which is seen as something that undermines the notion of the public realm as an open and accessible space.[29] The City of Stockholm's decision to continue to use public art in the form of traffic barriers reflects their idea that softer approaches can counter even terror.

This means that Stockholm's physical security measures should be seen as a work of art and, at the same time, as a way of cementing the idea of a public traumatized by terror. In this perspective, *Lions XL* represents something beyond a larger and heavier sculpture; it represents a notion of a kind of security that differs from the lightweight predecessor and points at an ambiguous ontological definition of public art. The lions are a direct response to the terrorist act, but they lack any notations or markings referring to this event. They are thus neither monuments nor memorials but rather establish a dialectical relationship between forgetting and remembering. Their physical form has incorporated the memory of the terrorist act. At the same time, the lack of any markings diverts attention from this very act and the trauma that goes with it. If the old lions provided a sense of safety by supporting the public's grief process in the immediate aftermath of the event, *Lions XL* symbolizes the political need to manifest not only the restoration of safety in the public space but the enhancement of security as well. To this end, public art has been updated for the age of terrorism, seeking to ensure

---

28   Erik Slottner, "När ska S börjar ta terrorhotet på allvar?" [When Will Social Democrats Start to Take the Terrorist Threat Seriously?], *Expressen*, 03/30/2018.

29   Schindler, "Architectural Exclusion: Discrimination and Segregation Through Physical Design of the Built Environment," op.cit.; Cozens & Love, "The Dark Side of Crime Prevention Through Environmental Design (CPTED)," op.cit.

that the social interaction, artistic ornamentation and commerce of the city streets can continue without dwelling on the trauma of the attack.

Light art in tunnels

> Here, in this government-improved and approved housing with too much man-made light, the moon did nothing kind. The planners believed that dark people would do fewer dark things if there were twice as many streetlamps as anywhere else. Only in fine neighborhoods and the country were people entrusted to shadow.30

I will now focus on the most extensive investment in light art as a measure for public safety in Sweden to date, which was realized in Gothenburg under the project *Safe, Beautiful City* (2005-2018). The project's overall aim was "to create safer and more beautiful places in the city through measures in the physical environment."[31] This involved several measures, and here I will discuss the investment in light art, which resulted in around ten art works in Gothenburg's tunnels during the project period. The light art was targeted at the city's so-called vulnerable areas. According to the governing red-green bloc (V, MP, and S), the project would strengthen residents' right to safe and beautiful environments in their neighborhoods. The placement of the light art in the suburbs was promoted as a democratic initiative based on the perception that the suburbs had been disadvantaged in relation to urban development in the central parts of the city. Another parameter cited was that residents in vulnerable areas were the most insecure.[32] Further background to the project was Gothenburg's aim to position itself at the forefront of the technological development of the smart, safe city of today. To this end, the light art in the tunnels was launched as the city's pilot project for *Lighting Urban Community*

30　Toni Morrison, *Love* (Knopf: New York, 2003), p. 39.

31　Municipality of Gothenburg, *Trygg, vacker stad 2005–2018* [*Safe, Beautiful City 2005-2018*]. Available at https://goteborg.se/wps/portal/enhetssida/trygg%2C-vacker-stad/!ut/p/z1/04Sj9CPykssy0xPLMnMz0vMAfIjo8ziTYzcDQy9TAy9_X18nAwcDZ2dgoL8Qg3dg430wwkpiA-JKG-AAjgb6XvpR6Tn5SRCrHPOSjC3S9aOKUtNSi1KL9EqLgMIZJSUFxVaqBqoG5eXleun5-ek5qX-rJ-bmqBti0Z0QXl-hHoKrUL8iNqPJJDXcEAHTKex8!/dz/d5/L2dBISEvZ0FBIS9nQSEh/ [accessed 11/26/2020].

32　Maria Börgeson & Mathias Stenback, *Trygg, vacker stad 2005–2018* [*Safe, Beautiful City 2005-2018*] (Gothenburg: Park- och naturförvaltningen, City of Gothenburg, 2019), p. 33, p. 4.

International (LUCI), a global network of cities working to promote the development of urban lighting.[33]

The light art in the tunnels was realized through a collaboration between *Göteborg Konst* (Gothenburg Art), a section within the Department of Culture, the Transport Department, artists, and the architectural firm White Arkitekter. The project focused primarily on artists who had completed their education and/or were residents in Gothenburg. As a result of the project's democratic aims, focus groups were created where residents were asked questions about their experiences of safety and insecurity. Some artists also established collaborations with schools and after-school centers and created workshops with residents in the areas concerned. The project's focus on social aspects and citizen dialogue in its work to increase safety can thus be seen as a literal example of the second generation of CPTED. Based on the qualitative and quantitative data collection, the City of Gothenburg formulated a concept of the unsafe tunnel that laid the foundation for the art commission. The unsafe tunnel was said to be characterized by "the difficulty of surveying the environment both inside and outside the tunnels, both during the day and at night, where they are used for drug dealing and/or sleeping, unauthorized traffic in the tunnels, dazzling and uneven lighting."[34] Here, insecurity (lack of safety) is defined as a combination of technical and social components. By improving lighting, art is offered as a way to help remove the social elements that give rise to insecurity in these environments.

The increased safety, which the artistically designed lighting in the tunnel was expected to create, was thus based on the exclusion of individuals and behaviors categorized as unsafe. This makes it possible to conceive of them as the negative target group for the project. It supports the view of criminologist Elen Midtveit that symbolic measures for situational crime control are not always less exclusionary. She discusses this by analyzing how opera music and Christmas carols were played at the entrance to Københavns Hovedbanegård in the early 2000s, which she understood as a targeted measure to remove drug dealers and homeless

---

33 https://goteborg.se/wps/portal/start/gator-vagar-och-torg/gator-och-vagar/belysning [accessed 11/26/2020].

34 *Trygg, vacker stad 2016* [*Safe, Beautiful City 2016*] (Gothenburg: Park- och naturförvaltningen, City of Gothenburg, 2019) p. 12. Available at http://www5.goteborg.se/prod/intraservice/namndhandlingar/samrumportal.nsf/93ec9160f537fa30c12572aa004b6c1a/d900d4206299b-850c12580b900358dbe/$FILE/%C2%A7%2029.3%20Bilaga%202%20Arsrapport%202016%20Trygg%20vacker%20stad.pdf [accessed 11/26/2020]

people from this place. This created a symbolic barrier, which according to Midtveit, was based on the notion that the undesirables did not identify with opera music and, because it was played at a high volume, made it unbearable for them to loiter for very long. She further assumes that this was not a measure to address the problems of drug dealing and homelessness but a deliberate attempt to use opera as a barrier to create safe spaces where these urban phenomena do not occur.[35] It was thus problematic that the exclusionary mechanisms of high culture were combined with technology to render vulnerable groups and social problems invisible. Similarly, according to Gothenburg municipality, the light art in the tunnels can be understood as a strategy to change the character of these areas, moving what residents had identified as insecurity factors out of sight.

Light art as decoy and exclusion

However, there is an incongruity between the municipality's assignment and definition of an unsafe tunnel, on the one hand, and, on the other, how this was subsequently implemented in the light art installation created within the framework of *Safe, Beautiful City*. Judging from my visits to the site, there are no artworks that functioned as the kind of exclusionary barriers that Midtveit discussed. Instead, the artworks had in common that they made the tunnels more familiar, often achieved by introducing abstract nature motifs and forms of interaction. Artist Marie Dahlstrand was commissioned to illuminate a pedestrian tunnel in Angered, an area in eastern Gothenburg that has recently attracted negative media attention as a center for organized crime and gang violence. The same year that Dahlstrand's *Pieces of time/Pieces of sky* (2017) was installed in a pedestrian tunnel connecting two schools, Angered launched a local urban development program that aimed in part to create more vibrant street environments to tackle widespread problems.

In the work, Dahlstrand has installed circular lights in changing colors at the tunnel's entrances and placed grey ceramic shapes over the interior walls like fragments of a dreamscape. I see her artistic design as an attempt to make the tunnel a pleasant environment and thus invite

---

35   Elen Midtveit, "Crime Prevention and Exclusion: from Walls to Opera Music," *Journal of Scandinavian Studies in Criminology and Crime Prevention*, 6:1 (2005), pp. 32-35.

more people to choose this route. Once inside the tunnel, the ceramic dreamscape lulls passers-by into a contemplative calm that is likely intended to reduce the anxiety of passing through the tunnel. Such use of light art to attract people into the tunnels is echoed in most of the works, although they employ different artistic strategies.

The artist Peter Ojstersek collaborated with lighting designers to create the light artwork *More Eyes* (2015) in a pedestrian underpass between the suburbs of Frölunda and Tynnered. The grey and bare tunnel walls have been covered with luminescent LED crystals that pulsate in different colors. During my visits to the site, I observed how these attracted children to explore their senses and play as they passed through the tunnel, which according to Kajsa Sperling from White Arkitekter, was one of the intentions of the work. She explains: "when people pause, the tunnel becomes more populated, making even more people want to use it."[36] The artwork is thus intended to delay the passage through the tunnel, which is thought to increase the flow of pedestrians. As we have seen, the aim of light art was more than just to improve the safety of the inhabitants. By increasing the circulation of people in these places, it was thought that groups and behaviors associated with insecurity would disappear, which is consequently interpreted as a desired negative function of this interactive artwork.

The light art in the tunnels does not evoke discomfort but invites moments of contemplation and interaction. It is not at the level of the individual work that the municipal security art assignment (keeping the homeless away) can be said to be realized. Instead, this can be seen as a potential consequence of the function as, on the one hand, a decoy, and on the other hand, a mechanism of exclusion. In this way, the light art actualizes what the architectural theorist Jane Jacobs in the 1960s called "natural surveillance."[37] Jacobs took issue with the trajectory of urban development in American cities, which assumed that inner cities needed regeneration, and also criticized the increased police presence. Instead, she suggested that policing should be built into the urban environment. Like the French philosopher Michel Foucault, Jacobs discerned a link between surveillance and discipline but argued that this was fundamentally desirable. Rather than funding major policing initiatives, Jacobs argued that cities could prevent crime just

---

36 https://whitearkitekter.com/se/projekt/ljuskonst-i-tunnlar/ [accessed 11/26/2020].
37 Jane Jacobs, *The Death and Life of Great American Cities*, 50th anniversary edition (Modern Library edition. New York: Modern Library, 2011).

as effectively by creating environments where the public was aware that their behavior was being monitored by what Jacobs called "eyes on the street."[38]

Jacob's perspective is, as I mentioned earlier, recognizable in the light art created under the auspices of *Safe, Beautiful City*. This is most evident in Ojstersek's work, whose title *More Eyes* is reflected in the eye-like crystals of light on the walls but also in the increase of the passing pairs of eyes that the project sought to achieve. Rather than being understood as a transport route, the municipality thus saw the suburban tunnel as strategically crucial for creating a safer and better monitored urban landscape. By inviting the residents to view light art, the municipality also encourages them to spend time in environments where they look and feel looked at by others.

The blood in us

The project *Safe, Beautiful City* was shelved by the center-right majority that took over the city council after the 2018 elections. The last light artwork completed within the project was Ola Åstrand's *Blodet i oss* (The *Blood in Us)* (2019), the theme of which differs from the other works and suggests a more critical, or perhaps even ironic, approach to the municipality's security art assignment. Since the absence of critique is a characteristic of much of contemporary safety art, which, as mentioned earlier, is characterized by its post-critical discourse in which safety/security-enhancing effects are central, I will analyze Åstrand's work in more detail in the following.

Åstrand has been active in Gothenburg's art scene for several decades and has always maintained a position as an outsider. In the 1980s, when Åstrand was a student at HDK-Valand – the Academy of Art and Design – he turned against what he perceived as the hegemony of postmodernism in art education. Instead of French philosophy, Åstrand turned to music and was a guitarist for some time in the punk band TT Reuter. Punk also found its way into his art, characterized by a firm rejection of conformity. In an interview in 2017, Åstrand was asked how he views art, to which he replied: "Art is a weapon to fight oppression and the bourgeoisie [...] not to make a social career or to

---

38 Jacobs, *The Death and Life of Great American Cities*, op.cit. chapter 1.

serve the rich."[39] However, creating municipally funded safety art for *Safe, Beautiful City* undeniably put the artist's punk self-image at risk. Åstrand's light artwork has been installed in a short pedestrian and car tunnel in Kviberg in eastern Gothenburg. Over the past decade, Kviberg has undergone extensive urban development with high-density housing and the opening of a large sports and recreation center. Socio-political tensions also characterize Kviberg. In particular, the area's flea market has been the subject of political debate, where voices from the Confederation of Swedish Enterprise and the Sweden Democrats claim that the market is being used for organized crime and have called for its immediate closure.[40] For a couple of years now, a non-profit cultural center has been operating at the flea market, emphasizing the market's importance as a socio-cultural hub and breeding ground for social enterprise. The social tensions in Kviberg attracted considerable media attention both locally and nationally when it was discovered that a housing association in the area had put up barbed wire on the side facing the neighboring apartment building. This action was justified by allegations of vandalism and can be seen as a literal example of how security is created through barriers that separate not only buildings but also social classes.[41]

---

39 "Konstens frågeformulär # 58: Ola Åstrand" [Art's Questionnaire # 58: Ola Åstrand] http://konsten.net/konstens-frageformular-58-ola-astrand/ [accessed 11/26/2020].

40 Henrik Ekelund & Per Geijer, "Ta itu med stölderna - stäng Kvibergs marknad" [Tie Up the Loose Ends - Close Kviberg's Market], *Göteborgs Posten (GP)*, 10/25/2019.

41 Lina Isaksson,"Taggtråd ska hålla hyresgäster borta" [Barbed Wire Installed to Keep Tenants Away], *Göteborg direkt*, 12/11/2018.

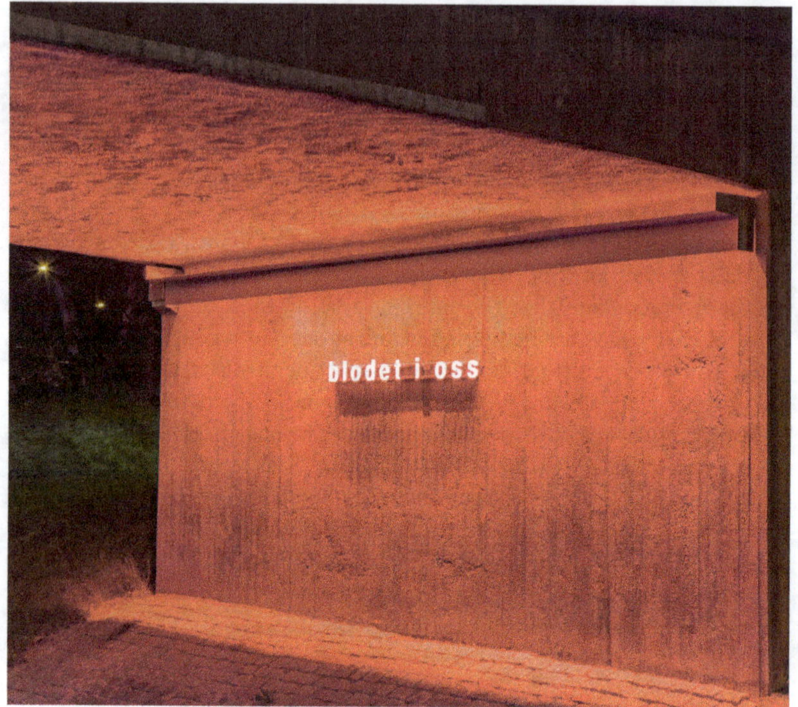

Ola Åstrand, *The Blood in Us*, 2019, Photo: Jan Peter Dahlqvist © Ola Åstrand / Bildupphovsrätt 2022

Bleeding

> I'm bleeding today cause I miss my bro / My girl still mad I ain't
> pick up my phone / My mama still think I ain't did nothing
> wrong / But I can't say the truth, so I sing this song.42

A few blocks away from the barbed wire fence, the walls of the Åstrand
tunnel glow with blood-red light, at least during the dark months
of the year. One wall reads "the blood in us" in LED letters. Blood is
probably not something most people associate with security/safety,
and the work challenges conventional notions of what it is to feel
protected. Although Åstrand explains in his project description that

---

42 Meron, *Bleeding (Ft. Ahdam & Ille Freeway)*, (video), https://www.youtube.com/
watch?v=LQmGufRy0TI. [accessed 11/26/2020].

his intention was for passers-by to feel embedded in a (mother's) body and to be struck by "a sense of something warm and inclusive," the work's text is sufficiently vague to evoke other associations.[43] Moreover, there is a rawness in the blood-red lighting that makes me experience the tunnel as a barren and rather bleak place.

The significance of Åstrand's *The Blood in Us* shifted when Swedish hip-hop artist Meron chose to shoot the music video for *Bleeding* (feat. Ille Freeway & Ahdam) in the tunnel. The video intersperses fast cars, crowbars, and a partying crowd with clips of musicians Ille Freeway and Ahdam miming the song's chorus with "the blood in us" in the background. The blood-red glow from Åstrand's work reappears in other scenes, setting the tone for the music video. The video contains several references to guns and drugs but also deals with losing a close friend ("Praying for my bro, he's gone it hurts / Trying to shed tears but it feels like I am empty"). In a scene set in the tunnel, Ille Freeway stands with his head bowed and prays, only to point his hand, shaped like a gun, at his head in the following clip. In this way, the video dramatizes the simultaneously raw and emotional mood that characterizes Åstrand's work.

In this example, public safety art has reached out and been renegotiated in its encounter with the suburbs' hip-hop culture. The work's formation of a blood fellowship is linked to the group of young black men who appear in the video. In this way, the subject matter that has underpinned the project and is represented in the more generic appeal of the other light artworks is undermined. It could even be said that Åstrand's work has attracted the unsafe/insecure behavior, particularly with regard to drugs and weapons, that the municipality would have preferred to make invisible. Instead, through Meron's appropriation, a sense of security is formed based on the group identity around hip-hop and gang culture. This is subversive, but it also creates new dividing lines. For example, in the song, "my girl" and "my mama" are excluded from the fellowship of young men, reinforcing the exclusion of suburban women, a group where insecurity is high. This occurs due to a series of interpretations and cannot be blamed on Åstrand's work. However, what can be said is that by not explicitly thematizing the insecurity of this marginalized group, the artworks in *Safe, Beautiful City* enabled such an outcome. Ultimately, this criticism should not be directed

---

43   http://olaastrand.blogspot.com/2019/01/utsmyckning-kviberg-goteborg.html [accessed 11/26/2020].

at the artworks themselves but at the project's initial invitation for proposals, as well as how the collected data was processed.

To call public light art racist would be an exaggeration. On the other hand, there is a reason, I believe, to examine the ideological underpinnings of the idea of light art as a security/safety measure in public spaces. Also missing from *Safe, Beautiful City* is a deeper problematization of the historical and political significance of sending artists to segregated suburbs to enlighten and beautify. Therefore, if light art is to be critically relevant, it would, I believe, require an in-depth analysis of the municipal and governmental visions to spread light and the belief that art can help to create a better future in these areas.[44] One path forward would be to think things the other way around, arguing that safety/security has less to do with lighting than with the right to darkness. The American writer Toni Morrison touches on this in the quotation from the novel *Love*, with which my analysis of light art began. She points to some of the prejudices that continue to find their way into current efforts of using light art as crime prevention and shifts the perspective so that lighting appears to be a threat. What is in danger of being lost, according to this view, is neither the safety/security of the individual nor private property but the lyrical sense of urban darkness as a safe, secure and communal space.

Another kind of security art?

In this article, I have raised several reasons to deepen and problematize public art's security/safety function, dealing with everything from terrorist threats to drug dealing and homelessness in recent decades. In the safety projects I have analyzed here, public artworks are used as interventions, while the artists have almost no say in the actual problem formulation, which in these cases has been decided at the level of local

---

44   The artist and researcher Monica Sand highlights this perspective on light art in her analysis of the light artwork that Alexandra Stratimirovic created in a collaboration between the City of Gothenburg and Public Art Agency Sweden within the framework of *Art is Happening.* What is missing from her account is a dialogue with those who, from decolonial and post-Marxist perspectives, have criticized the view of (European) Enlightenment as an emancipatory project. Monica Sand, *Tro, hopp och konst - konst som politiskt verktyg: forskningsrapport om Statens konstråds satsning Konst händer 2016–2018* [*Faith, Hope and Art - Art as a Political Tool: Research Report on the Public Art Agency Sweden's Initiative Art is Happening 2016-2018*] (Stockholm: ArkDes, 2019), pp. 103-113.

politics. The same can be said about the specific threats identified in these projects. In the case of light art in the tunnels, the threat was identified as darkness, as well as what the municipality of Gothenburg defined as behavior creating insecurity perpetrated by the homeless and other marginalized groups. This aligns with Listerborn, who also highlights the lack of critical perspectives as a pervasive problem in creating safer Swedish cities. As an alternative, she highlights the value of critically informed safety/security efforts that listen to, or rather are created by, minorities and other marginalized groups.[45] There are likewise good reasons to emphasize the necessity of a critical notion of security/safety in public art as well, which could result in projects that, rather than perpetuating and cementing normative ideas, can reshape what it means to feel secure. At the same time, the study shows how existing safety art has been renegotiated in the reception of the works, where works are associated with different kinds of security/safety and threats than those initially formulated by local politicians and even the artists themselves.

---

45 Listerborn, "Feminist Struggle Over Urban Safety and the Politics of Space," op.cit.

The Renegotiation of Care.
Contemporary Art and Research on a New Care Environment
//Pamela Schultz Nybacka

This chapter discusses the role and justification for art in a healthcare setting responsible for human health and well-being.[1] The importance of art in healthcare has received international and national attention, not least because of the construction of new hospitals and clinics, both private and public. Art theorist Andrea Phillips and architect Markus Miessen highlight how the neoliberal transformation of healthcare systems in the West has changed the way we think about healthcare. They argue that art, architecture and design can add perspectives and critique to help establish what they call "a culture of care."[2] Art placed in healthcare settings has mainly been examined and discussed in aesthetic terms.[3] As philosopher Boris Groys sees it, such a justification cannot support art, it instead works the other way round: "Aesthetic discourse, when used to legitimize art, effectively serves to undermine it."[4] The aesthetic attitude basically has no need for art. In terms of the aesthetic experience, Groys writes, most works of art cannot stand up against an ordinary sunset.[5] This draws attention to the fact that art in healthcare needs a different kind of legitimacy than the purely aesthetic, and my article is interested in the political and ethical dimensions that are formed around the idea of art as an aspect of care for patients, relatives and healthcare workers.

This chapter explores the emergence and renegotiation of contemporary art in healthcare settings through a case study of the Skandion Clinic, which was completed in Uppsala in 2014 and opened for patients the following year. The Skandion Clinic was created through a

---

1 The chapter is based on a research report from on-going evaluation and research regarding the project "Contemporary ART & CARE," funded by Akademiska Hus.

2 Andrea Phillips & Markus Miessen, *Actors, Agents and Attendants. Caring Culture: Art, Architecture and Public Health* (Berlin: Sternberg Press, 2011).

3 In addition to Rapp's account of the conditions in Sweden, see Jane Macnaughton, "Art in Hospital Spaces: The Role of Hospitals in an Aestheticised Society." *International Journal of Cultural Policy*, 13:1 (2005), pp. 85-101.

4 Boris Groys, *Going Public* (Berlin: Sternberg Press, 2010), p. 13.

5 Groys, *Going Public*, op.cit., pp. 12-13.

collaboration between seven regions with university hospitals. The clinic is the first of its kind in the Nordic region to specialize in proton beam therapy, which is a gentler, more effective and cost-efficient form of cancer treatment. The chapter focuses on the initial stage of the process of developing and renegotiating the artistic process with respect to the Skandion Clinic's different forms of care and considerations. The questions guiding the chapter are: How can art intervene and take form in a new healthcare environment? What is the relationship between art and the culture of care within the healthcare setting? How does art in a healthcare setting gain legitimacy and, if so, on what political and ethical grounds?

As a researcher with a background in organizational theory and user perspectives, I have had the privilege of following the work to develop an art program for the Skandion Clinic during the planning stage, as well as the renegotiations that took place during the process. The study resulted in a research report, and this chapter presents an abridged and revised version. The chapter begins with a brief introduction on art in healthcare as it occurs in Sweden, with an outlook on international examples. The chapter then turns to the case of the Skandion Clinic and the various decisions and interventions within the design project. This in-depth case study deals with the renegotiations and considerations that arose in choosing colors around the hospital environment by the artist Filippa Arrias.

Art in healthcare

In Sweden, research director Birgitta Rapp has conducted research and research programs on arts and culture in healthcare. Her book *Konst på sjukhus till glädje för alla (Art in Hospitals – For Everyone's Enjoyment)* describes the development and design of the healthcare system in Sweden, from the earliest reforms in the Middle Ages to the specialized large hospitals of the 1980s. Art first enters the healthcare environment in the 1930s with the breakthrough of functionalism and had a broader impact after the 1960s.[6] There was a clear political will to make art and culture available to citizens, which also left its mark on healthcare.

---

6   Birgitta Rapp, *Konst på sjukhus till glädje för alla* [*Art in Hospitals - For Everyone's Enjoyment*] (Stockholm: Raster förlag, 1993), p. 10.

The aim of art in a healthcare setting is, according to Rapp, "to be a source of enjoyment for everyone," that is, the three affected groups – patients, relatives and employees.[7] The cost-effectiveness of art in the healthcare setting is also something that needs to be considered.[8] Rapp argues that it is the combination of empirical studies, proven experience and even unwritten rules that informs or determines which art is considered appropriate in a public health care setting. In the following table, she compiles some criteria for the selection of what she calls "artistic decoration" in healthcare settings: [9]

7   Rapp, *Konst på sjukhus* [*Art in Hospitals*], op.cit., p. 197.

8   Birgitta Rapp, *Kultur i vården, visavi vården som kultur. Ett livsviktigt forskningsprogram med en tvärvetenskaplig syn på hälsa och livsvillkor i omvårdnad och åldrande* [*Culture in Healthcare, vis-á-vis Healthcare as Culture. A Vital Research Program with an Interdisciplinary Approach to Health and Living Conditions in Nursing and Ageing,*] Final Report (Stockholm: Stockholm County Museum, 1999), p. 36.

9   Rapp, *Konst på sjukhus* (*Art in Hospitals)*, op.cit., p. 213.

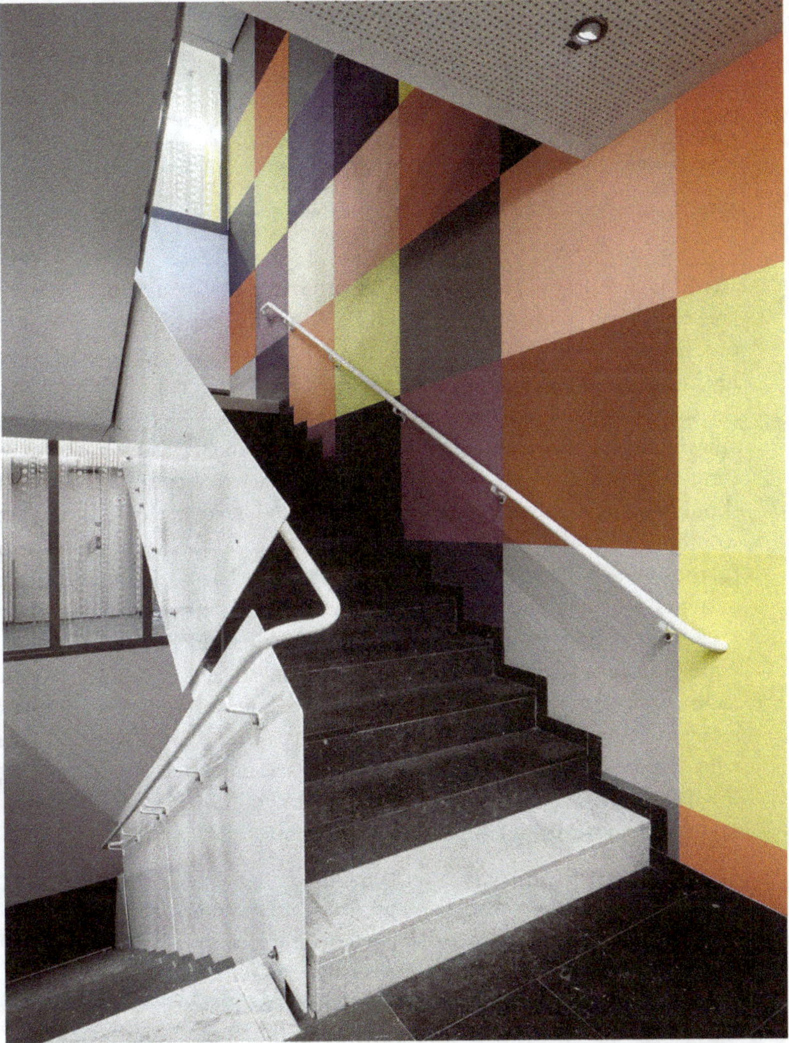

At the Skandion clinic the art was invited to intervene in the architect's vision about natural material and light transmission. The artist Filippa Arrias' coloration with bold colors in a health care environment was inspired by a study visit to Denmark.
Filippa Arrias, Skandionkliniken, 2014,
Photo: Pär Fredin © Filippa Arrias Filippa Arrias / Bildupphovsrätt 2022

Appropriate art	**Inappropriate art**
Good content	Inappropriate content
Good material	Inappropriate material
Easy-to-understand art	Difficult-to-interpret art
Calming art	Art with vortices, anxiety inducing
Art that calms, stimulates joy	Art that disturbs a tired, sick person
Quality art	Bad art/horror art
Art as an expression of enduring styles	Art as an expression of temporary trends

It is striking that Rapp does not consider that art is a form of production, i.e. something made and produced through different kinds of artistic processes. Instead, the selection of art is central for Rapp, reflecting her more traditional approach to public art as a form of decoration. As such, Rapp is also a proponent of Artotek, where patients are allowed to borrow their own artwork. Since, in her assessment, care should be based on the individual's needs, art in healthcare settings should also be flexible and individualized.[10] What seems to make the art 'appropriate' is that content and material is 'good,' without going into further details. Furthermore, Rapp prefers art that does not challenge patients, relatives and staff, but calms and stimulates joy. A relatively modest selection of traditional, figurative art seems to be the norm, while most contemporary art falls by the wayside.

In looking at the effects of the healthcare environment on people's recovery, Rapp refers to environmental psychologist Roger Ulrich, who has been very influential in international discussions on how the design of healthcare environments affects health. [11] Ulrich argues against the notion that all art is appropriate:

> It may be unreasonable to expect all art to be suitable for high-stress healthcare spaces, because art varies enormously in subject matter and style, and much art is emotionally challenging or provocative. [...] Interviews with patients suggested strongly negative reactions to artworks that were ambiguous, surreal, or could be interpreted in multiple ways. The same patients, however, reported having positive feelings and associations with respect to nature artwork.[12]

---

10   Ibid., p. 223.
11   Ibid. p. 206.
12   Roger S. Ulrich, et al. "A Review of the Research Literature on Evidence-based Healthcare

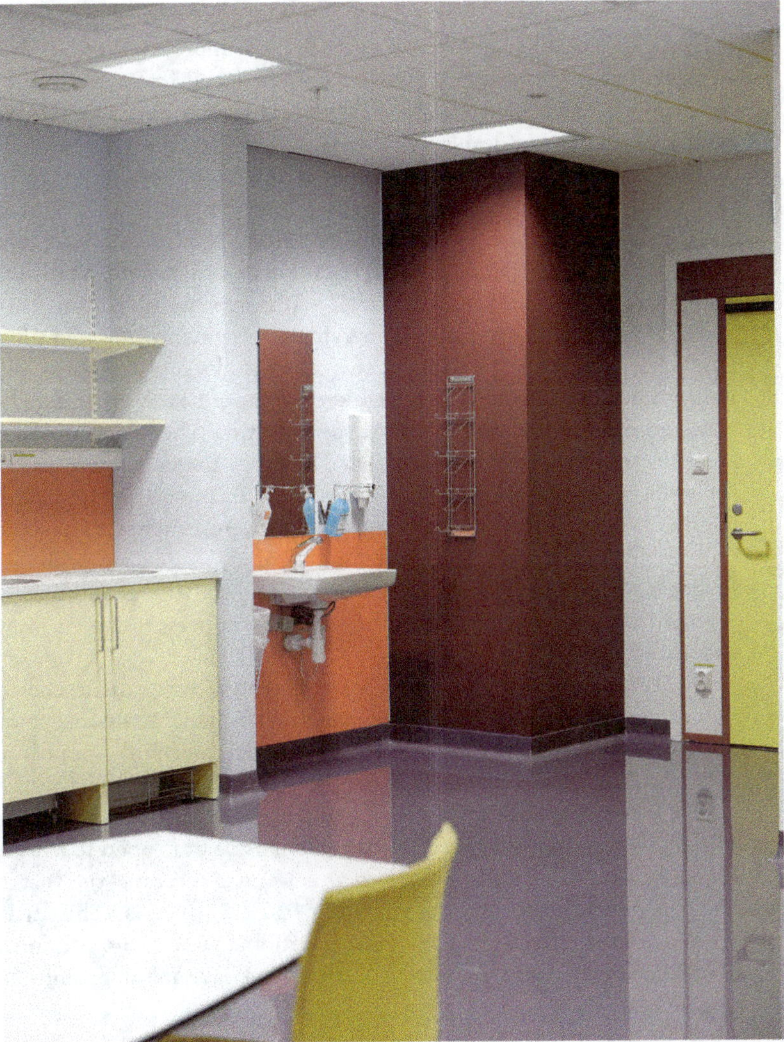

The adequacy of the oxblood red color in a health care environment returned in the discussions with in the project group and with the users. The color figure on walls and in details.
Filippa Arrias, Skandionkliniken, 2014,
Photo: Pär Fredin © Filippa Arrias Filippa Arrias / Bildupphovsrätt 2021

Design," *Healthcare Leadership.* 1:3 (2008), pp. 1-75.

The conclusion he draws from this evidence-based and instrumental perspective is that nature artworks are the most appropriate in hospital settings. In his view, nature art can reproduce and foster feelings of harmony, contributing to positive experiences and measurable effects, such as reduced stress levels in patients.

Since Rapp's report, healthcare systems in the West have, starting in the 1990s, been fundamentally transformed by the marketization, fragmentation and introduction of New Public Management governance.[13] During this period, healthcare has moved toward a performance and goal-based model, with increased measurability and customer orientation.[9] Ethnographer Annemarie Mol identifies a growing conflict between what she calls the abstract, economically motivated logic of choice and the concrete logic of health professionals based on practice and tradition.[14] At the same time, she underlines that care is a multifaceted concept that "provides ample opportunities for ambivalence, disagreement, uncertainty, misunderstandings and conflict."[15] Due to the considerable financial interests in healthcare, the "customer satisfaction" of patients has become the guiding principle in decision-making processes. According to Mol, the economically oriented market model stands in the way of other perspectives of what good healthcare can be.

Andrea Phillips points out that in the neoliberal, individualistic choice model that has also been implemented in hospitals, the concept of care is used as a rhetorical tool that in practice means the opposite. This gap, she argues, opens up critical angles on the role of art in the public sphere and calls for an in-depth discussion of the significance of care in contemporary art. Phillips urges artists not to operate within the margins of the public space, but to set out to recreate "the spaces and times that constitute what is public."[16] Here, there is a shift that follows from a resistance against the traditional view of art as a form of decoration, and where contemporary art can have an important role to play.

---

13   Maria Blomgren, "The Drive for Transparency: Organizational Field Transformations in Swedish Health Care", *Public Administration*, 85:1 (2007), pp. 67–82.

14   Annemarie Mol, *Omsorgens logik. Aktiva patienter och valfrihetens gränser* [*The Logic of Care. Health and the Problem of Patient Choice*], trans. Sven-Erik Torhell (Lund: Arkiv förlag, 2011).

15   Mol *The Logic of Care*, op.cit., p. 104.

16   Andrea Phillips, "Too Careful: Contemporary Art's Public Making," in *Actors, Agents and Attendants. Caring Culture: Art, Architecture and Public Health*, ed. Andrea Phillips & Markus Miessen (Berlin: Sternberg Press, 2011) p. 56.

The Skandion Clinic – a case study

The creation of the Skandion Clinic is a unique and advanced collaborative project in the Swedish healthcare system. In 2006, seven regions (then county councils) joined forces to create the *Kommunalförbundet Avancerad Strålbehandling* (KAS) (Joint Authority for Advanced Radiotherapy): Uppsala County Council, Östergötland County Council, Region Skåne, Stockholm County Council, Västerbotten County Council, Västra Götaland Regional Council and Örebro County Council. These regions are known for their university hospitals, which aim to be synonymous with excellence in care. The Skandion Clinic as a whole has both proven experience and innovation in technology, forms of care and delivery.

The Skandion Clinic would, as mentioned above, offer more gentle cancer care, namely, proton beam therapy for patients from different parts of Sweden.[17] During their hospital stay, patients and their families can stay at the Hotel von Kraemer, which was also planned for the building. In 2013, a stand-alone Ronald McDonald House opened nearby, where children under treatment can stay with their families. The plan was that all the country's children in need would receive proton beam therapy. The Skandion Clinic was thus of national importance for children and young people with cancer.

The building was designed by LINK Arkitektur AB. According to their vision, it was not meant to be perceived as a hospital. Thus the clinic was built primarily from natural materials, and the façade is perforated in a pattern. There is also a small courtyard, which faces the waiting room and the recovery department. Some parts of the clinic have a lower hygiene classification than is otherwise common in hospitals. The architectural design is intended to show consideration for patients' needs. The architect responsible for the proposal, Roger Larsson, stressed the importance of the architect empathizing with what it is like to be in the clinic as a patient, family member or staff member. In this context, Larsson emphasized the importance of symbolic value. This is directly visible in the building's location in the city, a prime location near the castle. The challenge, according to Larsson, was how to get the building also to symbolically express that it manages care for its users.

---

17 Proton beam therapy is certainly not a new phenomenon – an experimental facility has existed in Uppsala since the late 1950s – but a dedicated facility for clinical treatment had previously been lacking in the Nordic countries.

Although the Skandion Clinic was financed with public funds, with the state-owned Akademiska Hus as the property owner, the clinic was not a state project and therefore fell outside the scope of Public Art Agency Sweden's initiatives. Nor was the one-percent rule applied to the construction, resulting in a relatively small financial framework for investments in artwork. It was initially hoped that the art budget could be increased over time, including external funding, but this did not happen. In this context, it is nonetheless noteworthy that the Skandion Clinic contains large and prolific elements of art. In addition to Filippa Arrias' artistic color scheme, the sound art work *freq_out 1.2 ∞ (skandion)* by artist Carl-Michael von Hausswolff is located outside the building and was produced with 17 participating artists and musicians.[18] Adjacent to the entrance is a sculpture park, which was planned in collaboration with landscape architect Helena Jeppson and is home to the sculpture *Mor och barn (Mother and Child)* (1918) by Anna Petrus and works by three contemporary artists: the bronze sculpture *Winners* (2014) by Veronica Brovall, the light artwork *The Radiant Globe* (2014) by David Svensson and the sculpture *Lebenslauf* (2014) by Carl Boutard.

The artistic process

In the case of the Skandion Clinic, the art did not enter the process at its last stages, but was considered from the very beginning. From the outset, there was a private donation for the right to erect the sculpture *Mor och barn (Mother and Child)*, based on a plaster model by the artist Anna Petrus (1886 - 1949). The donation came from the first Director of the KAS, who was himself the son of the artist. This indicates an unusual personal commitment to the question of art in the clinic. The placement of the sculpture at the entrance to the Skandion Clinic takes on added significance as the country's children and young people suffering from cancer may be eligible for treatment.-

The art project at the Skandion Clinic was driven by the Joint Authority for Advanced Radiotherapy (KAS) through its director, both current and former, and by Akademiska hus AB Region Uppsala through the

---

18   Participating artists are Maia Urstad, JG Thirlwell, Anna Ceeh/Framz Pomassl, The Sons of God (Kent Tankred & Leif Elggren), Mike Harding, Christine Ödlund, Tommi Grönlund & Petteri Nisunen, BJ Nilsen, Brandon LaBelle, Jacob Kirkegaard, PerMagnus Lindborg, Finnbogi Petursson and Jana Winderen. See also http://freq-out.org/infinity/

project manager for the Skandion Clinic and an art consultant. Here the choice fell on Lotta Mossum, a freelance curator who was also a project manager at Public Art Agency Sweden. Mossum has a Master of Fine Arts (1998) and a one-year postgraduate degree in Architecture (2006), both from the Royal Institute of Art. She has extensive experience within process-oriented art and in working in close collaboration with artists, architects and users involved in such projects. She has also worked on new approaches to art in a healthcare environment within psychiatry. In her position at Public Art Agency Sweden, Mossum had previously been the project manager for building-related art projects and curated art collections for government agencies. As a curator, Mossum finds support in the psychoanalytic model of an *intervention*, seeking to translate how a psychoanalyst, with its outside perspective, advances claims that mirror the analysand so as to challenge the patient's ingrained beliefs and world of ideas.[19]

In her work on the Skandion Clinic, Mossum and the project's steering committee shared a vision that the art would function as a dialogue-based intervention rather than a stand-alone decoration. They felt that the art needed to be organized and formed in a way that challenged a more traditional understanding of art in a healthcare setting. According to the early plans, the Skandion Clinic's art initiative would characterize the clinic's entrance, lounge, therapy rooms, office, waiting rooms and hotel. The design of the building would thus be permeated by art, an overall vision which was expected to create positive effects for both patients and healthcare professionals. This approach was in line with the ethical stance of both the artistic and the humanistic workings at the clinic. Art was planned in particular for placement next to the treatment rooms in order to create an interaction with forms of care. The aim was to enable new ways of working for the staff, for example, by combining cancer care with artistic elements. This was expected to benefit the staff, whose skills would develop in dialogue with the art. In addition, the comprehensive support to art in the healthcare environment created the conditions for organizing public guided tours. All in all, the project exemplifies a high degree of

---

19   Lotta Mossum, "När sömmen får vara synlig. Permanent konst som intervention i samhället" [When the Seam is Allowed to Be Shown. Permanent Art as Intervention in Society], in *I det gemensamma. Konst, samhälle och komplexitet* [*In the Common. Art, Society and Complexity*] ed. ed. Lena From, Magdalena Malm, Anna Nyström & Anders Olofsson (Stockholm: Art & Theory, 2017), s. 122.

trust in the organizing power of art and its role in the care of children and young people.

In 2012, an open process group was established around the project with the artists, architects, interior designers, representatives of the users and other stakeholders, who gathered around invited guest experts on a specific artistic theme. The meetings were based on themes such as color, color/light, movement (i.e., passages such as entrances and waiting rooms) and sound. In her capacity as project manager, Lotta Mossum (together with myself in my role as a project researcher) was responsible for the organization, selection of scientific and artistic texts, documentation and compilation of the material. The overall theme in turn led to the formation of four artistic blocs. For each bloc, Mossum prepared a document concerning the selected artists and researchers and presented it to the art steering committee. These blocs constituted the backbone of the project's activities and contributed to the way the art program was ultimately implemented.

Art's intervention in the building started with Filippa Arrias' artful and pervasive use of color that has largely come to characterize the interior environment. Arrias has a degree from the Royal Institute of Art, where she was also a senior lecturer during her work on the Skandion Clinic. In addition to her artistic activity, she also has experience in scenography. The main reason she was chosen for this project, according to Mossum, was her "knowledge and experience in working artistically with color, with constructing spatial imagery and ambience".[20] The interior designers were involved only at a later stage, which is in line with the project's ambition to allow for art to come into play early in the process.

The research bloc as an intervention

The inclusion of research is what most clearly distinguishes the Skandion Clinic's artistic process from the norm in similar construction projects. The establishment of research as an additional bloc –that is, the research bloc – created a platform for exchange and dialogue between the various partners and stakeholders, as well as a common thread running between the different elements of the project.

The Skandion group went on a study visit to learn about both scientific and artistic research on art in healthcare. A delegation from the project

---

20   Lotta Mossum, art program 2012.

traveled to Umeå University in early 2012 to take part in an ongoing research study by design researcher Tara Mullaney. The study was based on evidence-based methodology (EBM), which has had a significant impact in both healthcare research and international studies of art in healthcare. The common argument for working with the EBM method is that it is expected to ensure that art contributes to measurably lower levels of stress among patients.[21] More specifically, Mullaney's study was concerned with measuring physiological responses to temporarily installed photo wallpaper and ceiling-projected nature images. Within the Skandion team, however, the visit to Umeå gave rise to a number of critical reflections, including the notion that such images cannot be equated with art, and that the emotional response to visual impressions is not easily captured by measuring instruments used in a medical setting.

Thereafter, on Mossum's initiative, the group traveled to a hospital in Herlev, outside Copenhagen, where in the 1970s the artist Poul Gernes created a grand color scheme that can be said to challenge the senses and interact with the healthcare environment. Filippa Arrias participated in the trip, which became a kind of exploratory study for her own art project. The group also met an open opponent of Gernes' color scheme from the medical profession, who preferred a traditional healthcare environment with white walls (without art) and grey floors. This criticism came to strengthen the support for contemporary art in the art steering group. The study trips laid the foundation for a collective view that artistic elements of a healthcare environment should not be reduced to an instrumental view of medical utility.

The establishment of the research bloc and its various activities was thus accompanied by a reorientation within the project team. It started to question the strictly scientific paradigm of the measurable effects of art on patients and instead to consider what role art could play in relation to healthcare as such. This reorientation also raised ethical questions about what actually characterizes good care. This is in line with Mol's critique of strictly evidence-based conceptions of healthcare, highlighting the capacity of good care to act as an "intervention."[22]

The research bloc within the Skandion project thus intervened in two ways: first, by actively participating in the construction project's

---

21 See, for example, Roger S. Ulrich, "How Design Impacts Wellness," *Healthcare Forum Journal*, 20 (1992), pp. 20-25.

22 Mol, *Omsorgens logik* [*The Logic of Care*], op.cit., p. 113.

planning of the art, and second, by contributing to a renegotiation of the role and significance of art in the context of good healthcare.

Another consequence of the two study trips was that the project team decided to seek out other relevant research studies that could support the project by opening up critical perspectives on the design of care environments. In my capacity as participant observer, I put together a compendium of relevant texts before each meeting. In the subsequent process, various guest lecturers were invited as experts, who in turn provided suggestions for other literature. In the selection of texts, I aimed to offer a balance between art, architecture and organizational theory. The project team thus reviewed scientific works (e.g., journal articles, extracts from dissertations, etc.), popular science articles, and texts of a more philosophical nature. The compendia were not intended to create a consensus among the participants but served as inspiration for new perspectives and to stimulate discussion.

Art as an intervention in the design of the building project

Initially, it was not clear on what basis and on what level art could be considered and influence the design of the clinic. It would of course have been interesting to follow the course of development if art and architecture had been planned at the same initial stage, and whether this would have influenced the dialogue between the actors involved. Since the art program was created when the construction process was underway, the art seemed to seek its *raison d'être* and legitimacy within the existing project framework from the outset. The interaction between the different stakeholders, and especially with the users, evolved over time. The research bloc's first color meeting was followed by meetings with a number of stakeholder representatives (the art consultant, the artist, the architects and user representatives). As a participant observer, it was interesting to see how differing views were expressed, considered and incorporated into the process of finalizing the artistic color scheme. During the second color meeting, the artist exclaimed: "Now it is a matter of getting the architects' approval". This could be interpreted as the artist wanting to get aesthetic approval from the architects for her intervention, something that was not formally required. This suggests a kind of uncertainty about the possibilities and the degree of integrity that art holds in the minds of other stakeholders.[23]

The overall project of implementing a dialogue-based and interventionist artistic design for the Skandion Clinic raised different stakeholder views, which, rather than being seen as a failure, is in line with Mol's definition of the practice of care. In one meeting, for example, KAS's planning manager asked whether the art program deviated from LINK's winning entry in the architectural competition. The consultant referred, among other things, to the prepared program documents and the design program, stating: "if there is that [difference], then I have to explain it [to the KAS management]." My understanding is that the very ambition to integrate the art gave the design manager cause for concern. However, its proposed impact on the expression of the project needed to be communicated and justified to management in order to achieve legitimacy. The architect stated matter-of-factly at the meeting that the artistic contributions would represent a departure from the previous plan. Whereupon the project's art consultant Mossum emphatically explained to the KAS design consultant that this was precisely the objective.

During the process, the art program evolved through political renegotiations in a decision-making process that arose from different perspectives about the different roles in the project. It moved away from the more aesthetically oriented aspects to develop a kind of shared poetics (in Groys' sense) where the focus was on the production of art itself: its creation and practical considerations. This was particularly evident in the case of the artistic use of color.

Color as an intervention

At the start of the project, artist Filippa Arrias was faced with an important choice: "What am I supposed to do? Art or color?"[24] The question had no predetermined answer, and in fact it evolved through an interplay between these two alternatives. For Arrias, color was more about responding to the architects' visions, while the role of color in art was more about evoking other kinds of moods and emotional states. The study trip to the hospital in Herlev made a big impression on Arrias, since she felt she had found effective strategies for combining art and architecture.

---

23 Arrias, 08/24/2012.
24 Arrias, 06/19/2012.

Together with her assistant, artist Malin Holmberg, she formulated a vision for the color selection process:

> We want to work with color in a way that will stimulate the experience of being present and feeling cared for. Consciously choosing color with an artistic design means that the choices have to pass through emotion and thought, the complex process of choice.25

This expresses the view in which the choice of color aims to reinforce physical presence and the sensation of being in a secure care environment. It is described in terms of both emotional and cognitive aspects. In addition, as an artist, Arrias needed to learn to navigate a complex environment that included staff, patients and family members. After working with Holmberg, Arrias went with warm colors including yellow, violet, gray and different shades of red.[26]

In a hospital, choice of color is important. It is considered to have an impact on the well-being of the patients. In this connection, it is interesting that the Greek word *pharmakon* means both remedy, medicine and color.[27] Filippa Arrias' color scheme proposal for the Skandion Clinic was presented during a meeting where the invited guest lecturer, color and light researcher Ulf Klarén, participated in the role of expert. He stated that it was "very brave to use such a colorful palette in this way." He also wondered where the pauses were, where one could rest one's gaze? The interior designer then suggested that Arrias should adopt an even clearer user perspective on the color scheme, to which she replied that the architect and preferably a representative of the client (Akademiska Hus) should be brought in instead to continue the discussion.

Once again Arrias perceived it as if the basis for the acceptance and possible legitimacy of the color scheme lay with the architects. At this stage of the project, the users themselves were still relatively far off from being real. With the support of the process, user participation and learning over time, Arrias hoped to adapt the project plans to the views of the process group and clearly incorporate the user perspective.

---

25 Mossum meeting notes (user theme), 09/20/2012
26 Arrias, Art Program, 09/20/2012.
27 Jacques Derrida, *Colour: Documents of Contemporary Art*, ed. David Batchelor (London: Whitechapel, Boston: MIT Press, 2008).

Ideally, without compromising her artistic integrity in favor of what she understood to be a limited view of the function of art in the care environment.

Perspectives and experiences of user representatives

Artworks are not always noticed by patients in healthcare environments, writes Birgit H. Rasmussen, a professor of nursing science at Umeå University with a background as a nurse.[28] According to Rasmussen, good art in the care environment does not always have to be directly visible to the patient, but a pleasant, caring atmosphere, is appreciated. However, patients clearly sense and react when art is missing, or lost. Rasmussen takes the example of a patient who saw the same empty picture hook on a wall every day, and who eventually wanted to be relocated. At the same time, there is no guarantee that the presence of art in itself creates a good care environment. There are many examples of hospital corridors that are perceived as desolate and uncomfortable, despite the fact there are paintings on the walls.

Purely decorative art does not work well in a hospital environment, at least according to the experience of the review panel of health care professionals. When the "beauty" on the walls does not harmonize with the surroundings and its ambience, it creates a contrasting effect that, in their opinion, does not work. At a meeting in connection with the use of sound, the staff explained that there had been previous experiments with images of nature and nature sounds in cancer care, including an environment with plants and water. However, this attempt to make a pleasant natural environment failed because the machines made too much noise and took over sensory impressions.[29]

Our interviews revealed that healthcare workers often associated the art found in the care environment with the disease on a symbolic and metaphorical level, such as "going to the grave." That is not very good art, according to the healthcare workers, because it is associated with suffering and death – the ultimate failure of the care intervention.[30] From this it can be deduced that what is required is a form of artistic expression that neither beautifies nor expresses pity.

Staff representatives also shared their view on developments over

---

28   See also David Edvardsson, *Atmosphere in Care Settings. Towards a Broader Understanding of the Phenomenon*, doctoral thesis (Umeå: Umeå University, 2005).
29   Sound bloc, process meeting, 11/09/2012.
30   Birgit Rasmussen, process meeting, 11/09/2012.

the previous five years, commenting that the former normative phenomenon of art for art's sake has lost its hold. Instead, the focus has shifted to technology and digitalization. For example, they highlight tests with diodes and ceiling projections where the entire ceiling is transformed into a film. However, as staff representatives noted, in practice, patients are not so interested in this, with experiments using this type of technology not being well received. If this is true, perhaps it is because patients have not been offered anything else? Maybe, what is needed is a new approach to art in healthcare. Regarding the user perspective, the project team had clear ethical concerns about involving in the study children and young people diagnosed with cancer. At the same time, there was a strong desire to weave their crucial experiences into the ongoing work. To resolve this dilemma, we chose to turn the focus of the research bloc toward the perspective of the children's next of kin. This is in line with a general trend in art in care settings where in recent decades the next of kin have also been given a stronger position in legislation.

Via my role as a researcher, the project team came into contact with a parent of a three-child family with a severely ill child, who was at that time ten years old. The woman (also referred to here as VS) came to represent her son in matters concerning the care environment. With her background as an engineer, and as an art school student in her youth, she had a favorable insight, from our perspective, into both technical and artistic fields. When asked about the role of art in healthcare, she responded based on the family's previous experiences: "Exciting project. The art in the hospital receives a lot of comments. The children react and it is scary and not adapted for children."

Since art in previous care settings has made such a negative impression on her children, VS had many questions for both nurses and play therapists, who explained that special arts councils are responsible for the art with hospital staff not involved in the selection process. This experience underlines the importance of investing in as open and inclusive process as possible, ensuring that representatives of patients and relatives for the Skandion Clinic's art program as well as staff members are themselves included in the ongoing dialogue.

From nature images to structure, rhythm and movement

The woman with the cancer-stricken son initially confirmed the widely held belief that art depicting nature is perceived as restful in the care environment. She says that during her child's illness she often lost track of time and therefore found it nice to look out of the window and follow the rhythm of the seasons. In group conversation, VS became increasingly sympathetic with Klarén's analysis that it is mainly the structural elements of nature's colors, alongside the play of light, that appeal to our human senses. She mentioned that the view of the motorway at Astrid Lindgren Children's Hospital was just as restful as natural images. Through my conversations with this mother, I came to see that calmness and restfulness do not necessarily arise from nature or harmonious colors but can also emerge in the contemplation of the rhythm and movement of the motorway. This example highlights how conversations with family members can open up a reinterpretation of what kind of art is appropriate for healthcare environments, in this case, by challenging prevailing norms.

During the conversation with VS, she remarked that as a parent she sometimes finds the art displayed in hospitals inappropriate and that she, along with other parents, sometimes hides it from their children. Not because it is too difficult to interpret, as Rapp argued in her classic history of hospital art. Rather, it is the opposite. The woman said that she perceives the art at Astrid Lindgren Children's Hospital as closed, where someone has "thought out and interpreted" what the patients should feel and think. In several cases, the art is presented to the children in a way that is considered "clarified." Based on this reasoning, Mossum raised the question whether in a care environment, this kind of art is perceived more as a symbol of care, rather than an expression of genuine care. This is in line with the woman's view that the kind of art that works well is art "that doesn't tell an exact story" but is open to interpretation and creates a space to discover things afterwards: "That's what the children need! [...] More playful and abstract! Let us interpret for ourselves."[31]

---

31   Process meeting, 09/28/2012.

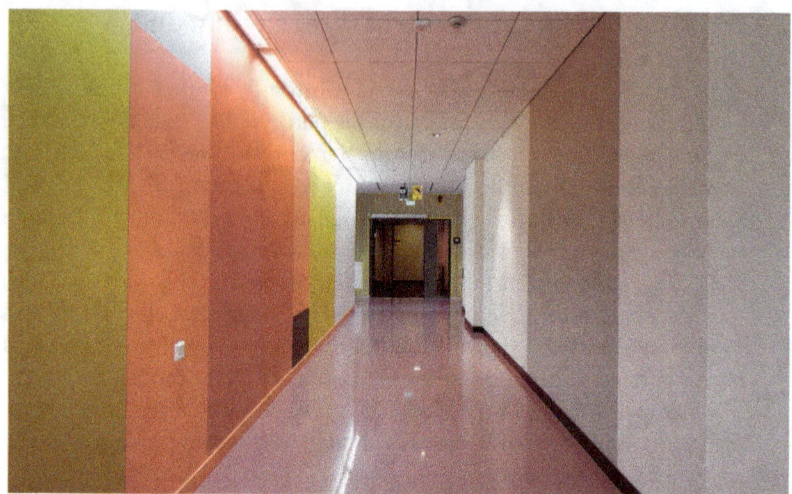

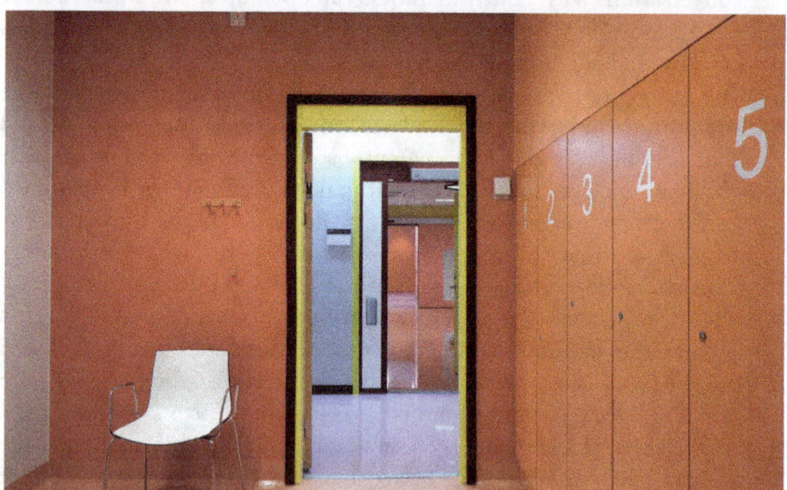

Art and the colors creates orientation in the health care environment. In the image below, the red color shows the direction to the treatment room. The floor paint in pink and violet was developed specifically for the clinic.
Filippa Arrias, Skandionkliniken, 2014
Photo: Pär Fredin © Filippa Arrias Filippa Arrias / Bildupphovsrätt 2021

Art's intervention against symbolic orders

In the fall of 2012, the project team and staff representatives gathered in
Arrias' studio for a review meeting to present their artistic design to
the users. The views of the caregiver documented above attended the
meeting and her feedback was recorded by the art consultant. After
receiving the proposal, the woman described her feelings about the
different colors used in the design, how they took on the character
of "guideposts" helping her to navigate the environment. The color
scheme is thus not a static backdrop, but has a practical function:

> The color reflects that things are happening, changing your ex-
> perience as you move. [...] very positive about the play between
> the opaque and transparent in the horizons, corridor between
> CT room and gantry. There is suddenly soul here. A dreamy
> sense, a bit of a spa feeling. It lets the viewer have their own and
> open interpretation. Positive that you can see here the trace
> of a human action, handwriting. [...] If it's well thought out, it
> gives a sense of caring. That's the difference from coming to a
> standardized place. You feel that someone has made an effort,
> put in the time.

The woman was however apprehensive about a color that Arrias called
"wine red or oxblood red",[55] but which changed its name during the
course of the project:

> [The woman] questions the Falu red color of the corridor. Cor-
> ridors are difficult by default, very long and narrow. [The wo-
> man] fears that the red color may be perceived symbolically,
> that the dark red is associated with blood. [She] thinks one
> should be careful so that the color of the floors doesn't make
> the corridor even longer.

The association with blood brought out the symbolic and affective
qualities of the color. These were considered disturbing, thought to
give rise to uncomfortable thoughts. The woman's point of view was
recorded in the meeting minutes, but no responses from the other
users were noted. On another occasion, Arrias asked a few questions to
the health care representatives about the red color. She asked, among
other things, whether they thought it was too dark and whether this

color scheme could be considered problematic by creating negative associations.[32] The respondents felt that the color could be considered too dark but pointed out that this was difficult to determine without seeing it in place. On the second question, the group was less hesitant. On the contrary, the interior designer was favorable toward the wine-red floor color, which he felt was in keeping with the artist's vision of red, glossy floors. The staff representatives present at the meeting – the head of the department and the nurse – considered it not to be a problem either. It was also pointed out by the planning manager, the consultant to KAS, that a dark red color is tried and proven in public spaces.[33] The stakeholders in the group were thus able to work together to clarify the relationship between the color scheme to both the symbolic experience of the healthcare environment and to the institutional conditions in the planned building. In this way, the perspective of the relatives was taken very seriously, but was later sidelined in the encounter with other stakeholder perspectives. The artist's original concept was thus explicitly supported, and the artistic process more deeply embedded in the building project. The architects at LINK, in particular, provided valuable assistance and support to Arrias and the art in the various phases of the process.

In connection with the realization of the color program, however, Arrias had to change the color of the floors. Hence, the oxblood red color can be seen mainly on doors and in details. There were only a number of standard colors to choose from in the required material; it was not technically possible to achieve full-color floors in the selected red color. The solution was for Arrias to work with the flooring manufacturer to develop a composition of pigments that would shift as far as possible from grey towards shades of pink and violet. The cost of the material samples initially fell in-between the budgets of the art project and the architecture, but the architects stepped in and took it upon themselves to get the project moving. Arrias then had to change, once more, the entire of the color scheme. In the final stages, a new user representative objected to the darker color schemes, reasoning that they would appear dark and threatening to those in the building. Given the perceived relevance of the criticism, Arrias adapted the color in accord with the user's criticism. In retrospect, Arrias notes that there is nevertheless a lack of register in the color scheme as a whole.

---

32   Process meeting, 10/15/2012.
33   Mossum, notes, 08/24/2012.

During any dialogue with citizens and users, architectural theorist Sofia Wiberg has stressed the importance of the practice of listening. She argues that good listening can paradoxically be said to be both active and passive. Philosopher Jonna Bornemark explains this by way of *pactive listening*, which she defines as encompassing both sensitivity and judgement.[34]

One particular area where the design process was gradually adapted to the users was in relation to children. One environment where art went through different phases of negotiation was the anesthetic room. Arrias describes this process as follows: "this room was initially perceived as passive and calming, but after being made aware that it is mainly children who will be passing through, we have chosen a brighter and 'happier' color scheme."[35] However, during the follow-up visit, the user representatives told us that the children in this room are in a particularly vulnerable situation and further reflection was required:

> Often the child has been sedated before being anesthetized and the environment in the room should have a calming effect rather than the other way around. Most children are sensitive to impressions in this situation. For example, it is a good idea to have acoustic tiles on the ceiling to muffle sounds. [36]

Arrias took the feedback to heart, proposing that instead she creates a softer color scheme for this room, with finer details in bright colors that the children could focus on while undergoing anaesthetic. The CT rooms would also be given a more limited but thoughtful color scheme in the form of a kind of "color chord," which was expected to counteract fragmentation and strengthen the sense of coherence. In this way, Arrias also tried to incorporate the aforementioned criticism that her coloration had a lack of "pauses." Accordingly, and by virtue of what I (in line with Bornemark) call pactive listening, Arrias was able to adapt to the patients' conditions in specific spaces without compromising her artistic integrity.

One aspect of the art program that was particularly appreciated by the

---

34 Jonna Bornemark, *Horisonten finns alltid kvar* [*The Horizon Always Remains*], (Stockholm: Volante, 2020), pp. 76-77.
35 Arrias, 09/20/2012.
36 Mossum, notes, 10/05/2012.

staff representatives was its concrete execution.[37]

> Some parts have been painted by professional painters and oth-
> ers are painted thinly on top (the glazing technique) by hand
> ... to create a shimmer of light and associations with the view
> of a horizon. This becomes the expression of a little something
> extra. Like handwriting; the trace of a human hand. [38]

By adding a human touch to the painting, the concept of being "cared for" is given a concrete artistic expression.

Conclusion

The case of the Skandion Clinic and the formation of its art program can be interpreted as an example of how art is given a place in the public sphere through a long series of decisions and renegotiations. But it is also an example of how various actors seek to justify art's ability to contribute to the design of healthcare environments and not merely function as a decoration created at the end of the process. In this context, art in hospitals is a phenomenon that is both relevant and contested. My chapter presents examples of how the presence of art can contribute to a more humane environment and play an active role in the creation of a culture of care. Furthermore, I have taken a critical look at an instrumental approach to art in the care environment that can be said to reflect the pervasive commercialization of Western care systems, and that in recent decades have moved toward a market model with demands for results-based governance, strictly measurable evidence and guaranteed customer satisfaction. In this context, a tug-of-war is created around the question of what kind of art is considered appropriate and what is not. The mainstream perspective is based on a very narrow view of art, while my article stresses the need to safeguard the expression of contemporary art and the integrity of the artist. In the words of Boris Groys, this can be described as a shift from a purely aesthetic understanding of the function of art in healthcare to a model that focuses on the integrity of art, as well as its poetic and organizational agency.

---

37 Ibid.
38 Ibid.

Finally, the study of the Skandion Clinic shows that it is of the utmost importance in a care environment that art does not symbolically express an imposed sympathy for the patients' situation. When this happens, art appears as a kind of a contrived symbol of care, rather than good care in practice. Well-executed contemporary art can, however, offer resistance to both purely decorative and overly direct symbolic elements. In addition to contributing to the practical dimension of care, it is necessary, in my view, to have faith in the ability of artists to deal with ambiguity and contrast, and to show other worlds and ways of being to patients, their next of kin, and caregivers.

Temporary Liaisons and Far-reaching Convergences.
Public art under municipal auspices

//Håkan Nilsson

Ars longa vita brevis

On a late summer's day in 2020, as I pass over Odenplan in Stockholm, a grove of deciduous trees has vanished. Instead, there is a sort of arrangement of conifers and autumn flowers. Soon they too will give way to a few spruce trees, which after a few months will in turn be replaced by new (or perhaps the same?) deciduous trees. At the same time, a section of a nearby street has been turned into a playground, but that too will be removed within a few months. *"Ser du möjligheterna?"* (Do you see the possibilities?) asks a sign from the City of Stockholm. Do I? I certainly see how the temporary has become an increasingly common feature of our public space. Meanwhile, in the schoolyard of Gustav Vasa's School in the same area, there are a couple of portacabins placed to alleviate the lack of space in the city's schools. They have been there on temporary building permits since 2009. What exactly is "temporary" and what role might it play in public art?

School portacabins are a reminder that the "temporary" can be a way of circumventing the rules that apply to the permanent. This aspect of the temporal, as a suspension of the permanent, can be understood by what philosopher Giorgio Agamben has called the state of exception, where regulations are set aside to protect what the regulations came into being to protect.[1] But as such, it also needs a time limit. In the case of the school portacabins, the City Planning Department has provided me with a definition: temporary permits are granted for up to five years and a maximum of three times, after which they are considered permanent.[2]

However, it is not a state of emergency that the municipality wants to signal with its temporary playgrounds and decorations of public squares, but flexibility and possibilities. Why should urban space not change with

---

1   Giorgio Agamben, *Undantagstillståndet [State of Exception]*, trans. Sven-Olov Wallenstein (Stockholm: Axl Books, 2009).

2   Mail from the City Planning Department to the author 11/06/2020.

time and demographics, needs and demands? When it comes to public art, the question has recently come to the fore. Public art, which has long been associated with monuments and/or memorials, goes against the idea of the flexible. Here, if it is not the eternal, then it is at least long-term values that are at stake. Today, many see this approach as more or less obsolete. According to this view, traditional public works of art cannot (any longer) lay claim to the eternal. It is partly a question of different levels of relevance. Permanent art is gradually being forgotten. The person the sculpture depicts is forgotten. The artist is forgotten. The statue, although it remains where it stands, is forgotten. In the end, it pleases only the doves. But it is also a question of what is to be remembered. Values change, places and their significance change, people, events and governments change.[3] Not even the hardest bronze can alter these empirical realities.

Ars longa, vita brevis: Art endures, life perishes. As far as public art is concerned, Hippocrates' maxim is no longer a given. The changing view of eternity is one of the reasons why public art in recent decades has taken on changing and sometimes transitory forms. "No more statues in the square" has become a mantra to explain the change.[4] Everything that is permanent, evaporates. Instead, the square becomes a changing place, with temporary elements, such as when the artist Santiago Mostyn positioned himself on Möllevångstorget in Malmö one fall day in 2016, accompanied by a cello and violin, to painstakingly memorize and finally sing the entire Swedish national anthem.

In this text, I will discuss the approach to temporary public artworks at the municipal level. Through a questionnaire sent to the 20 largest municipalities in Sweden, I have tried to get a picture of how much of the public art at the local level is actually temporary and how those responsible for public art in the municipalities view this, both in terms of opportunities and concerns.[5] Of the 20 municipalities, 19 responded (Gävle was, at the time of writing, in the process of restructuring its public art administration and was therefore unable to participate).[6]

---

3   The most intense debate on public art in Sweden in 2020 was undoubtedly the one that high-lighted Carl Linnaeus' background as the founder of racial biology rather than the Enlightenment scientist he had otherwise been remembered for.
4   That the "statue on the square" is resigned to become a remnant of a bygone era is of course not self-evident, as Anna Rådström's chapter on Umeå's "#MeToo cougar" in this volume shows.
5   The questionnaire is available as an appendix at the end of this text.
6   I am grateful that so many busy officials have taken their precious time to answer my questions. A sincere thank you to: Anja Boman, Art Secretary, Umeå; Olof Ahlström, Curator of Public

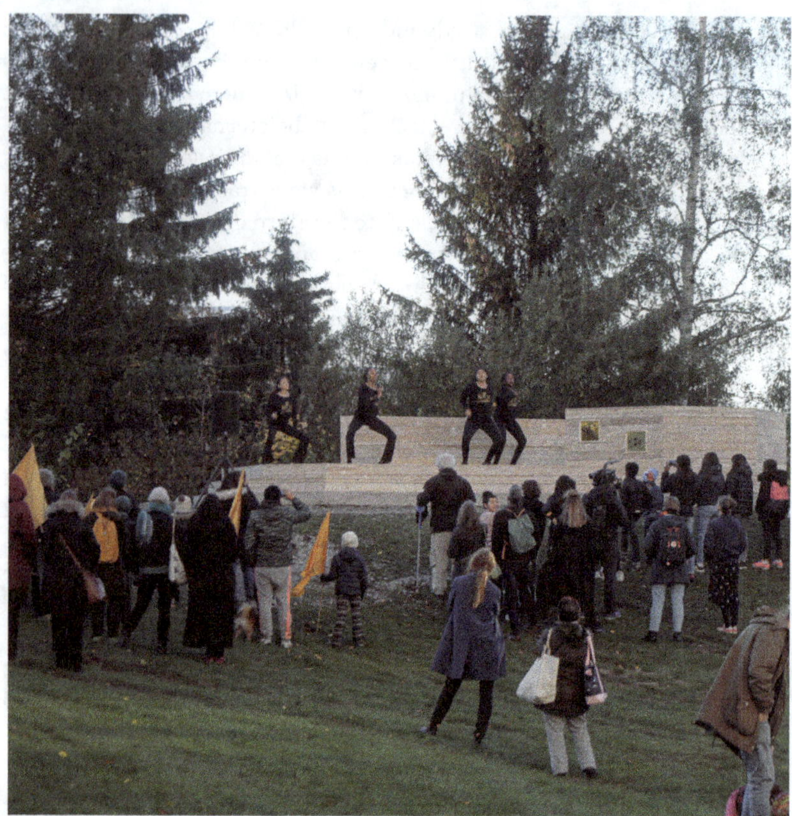

Open process. When Ruben Wätte was commissioned to create public art in the district Årby in Eskilstuna he opted for a permanent piece, which could form a meeting point in the public sphere for teenage girls. The piece was shaped in collaboration with the local dance group Royal Sisters. It resulted in the work Just to be (Here and Now), a kind of stage for performances and meetings. Images from the inauguration.
Photo: Ruben Wätte

Art, Sundsvall; Anna-Karin Wulgué, Art Gallery Director, Örebro; Anna Ehn, Head of Public Art, Uppsala; Anna Wignell, Curator, Process Manager New Public Art, Västerås; Josefine Bolander, Curator of Public Art, Eskilstuna; Stefan Hagdahl, Head of Stockholm Art, Stockholm; Peter Bergman, Curator at Fullersta Gård, Huddinge; Fredrika Friberg, City Creator, Nacka; Joanna Sandell Wright, Art Gallery Director, Södertälje; Mattias Åkeson, Curator of Public Art, Norrköping; Camilla Lothigius, Project Coordinator Public Art, Linköping; Sarah Hansson, Process Manager Public Art, Gothenburg; Joacim Eneroth, Curator Public Art and Collection, Halmstad; Filip Zezovski Lind, Art Director, Jönköping; Eva Eriksdotter, Museum Director, Borås; Joanna Thede, Deputy Curator of Public Art and Gunilla Lewerentz, Director of Dunkers Kulturhus, Helsingborg; Emil Nilsson, Curator, and Åsa Nacking, Museum Director, Lund; Anna Wahlstedt, Manager of Image and Form, Malmö and all the others who helped me to find the right people.

For a reflection on the role and effects of temporary art, I consider two relatively early works (from 2006). *The Voice* by Lisa Jevbratt, which was a net-based work that existed as a counterpart to Public Art Agency Sweden's website, and *Taxinge Piazza*, where the art groups' International Festival and Front converted a parking lot in the Stockholm suburb of Tensta into a public square. I further discuss the concepts used in the art world to describe temporary (temporal) art, and moreover discuss the emergence of temporary art in the 1990s in order to highlight the issues that have always accompanied it. This chapter will conclude with a discussion of how critical/activist art can be accommodated within public art initiatives. My conclusion is that temporary art must submit to a litany of rules, regulations and expectations when it becomes part of the public art system, but in doing so, it also plays a role in transforming this system from within. I suggest that the relationship between the system and (temporary) art can best be described as one of convergence, and which media theorist Henry Jenkins defines as a process in which different quantities, by coming closer together, also undergo mutual change.[7]

Opportunities

Where the city of Stockholm sees opportunities by seasonally changing street environments and spaces for play, Santiago Mostyn occupied the square in Malmö with a temporary artwork whose clear but subtle political message was about inclusion and belonging – qualities that allow us to just *pass by*, more or less unnoticed, as we stroll across the square. But for the work *The Repetition* to have that effect, it cannot be permanent: it needs to break with the familiar, it needs to surprise in order to make visible everything that lies at the subtextual level. Recurring references in these contexts are French radical art groups, such as the Lettrists and the Situationists who followed later. The latter, with the concept of *détournement* (French for "redirection" or "hijacking"), attempted a kind of "double negation" in which the classic avant-garde strategy of sensational scandals was abandoned for a different kind of displacement, in which the conflation of elements was thought to create new political situations, which could not be dismissed as mere art.[8]

---

7   Henry Jenkins, *Konvergenskulturen. Där nya och gamla medier kolliderar [Convergence Culture. Where Old and New Media Collide]* (Gothenburg: Daidalos, 2008).

8   See Guy Debord & Gil Wolman "A User's Guide to Detournement" (1956) from *Situationist*

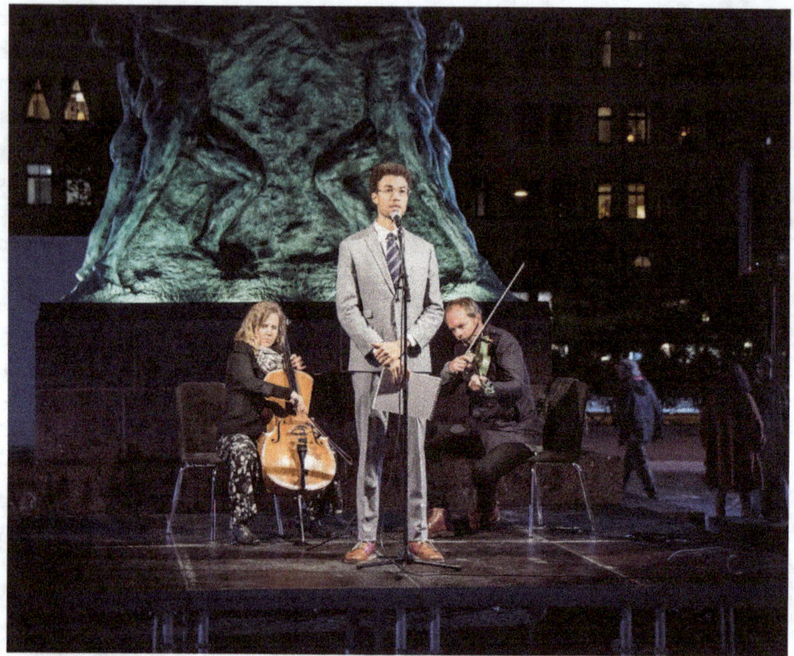

Santiago Mostyn, The Repetition, 2016, Photo: Ricard Estay/Statens konstråd

Though not quite as politicized as Santiago Mostyn's *The Repetition*, making the invisible visible, "creating a rupture in the everyday" as the aesthetics professor Cecilia Sjöholm puts it, is one of the qualities usually emphasized in an argument in favor of temporary art.[9] The temporary "awakens" the viewer, and as the art gallery director Eva Eriksdotter in Borås points out, the same thing happens when something permanent is removed.[10] Her insightful observation shows that the "invisible" is visible, though we need to be reminded of it. In an attempt to awaken not only the viewer but also invisible art,

International online https://www.cddc.vt.edu/sionline/presitu/usersguide.html [accessed 02/04/2021]

9   Cecilia Sjöholm: "Sann konst? Konst och offentlighet på 2000-talet" [Real Art? Art and the Public Sphere in the 21st Century] in *I det gemensamma: konst, samhälle, komplexitet [In the Common: Art, Society, complexity]*, ed. Anders Olofsson & Anna Nyberg (Stockholm: Art and Theory Publishing, 2017).

10   In this and the following references to those responsible for public art in Sweden's largest municipalities, I have based my text on responses given in the abovementioned survey. All responses were received September-October 2020.

Stockholm Konst (Stockholm Art) has begun to invest in new works whose role is partly to activate already existing art by initiating a dialogue with it. This strategy has been important in a broader field as well and has gained renewed relevance for many temporary projects in art, architecture and design since the turn of the millennium.[11]

The Repetition was funded and commissioned by Public Art Agency Sweden, an agency that has been a driving force in temporary public art over the past decade. Public Art Agency Sweden's work in this direction was intensified in 2012 when Magdalena Malm took over as its director. Malm came from the curatorial project MAP (Mobile Art Production), an organization that has been working with temporary art in public spaces since 2007. When I ask Martin Sundin, who was the Head of Unit at the Ministry of Culture when Malm was appointed, whether her experience with temporary art was important for the appointment, he replies that it was not decisive in the recruitment.[12] He notes, however, that once Malm took up the post, she was able to push through changes in that direction. The Ministry of Culture's readiness was partly due to their desire to see a renegotiation of what public art could be. It was also due to a changed view of where Public Art Agency Sweden should operate, the result of which was to encourage collaboration with both private and public actors.[13] It was also the case that the role of public art , after deregulation and the reframing of Public Art Agency Sweden's *raison d'être*, had been under discussion for some time. When the state sells off its real estate, not only does it divest a stock of building-related art, it raises questions about whether public art will be needed in the future too. Both the Swedish Agency for Public Management's *Nya former för Statens konstråds verksamhet* (*New Forms for Public Art Agency Sweden's Activities*) (2005) and the *Kulturutredningen* (*Culture Inquiry*) (2009) advocate a fundamental change in Public Art Agency Sweden's

---

11 The Situationists are referenced again in Claire Bishop's *Artificial Hells: Participatory Art and the Politics of Spectatorship* (London: Verso, 2012) as well as in her "Participation and Spectacle: Where are We Now?" in *Living as Form: Socially Engaged Art From 1991-2011*, ed. Nato Thompson (Cambridge, MA: MIT press, 2012). Similar reasoning for architecture can be found, for example, in *Instant Urbanism: auf den Spuren der Situationisten in zeitgenössischer Architektur und Urbanismus [Tracing the Theories of the Situationists in Contemporary Architecture and Urbanism]* (Basel: Christoph Merian, 2007) and in Magnus Ericson & Ramia Mazé, *Design Act: Socially and Politically Engaged Design Today – Critical Roles and Emerging Tactics* (Berlin: Sternberg Press, 2011).

12 Interview with Martin Sundin 11/03/2020.

13 Malm took office during Fredrik Reinfeld's (M) second administration (2010-2014) when Lena Adelsohn-Liljeroth (M) was Minister of Culture.

activities. The former proposes, for example, that activities related to art should be placed under the auspices of the Moderna Museet and that Public Art Agency Sweden should thus be dissolved. [14]

In 2020, temporary projects coexist with permanent ones in Public Art Agency Sweden's supply. Contrary to what it may seem, a turn toward the "temporary" has never been a question of consciously choosing a particular path, something that Magdalena Malm has also pointed out on several occasions. In an interview in *Kunstkritikk*, for example, she stressed that for her there was no "contradiction between permanent and temporary projects."[15] Perhaps the difference between these two concepts is smaller than it would first appear, at least when it comes to public art funded and commissioned by the public. In the present study of the position of temporary art at the municipal level, I find plenty of hybrid models in which the value of the dialogue itself varies. The interaction that "temporary" art often entails is partly related to, or at least coincides with, the fact that public art is partly seen through different eyes and partly given different tasks, a change that Malm can be seen as both a symptom of and a driving force behind.

Municipal interest

Responses to the survey I sent out to the country's municipalities varied. Some gave extensive answers, while others were more brief. This creates an uneven balance, and the answers are therefore not always comparable. However, overall, the survey responses provide at least a tentative picture of the current situation.

When asked whether the municipality invests in temporary art, 14 out of 19 answered yes. Some variation in responses may be due to how the question was interpreted. Both the term "invest" and especially "temporal" can have different associations, which also leads to a discussion of the latter term later in the text.[16] What can be inferred from the responses of the (few) municipalities that do not "invest"

---

14 *Nya former för Statens konstråds verksamhet* [*New Forms for Public Art Agency Sweden's Activities*] (Stockholm: Swedish Agency for Public Management, 2005), Government Inquiry 2009:16, *Report of the Swedish Committee of Inquiry on Cultural Policy 1, Base Analysis.*

15 Frans Josef Petersson "Satsar på konst i miljonprogrammet" [Investing in Art in the Million Program] 12/01/2015: https://kunstkritikk.se/satsar-pa-konst-i-miljonprogrammet/ [accessed 10/09/2020].

16 The question in the survey was formulated as follows: Do you aim to incorporate temporary and/or process-oriented/dialogue-based art as part of public art?

directly, is both that they have an ambition to do so in the future and that they refer to artistic projects not directly part of the municipality's public art, but do take place in the public space and with the municipality's support. From Umeå, art secretary Anja Boman replies that they have been working with temporary projects throughout the 2000s, but that commissioning and placing these kinds of artworks in public space is rare. Other occasions and paths are found; for example, temporary artworks can be combined with permanent expressions, such as with the inauguration of *Listen!* (the #MeToo Monument) in 2019.[17] In Helsingborg, Joanna Thede, acting curator for public art, answers no to the question of whether they invest in temporary art, but refers to an investment in street art through the City Planning Office, which means that the municipality does, to some extent, support temporary art in public spaces. In Halmstad, Joacim Eneroth, curator of public art and collections, notes that works of this kind are mainly produced in collaboration with external partners. Peter Bergman, director of Fullersta Gård in Huddinge, says that the municipality lacks a strategy and organization to work with such issues, but that they do see property owners and the community planning department starting to incorporate process-based artworks in their planning. The administrator for *Bild och Form* in Malmö, Anna Wahlstedt, says that they are in the process of a reorganization, but writes that they intend to invest in temporary art. At the moment, however, there is no budget for public art; each project has to go through an application process, which makes questions about the quantity of temporary art difficult to answer. Other municipalities express an ambivalent position as well. Mattias Åkeson, responsible for public art in Norrköping, writes that they lack an "explicit strategy" and that they, like Malmö, must apply for funds for each project. They apply every year for SEK 1.5 million for investments, maintenance and restoration, but nothing specifically for temporary projects.

All municipalities report an ambition to work with temporary art, but there are great differences with respect to the conditions for doing so. It is a question of finances: some municipalities have a budget for public art, others have to request it. Most municipalities apply the 1% rule, but when this is applied, it is often difficult to commission temporary art, depending on the nature of the governance

---

17   Anna Rådström discusses this relationship in "*Listen!* A Sculpture in the Square and a #MeToo Monument" in this anthology.

documents.[18] Many of those responsible for public art also testify to the pedagogical challenge of getting both politicians and property companies to invest in temporary projects. This also highlights the difference between different types of funding, such as operating or investment budgets, or collaborative projects between several municipalities and/or regions/state. The home of public art within the municipal organization is also important. In many municipalities, public art is tied to or falls under the municipal art gallery, others have their own departments (as is the case for large cities such as Stockholm and Gothenburg, but also Uppsala) and still others are under the city planning office or equivalent (such as Nacka) and thus have little or no contact with the municipal art gallery's exhibition activities. I will come back to this point.

One stumbling block municipalities face is the question of whether a work of art funded through taxation must manifest in the form of a physical object. As Anna Ehn, head of public art in Uppsala, reports, the money spent must result in something physical that abides, but she also argues that this can be a documentation of, for example, a performance. Regarding performance, several write that it can be part of a larger project, as has happened in Umeå and Jönköping. Short-term art projects, such as performances, thus have greater opportunities if they can be linked to something else to which they call attention. At the same time, documentation is seen as having an intrinsic value; for example, Joanna Sandell Wright, head of the art gallery in Södertälje, argues that some temporary art projects circulate in magazines and books by virtue of documentation, thus contributing to public awareness of the place where the work is located.

Others explain that they can take a process-like approach and still end up with an art object. Josefine Bolander, curator of public art in Eskilstuna, explains that the municipality has opened up a sketching process, so that at this stage artists can engage citizens in a long-term dialogue, which in turn results in a work of art. Mattias Åkeson explains that they are working with similar solutions in Norrköping.

Sarah Hansson, curator at *Göteborg Konst*, also points out the importance of how an art project is formulated. They see a need among clients

---

18   For a more detailed discussion on the 1% rule and its application in Swedish municipalities, see *1% för konstnärlig gestaltning av offentlig miljö. En komparativ studie av enprocentsregeln i kommuner och regioner 2012 och 2018* [*1% for Artistic Design of Public Spaces: A comparative study of the one-percent rule in municipalities and regions in 2012 and 2018*], ed. Anna Söderbäck (Stockholm: Arts Council, 2020).

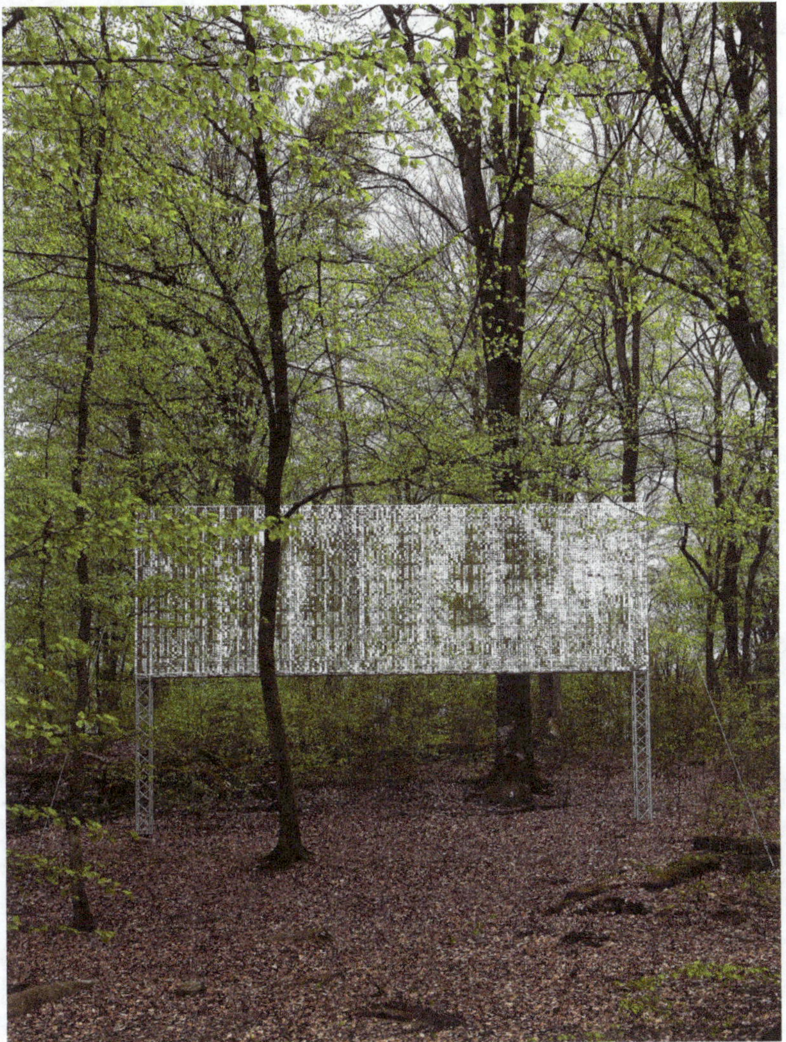

Re-installed permanent art. Katarina Löfström's piece Open Source in Wanås Konst Sculpture park was reinstalled after the original work had been severely damaged by a fallen tree.
Photo: Mattias Giwell/Wanås Konst

that process-oriented/dialogue-based art result in a physical work, but also believe that if processes and performances are instead described in terms of "events," then an understanding that the work is not permanent increases. Joanna Thede in Helsingborg reflects similarly on the use of language, writing that projects of this kind are more easily accepted if they are called "theater" or "sound projects." According to art curator Filip Zezovski Lind in Jönköping, more traditional terms such as "gestalting" (design) and "löskonst" (a term referring to a collection of movable, often wall-hung pieces) are avoided in order "to seek a language that does not limit the freedom of art from the outset."

Temporary art and the institution

When asked how long the municipalities have been working with temporary art, different trends can be discerned. Those that see little or no investment at all, have no history of adopting this approach (e.g. Huddinge, Helsingborg and Malmö where the latter is in a process of transformation where the ambition is to work with temporary art in the future). Most respondents speak of it as a relatively recent initiative. It has been happening since the mid-2000s, remarks Mattias Åkeson in Norrköping. Anna Ehn writes that Uppsala has used this approach since 2014, but also points to a large temporary exhibition on the castle hill in 1998. Those responsible in Gothenburg, Västerås, Eskilstuna and Jönköping responded that they have worked with temporary art since 2015; Joanna Sandell Wright in Södertälje states that they have done so since 2017 (but also mentions previous municipal investments in street art) while Olof Ahlström answers "3-4 years" for Sundsvall. Others report a longer history. In Umeå, for example, cultural secretary Anja Bohman answered that they have worked with temporary art for the twenty years she has worked there. Stockholm Konst replied that they have been doing so since they were established in 2008, but that similar projects were already carried out during the Capital of Culture year in 1998.

From Lund, Emil Nilsson mentions that public art has been included under the auspices of the municipal art gallery since 1996, further commenting though that it is a bit unclear how long process-based art has been part of the municipality's public art initiatives: "events have taken place, but they have not always been defined as public art." Örebro points to a work by the group Love & Devotion from 2005 as the earliest work, but also mentions the city's biennial *Open Art,* which started in 2008.

Like Emil Nilsson, Anna-Karin Wulgué, director of the Örebro art gallery, writes that it is also a question of how we understand "public art" and describes the biennial as a special case. Many municipalities work with or are involved in similar events where the question of their involvement with temporary art becomes difficult to answer. Borås, which has held its international sculpture biennial since 2008, argues along similar lines as Örebro, as does Halmstad, where we find *Art Inside Out* (since 2015) and *x-sites* (2017-2019, turning into a biennial in 2020) and in Helsingborg, which has held its annual street art initiative *Artstreet Hbg* since 2015. These biennials are examples of hybrids in which the municipality's public art department is involved to varying degrees.

Art Inside Out is a residency activity and a collaboration in Region Halland that moves between all the municipalities in Halland. Skåne has similar regional initiatives in NOKS, *Nätverket för Offentlig Konst i Skåne* (Network for Public Art in Skåne). Several municipalities also show other co-financed projects, for example EKFA was a project organized by Västerås Museum, which was co-financed by the Swedish Arts Council (50%) and Region Västmanland (25%) with the remaining 25% coming from the different municipalities. The advantage highlighted here is that this project was not influenced by local public art policy documents, and therefore offered greater freedom regarding the selection of art. Several mention individual projects: Malmö cites the so-called tripartite funding of the City Tunnel as an example but sees this more as an exception than a rule.

In the responses from both Lund and Umeå, public art is balanced against what happens at their respective municipal art spaces. Umeå, for example, describes how performance is a "natural feature" of municipal art spaces and Lund refers to a tradition that goes back to the 1960s. Questions about municipal art spaces as "semi-public" environments (as art historian and curator Nina Möntmann has called it) and whether the exhibitions that take place there are to be understood as "public," constitute an important field of inquiry.[19] However, for the purposes of this study, it is more interesting to

---

19 Nina Möntmann "Art Institutions and their Publics: On Relational Strategies," *Placing Art in the Public Realm*, ed. Håkan Nilsson (Huddinge: Håkan Nilsson (Huddinge: Södertörn University Press, 2012).

address what role the municipal art gallery plays in relation to public art, a question asked directly in my survey.

When asked about the role of municipal art spaces, Jönköping replied that there is no such thing while Helsingborg stated that it has been deprived of its official mission. In Nacka, public art is part of urban planning, and therefore have little contact with the municipal art gallery, while Stockholm, Uppsala and Gothenburg, as mentioned above, have their own public art departments. Stockholm writes how the art gallery (Liljevalchs) and Stockholm Konst "support each other," even if they do not work together very much. When Stockholm Konst started in 2008, it was part of Liljevalchs Konsthall and the links were stronger then.[20] Among other things, a part of the art gallery's new pavilion was designed to showcase ongoing public art initiatives. Such a space exists in Uppsala, but it is currently located in the same building as the city theater, not at the art museum. Sarah Hansson, process manager for the 1%-rule at Göteborg Konst, replied that the municipal art gallery has a public art activity, but that it is in the process of being reshaped and currently has a marginal collaboration with Göteborg Konst. On the other hand, the municipal art gallery runs its own project, Urban Konst, which aims to create and promote public art in the city.

In other municipalities, the link between public art and the municipal art gallery is generally tighter. Public art is organized either together with the municipal art spaces or under its auspices. This is also reflected in other responses. In Eskilstuna, it is reported that public art initiatives are regularly arranged at the art gallery, and the art managers in Halmstad describe the municipal art space as having a close relationship with public art. Peter Bergman, museum director at the gallery in Huddinge, emphasizes the expertise of the art gallery, and Västerås, Borås, Eskilstuna, Sundsvall and Södertälje respond that public art in the municipality is arranged through their art spaces, while Örebro speak of their art gallery having a "decisive influence." Malmö, which is currently undergoing a reorganization, also emphasized the importance of the gallery for this purpose.

It is not possible to make any sweeping conclusions based on these differences, though it is clear that those municipalities with close collaborations with local art spaces also see the gallery as part of their

---

20 Since 2019, it has been part of the Museums and Art Department, together with the City Museum and the Medieval Museum, among others.

overall work with public art, whether it is a question of using the site as a forum for performances or as a place where a discussion about temporary art can be held.

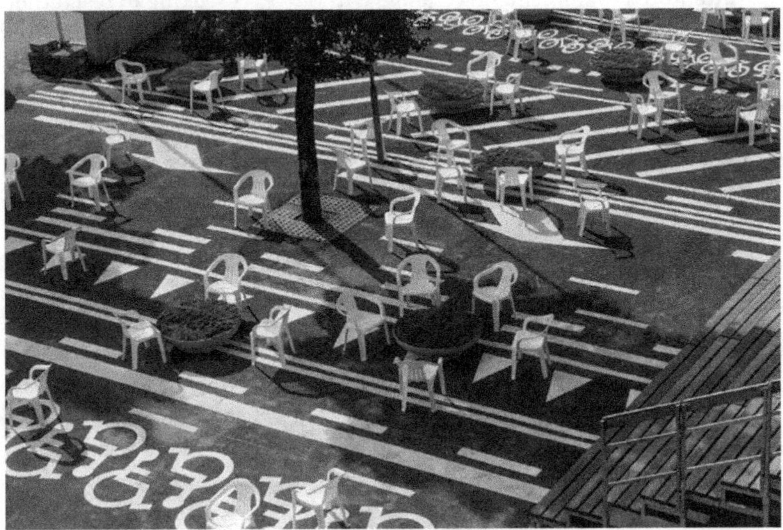

International Festival / Front, Taxinge Piazza, 2006, Photo: Tor Lindstrand

Temporary site-specific art: two examples

It is easy to associate temporary art with things that only exist for a certain period of time or in the context of a defined process. But "temporary" can also mean that the life of the work or process is uncertain, as is the case with the Helsingborg Street Art Festival. The works produced in this festival last for a while, but erode over time. These works can be said to exist in a kind of extended now, where a deliberate non-maintenance allows them to weather away rather than be completed or dismantled.[21]

Another example of a temporary yet long-lasting work is *Taxinge Piazza*, which was created in 2006 when the performance collective

---

21   But the outcome is not always certain. As Joanna Sandell Wright of Södertälje Konsthall notes, the tradition of 'the permanent' is strong, which also implies a desire to preserve the temporary, thus going against the very intention of the work.

International Festival and the design group Front were given the opportunity to redesign the space outside Tensta Konsthall in Stockholm. The municipal art space awarded International Festival a grant, which was invested in working out an application to transform the parking lot outside the municipal art space into a public square. What began as a sort of extended performance in which the group attempted to implement a change without ever seeking to reach their goal, ultimately resulted in the city planning office getting involved in the issue and, against all odds, carrying out the project. The new budget was limited, so it was decided to maximize outcomes by finding the cheapest and most sustainable (i.e. durable) solutions possible. It was decided to design the new plan with road markings, using road marking paint, and to fill the square with lots of plastic chairs.

Taxinge Piazza highlights a number of aspects of public art that are relevant to my investigation. Partly because of budgetary constraints, and the way the application process was integrated into the artistic one, but also because the artists were comprised of a performance group and a design collective.[22] It is also interesting that the initiative originates from the local municipal art space, which, so to speak, turned outward toward the public.[23] The work was conducted outside Stockholm's "public" art and was never intended to be understood as permanent. But since these kinds of markings are quite durable, they were left to slowly wear away.[24]

If *Taxinge Piazza* slowly disappeared, there are also works that are based on a continuous inflow and interaction. In these cases, the work ceases to "exist" whenever this flow is impeded. Lisa Jevbratt's *The Voice* (2006-2009) is such an example. *The Voice* does not have a municipal commissioning body, it was commissioned by Public Art Agency Sweden, and existed in what was then a fairly new part of the public space, namely, a government website. The work was transformed by the searches individuals made on Public Art Agency Sweden's website

---

22 For a discussion of this, with an emphasis on International Festival, see "Too Much Too Soon: Tor Lindstrand's and Mårten Spångberg's International Festival" in *Empty Stages, Crowded Flats: Performativity as Curatorial Strategy*, ed. Florian Malzacher and Joanna Warsza (Berlin: Alexander Verlag, 2017).

23 Tensta Konsthall's outward turn can be seen as part of a broader movement among many publicly funded art institutions in the late 1990s and early 2000s, which the Norwegian critic and curator Jonas Ekeberg described as "New Institutionalism." See, for example, *New Institutionalism: Verksted #1*, ed. Jonas Ekeberg (Oslo: Office for Contemporary Art Norway, 2003).

24 Interview with Tor Lindstrand May 15, 2020.

(and searches that led there via other search engines). In simple terms, the work consisted of the search terms used, which, using typographic size differences and different frames around the words, provided information about parameters determined by the artist, such as how often a word was searched for or how frequent it appeared on the website. In other words, the work was interactive. Nonetheless, it still broke with existing conventions in that the interactivity was not visible to all users (since people were interacting with the search engines, not because they wanted to be incorporated into an art piece, but simply because they were seeking information) and in that the result of the search was delayed so that the output was not displayed in real time. The work aimed to make visible what was being searched for, and not invite analysis of the algorithm itself.

In this way, the result was a kind of portrait of what applicants expected to find on Public Art Agency Sweden's website, and thus also a picture of hegemonic structures, both perceived and actual. What the visitors searched for not only shows who Public Art Agency Sweden represented, but also makes the visitors' expectations visible. *The Voice* can thus be said to be site-specific, not only because it was associated with the website, but also because the work depicted (without evaluating) the different art-political, sociological and economic conditions that prevailed at that point in time.[25] However, *The Voice* existed in this form for only a few years. This was mainly due to the fact that the website was constantly being rebuilt and the work therefore needed to be constantly updated to maintain its function. This was both a costly process and labor intensive for the artist.

The examples I have presented above show that maintenance issues are important even for temporary art, a point rarely discussed. This is certainly a problem that all kinds of public art encounters, as Karin Hermerén shows in *Offentlig konst - ett kulturarv* (*Public Art - A Cultural Heritage*).[26] Among other things, Hermerén touches on the issue of responsibility for the many works of art included in the corporatization and selling of State agencies to private actors,

---

25 Both Miwon Kwon and Douglas Crimp emphasize that "site specific" entails links to a site's social and economic conditions. For an introduction to this, see Miwon Kwon, "One Place after Another: Notes on Site Specificity", *October*, Vol. 80. (Spring, 1997), pp. 85-110, and Douglas Crimp "Redefining Site Specificity" in *On the Museum's Ruins* (Cambridge: Mass.: MIT Press, 1993).

26 Karin Hermerén & Henrik Orrje, *Offentlig konst - Ett kulturarv. Tillsyn och förvaltning av byggnadsanknuten konst [Public Art - A Cultural Heritage. Supervision and management of building-related art]* (Stockholm: Public Art Agency Sweden, 2014).

including buildings and the art they hold. Hermerén shows, for example, that in 11 of 25 case studies, the buildings (and the art) have changed hands at least once since they were commissioned.[27] The examples I present here highlight another aspect of time, namely how slow change and weathering can be part of the work itself, and how change can be repeated and occur at the rapid speed of digital technology. The predetermined lifespan of *The Voice* meant that the art had to relate to this very fact, which also illustrates how flexibility (and time constraints) has become an increasingly common issue for public art.

The duration of *The Voice* was regulated in a contract, and only months after the contract expired, Public Art Agency Sweden changed its internet provider and suddenly. The outcome was that all contacts between *The Voice* and the website were instantly broken. This highlights another interesting aspect of the public sphere. Public Art Agency Sweden's website, a public environment, is owned and managed by a private company. But this company is periodically changed as a result of the dictates of the procurement process. The publicly funded public sphere thus steers art more towards the temporary, rather than the permanent.

The boundaries between the private and public sectors have long since been blurred. This of course also changes the conditions for publicly funded art. The survey reveals other hybrid arrangements between private and public, where, for example, municipal expertise is consulted when private companies are building residential areas on the basis of land allocations they have received from the municipality, and where the municipality procures private art consultants to produce suitable proposals for artists.

Even the question of a work of art's regulatory compliance has become incorporated into issues that are regulated from the outset. If the deregulations of the 1990s had surprising consequences in terms of permanent art, public art commissioning bodies have a greater awareness today. In an interview, Anna Ehn in Uppsala explains how, even early on when commissioning public art for a municipal building, they already consider what will happen to the work if the site where it is displayed or performed is decommissioned .[28] In general, many of the municipalities interviewed testify to the fact that in recent

---

27 Ibid., p. 290.
28 Team meeting on October 8, 2020.

decades the process of commissioning a work of art has become more professionalized and bureaucratized.[29]

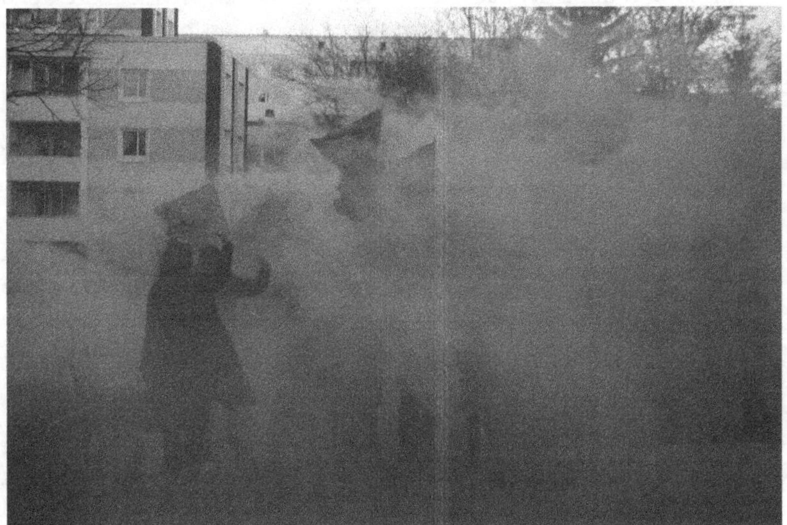

Just to be (Here and Now) a kind of a stage for performances and meetings. Image from the inauguration. Photo: Ruben Wätte

Temporary art and commissioning bodies

The temporary art of today often involves dialogue with citizens. It can be seen as an attempt to move beyond what the art historian and critic Alexander Nagel has called *plop art*, the kind of art that is suddenly just sitting there in the middle of the street, without anyone in the neighborhood being asked or even told about it.[30] Nagel's comment is

---

29 The same conclusion is reached in Söderbäck 2020. See also the reference to the private art consultancy *ArtPlatform* in "Public Art – An attempt to navigate" in this volume where they state that they started to work with municipal public art commissions in 2016, a decade after the consultancy was built. Four years later, municipalities are the commissioners in four out of five projects.

30 Alexander Nagel, "ON DEMAND. Alexander Nagel on Reclaiming Art/Reshaping Democracy," *Artforum*, November 2017.

based on French artist Xavier Veilhan's sculpture *Le monstre* (2004) in Tours.[31] Nagel initially sees this as a textbook example of plop art, but changes his mind when he learns about the process behind it, where the local community had a major influence on the artistic process and its final outcome. Veilhan's sculpture was commissioned by *Nouveaux Commanditaires*, a French public art organization (though not publicly funded) that operates based on the assumption that the need for and commissioning of a work of art must come from the local community, not from either the state or municipality. The "protocol" that stipulated the process underlined the shared responsibility of all stakeholders.[32]

The questionnaire asked the respondents to comment on why they wanted to work with temporary art and with what value they felt it contributed. As many as 80% responded that this art opened up to dialogue with the intended users, either because it opened the door to discussion or because it is easier to anchor locally. "An opportunity for people to become involved in the development of the city," writes art manager Josefine Bolander in Eskilstuna, and art gallery manager Eva Eriksdotter in Borås mentions "social sustainability" as a motivation for this approach. The municipalities' responses also indicate that these works were considered better at capturing current issues and provide insights into and knowledge of artistic processes. Temporary art creates greater equality between the viewer and artist and an "[a] ctive versus passive consumption of art," according to Olof Ahlström, curator of public art in Sundsvall.

By involving the intended viewers, the users, the municipalities claim that other ways of looking at art, differing from how traditional art is viewed, are enabled. This may require that users have an influence, a kind of municipally organized grassroots perspective. But they can also come up with ideas for completely different uses and new questions regarding "utility." Emil Nilsson, curator of public art in Lund, echoes these ideas when he links the development of art to social change. In the service economy, art is moving more towards event-based work, he says. However, a few municipalities see a potential danger in participatory art being instrumentalized in this way. There is a strong

---

31 In 2020, the French artist was featured in Stockholm's public art with *Vårbergs jättar* (*Vårberg's Giants*), a public work in the Stockholm suburb of Vårberg inaugurated in October 2020.

32 See Estelle Zhong Mengual & Xavier Douroux, *Reclaiming Art/Reshaping Democracy: The New Patrons & Participatory Art* (Paris: Les Presses du Réel, 2017). The protocol for the process is described by the initiator François Hers on pp. 421-422. See also http://www.nouveauxcommanditaires.eu [accessed 02/04/2021].

awareness in the construction industry that the use of a building may change. Permanent art then risks reflecting a situation that no longer exists and thus hinders the building's reprogramming. Temporary art simply responds better to this need for flexibility, say curators Sarah Hansson in Gothenburg and Anna Wignell in Västerås. On the other hand, others think that temporary art may have a greater critical potential, since it is not subjected to the same conditions as a permanent work.

The responses show that temporary art can help activate and engage citizens, but they also show that this kind of temporality, even when it includes participation, can be driven by other agendas. Ultimately, the question of the capacity for art to engage effectively, returns, which, in Alexander Nagel's view, may well result in something looking like "plop art" without in fact being so.

Getting involved

The examples I present above, *Taxinge Piazza* and *The Voice*, show that permanence and transitoriness are best viewed as approximations in a reciprocal relationship. The concepts are thus not mutually exclusive since what is temporary is always permanent to some degree, and the permanent always temporary. This is also true of legal definitions. Temporary building permits are valid in the municipality of Stockholm for a maximum of five years and, as mentioned above, they can only be renewed a certain number of times before they become permanent. Permanent art, on the other hand, comes with a promise to be sustainable for a certain number of years. For Public Art Agency Sweden, the minimum is five years (depending on the situation and technique), while 20-30 years is usually considered the norm for building-related art.[33]

Taxinge Piazza and *The Voice* also shed light on the role of participation. If *Taxinge Piazza* ceased to exist because of the activity of the participants (i.e., it was worn down from their visits), *The Voice* ceased to exist as soon as participation was no longer active. Only traces remain, memories of an activity. Both artworks thus raise questions about what participation actually is: in neither case were the participants directly aware of their importance to the existence of the work. Yet the artworks were unthinkable without them.

---

33 According to an e-mail from Henrik Orrje, Head of Operations 12/11/2020.

What it means to be involved can thus look very different in different works and the relationship can consequently be described by a variety of terms: interactive, immersive, practicable, relational, performative, participatory, dialogical or even unconscious. What these terms have in common is that they point to phenomena that unfold in a temporal process, which also means that some works of art are readily identified by this characteristic; they may, for example, be called processual, temporary, temporal-based or time-based. The concepts themselves are multifaceted: interactivity can be human-human, human-document or human-system, for example, and under all of these there are subdivisions and degrees of participation. Leafing through a book is interactive in a certain way, being involved in designing it is another.[34] An activity can also have different degrees of activity. Both listening and seeing more or less actively is central to the philosopher Jacques Rancière's concept of the emancipated spectator when he writes that "viewing is also an action that confirms or transforms..."[35] As Rancière tells us, experiencing and interpreting a work of art can be engaging.

Active listening involves more stakeholders in public art, particularly in relation to participation, where it is important for both the commissioning body and the artist to listen to both those affected by the art, without losing artistic integrity in the process.[36] The process leading up to a completed public artwork is really a chain of decisions, all of which involve varying degrees of participation. Anna Ehn in Uppsala, for example, outlines a multi-stage process in which participation comes into play even before an artist is consulted, as was the case in the Gothenburg municipality's *Safe, Beautiful City*, discussed and problematized in Oscar Svanelid's chapter in this anthology.

The position of the artist in public art in general, and participatory art in particular, is thus (at least in theory) different from the situation in

---

34 For a discussion of these concepts, see Peter Mechant & Jan Van Looy, "Interactivity" in *The Johns Hopkins Guide to Digital Media*, ed. Marie-Laure Ryan, Lori Emerson & Benjamin J. Robertson (Baltimore: Marie-Laure Ryan, Lori Emerson & Benjamin J. Robertson (Baltimore: Johns Hopkins University Press, 2013). See also: Jens Jensen, "Interactivity: Tracking a New Concept in Media and Communication Studies," *Computer Media and Communication*, ed. Paul Mayer (Oxford: Paul Mayer (Oxford: Oxford U.P., 1999), pp. 160-187.

35 Jacques Rancière, *The Emancipated Spectator* (London & New York: Verso, 2011), p. 13.

36 Sofia Wiberg, *Lyssnandets praktik. Medborgardialog, icke-vetande och förskjutningar [The Practice of Listening. Civil dialogue, unknowing and displacement]*, doctoral thesis (Stockholm: Royal Institute of Technology, 2018)

his or her own studio. A recurring concept here is "criticality," which attempts to carve out a position between, on the one hand, a kind of dependence/loyalty to the art and a critical distance toward it. [37]

The many concepts I introduced above are sometimes interrelated, though sometimes they are mutually exclusive, for example, the relationship between the work and the viewer. "Immersive" is a term which (like many others) is used in interactive media and computer games and describes the situation that arises when, for example, the player is immersed in the game and feels that he or she "exists" in the world.[38] On the one hand, such a situation may seem to be incompatible with a critical distance, since the viewer is more or less in the hands of the storyteller; on the other hand, it describes what it is like to participate in Taina Ruiz Guiterrez's video walks, *Örebro Variations*. In Guiterrez's work, the viewer follows a pre-recorded walk using a phone and thus occupies one and the same place, but in two different ways. The work allows the viewers to see a different story unfolding in the place where they are, as if in a parallel universe. It is an example of how immersive works can 'absorb' the viewer while the physical place they occupy continues to be present but in a different way.

Immersive works are also often "practicable," requiring the viewer to move around an area. Practicability is a term introduced by researchers Samuel Bianchini and Erik Verhagen, who use it to describe art that can or should be touched (and thus need not be public). "We describe them as 'practicable' because their defining characteristic is the ability to generate an activity that can transform both the works themselves and their audience."[39] This leads them to discuss artwork as a kind of initiator, a dispositif, a term developed by Michel Foucault to describe how an "apparatus" (*dispositif*) initiates and shapes human activities. The idea here is that the "practicable" artwork functions as such a *dispositif*, that it actually requires some form of interaction by the viewer to exist at all. The concept of *dispositif* also points to the need for critical examination of the "performance" itself. For Foucault, the term also denotes the strategies of modern power structures to

---

37   See the discussion in the chapter "Public Art: An attempt to navigate" in this anthology. As well as Irit Rogoff "From Criticism to Critique to Criticality": eipcp 1/2003, http://eipcp.net/ transversal/0806/rogoff1/en.html [accessed 03/17/2020].

38   Janet H. Murray has discussed the relevance of this concept for storytelling in digital worlds in her *Hamlet on the Holodeck: The Future of Narrative in Cyberspace* (New York: The Free Press, 1997).

39   *Practicable: From Participation to Interaction in Contemporary Art*, red. Samuel Bianchini & Erik Verhagen (Cambridge, Massachusetts: The MIT Press, 2016).

control and discipline individuals.40

"Practicable" art also creates a kind of bond between participant and artist, which is reminiscent of the way art theorist Nicolas Bourriaud conceived of the concept relational aesthetics.41 The traditional artwork, as Bourriaud argued, creates a relationship between artist and viewer. In relational aesthetics, it was precisely this relationship and this encounter between artist and viewer that characterized the work of art itself. Bourriaud has been the subject of criticism for his idealized way of describing the relationship between viewer and artist (in which the former at worst becomes the latter's "material"), but here it may suffice to note that he downplayed the object in favor of what the work itself makes the participants do, that is, what kind of interaction the work/situation evokes.

Another way of approaching the complex issue of participation/involvement is to consider that when individuals other than the artist have influence over the production itself, hence the concept of "prosumers", the distinction between consumer and producer seems to disappear. Participation in this respect requires a different level of engagement than what is commonplace in mainstream spectator culture; "no one protests if you walk out of the cinema," as Haggren puts it in the book *Deltagarkultur (Participatory Culture)*.42 Not that this means that the situation is entirely egalitarian; in every situation where there is participation, there is also a tacit agreement. If these agreements stipulate active participation (e.g. prosumers), passive viewing is not always acceptable (those who participate without participating are called lurkers). Identifying what these agreements are and how they are to be respected therefore becomes crucial for dialogue-based art. What will the dialogue lead to and who is it for?

Works where the creation process involves participants are therefore sometimes described as "process-based," because they are characterized by dialogue. Insofar as the dialogue is to be considered as the work of art itself, the work is thus temporary. However, this does not mean that all temporary works are dialogue-based. Performance, for example, is an art form that takes place over a stretch of time but does not need

---

40   Michel Foucault, "The Confession of the Flesh" (1977) in *Power/Knowledge Selected Interviews and Other Writings* ed. Colin Gordon (New York: Pantheon, 1980).

41   Nicolas Bourriaud, *Relational Aesthetics*, trans. Simon Pleasance & Fronza Woods (Dijon: Presses du réel, 2002).

42   Kristoffer Haggren et al, Deltagarkultur *[Participatory Culture]* (Gothenburg: Korpen, 2008), p. 60.

to involve the viewer more than as a spectator (which, according to Jacques Rancière's argument above, can be quite interactive). In this respect, this kind of performance is more similar to other art forms that unfold over time without the direct need for viewer interaction, as is the case for much of today's video and sound art, which is why time-based is a more appropriate term than temporal in these cases.[43] Of course, there is no obvious distinction, as a work that is on display for a certain period of time (for example, during a biennial) is temporary without being either time-based or dialogue-based. However, temporary and/or temporal here refers to art that plays out over time and is often performed dialogically between artist and participants.

As this exposé demonstrates, what involvement actually means is extremely complex and the question of what it might lead to needs to be preceded by a critical examination. I have also aimed to demonstrate that the dividing li<<<ne does not run between temporary and permanent, which themselves are not static concepts. Moreover, the analysis shows that participation and transitoriness are not synonymous or symbiotic; for example, participatory processes can lead to permanent works. We also saw examples of this in my analyses of the municipal investments in temporary art, where, for example, we encountered a strategy of creating dialogue to increase participation in the creative process itself by opening up the part of the procurement called the "sketch assignment." An artwork with an objective that creates a permanent outcome can increase the participant's understanding of their own involvement, whereas temporary art can create participatory processes that do not contribute to activity. And vice versa.

Temporary art: concluding discussion

Some municipalities report that the fact that state institutions have started to work with temporary art has had an impact on its implementation. Another reason municipalities reported for wanting to work with temporary art is that it was seen to reflect what contemporary art looks

---

43　It should be stressed that I am not suggesting that "temporal" art has a higher value or that it is better suited to make an impact on viewers or "spectators." But that is not the subject of this text. For a discussion of the transformative capacities of sound art, see Åsa Stjer's *Before Sound: Transversal Processes in Site-Specific Sonic Practice*, doctoral thesis, (Gothenburg: ArtMonitor, 2018).

like, and they do not want to separate out public from contemporary art. They see it as their mission to "show the breadth of what the art world encompasses in an accessible way," as Anja Boman in Umeå puts it, while Joacim Eneroth in Halmstad stresses the importance of showing "more kinds of artistry and more kinds of art." Similar perspectives emerge in the responses from Jönköping, Stockholm, Gothenburg and Västerås. Anna-Karin Wulgué in Örebro replies that temporary art is more in demand today; after being very much about function in the past, it is now more about "participation and openness towards an undefined result."

It is evident that an important and central part of contemporary art has oriented itself toward participation and dialogue. This "turn toward the social," as Claire Bishop calls it, has a chequered history that is worth touching on briefly here.[44] In Sweden, this turn toward the social is best exemplified with an exhibition curated by Ulrika Léven, Åsa Nacking and Mats Stjernstedt at the ICA store Malmborg Caroli in Malmö in November 1993. Elin Wikström, among others, participated with her work *Hur skulle det gå om alla gjorde så? (What Would Happen if Everyone Did This?)* in which she slept in her bed in the shop during opening hours.

But as Lisa Jevbratt's aforementioned artwork reminds us, process-based art also has other genealogies: interactivity has been a central factor in digitalized art since at least the middle of the last century. The similarity between dialogue-based art and internet art became increasingly evident with the first generation of "net artists" around the mid-nineties, where the interaction between artist and viewer often moved between the public space and the digital sphere. If such a distinction can be made, then we can say that *The Voice* was enacted in the part of the public sphere that exists in the digital world. Net art depends on its viewer/user to exist and thus (partially) dissolves the boundary between artist and viewer, another recurring theme we see in process-based art.

It is perhaps serendipitous that the art field moved toward dialogue-based art at the same time as net art was established. But another, common cause for the emergence of both, and which is usually discussed, relates to larger, societal changes such as the financial crisis of the 1990s, the deregulation that took off with the emergence of neoliberal politics and the accompanying notions of the "creative class." Major issues

---

44   Bishop, *Artificial Hells: Participatory Art and the Politics of Spectatorship*, op cit.

such as globalization, political shifts and various economic crises are, of course, relevant in some sense to all artistic activity. What set dialogue-based art (and net art) apart was that it so clearly tried to find forms that could respond to the consequences of globalization. It did not seek to make objects for an art market but, on the contrary, to use art to bridge the social gaps widened by including the viewer. Both dialogue-based art and net art held the promise of strengthened democratic institutions in which the participators were involved in a more direct way.

Dialogue-based art is therefore often presented as part of a broader form of activism. Curator Nato Thompson describes how socially engaged art is closely intertwined with movements such as AIDS activism, the women's rights movement, etc.[45] Artist and activist Gregory Sholette has discussed the emergence of a variety of socially engaged art groups from the 1980s to the present day.[46] Theorist Grant Kester also discusses the art scene's turn toward dialogue-based art, taking on the issue of what happens when an artist acts on behalf of someone else without any point of anchorage.[47]

Much has been written about this, and it would be beyond the scope of this study to explore all the complexities. However, two points are relevant to my discussion here. One is about how temporary, dialogue-based art relates to the art world. Theorists and critics such as Maria Lind, Nato Thompson and Claire Bishop have pointed out that the emergence of this kind of art is often based on the hope that art can offer a counterweight to the world's increasing commodification where citizens are turned into passive consumers,[48] as well as a turn away from the art market's focus on the genius of the individual artist's product,[49] and that this also comes with the justification that art should act and activate people where the state has failed.[50] They all point to the risk that the new strategies will be "captured" and commodified. On this point, Lind writes: "Here, activism's idealistic

---

45 Nato Thompson, "Living as Form," in ed. Nato Thompson, *Living as Form*, op.cit. , p. 21.

46 Gregory Sholette, *Dark Matter: Art and Politics in the Age of Enterprise Culture* (London: Pluto Press, 2010).

47 Grant Kester, *Conversation Pieces: Community and Communication in Modern Art* (Berkeley: University of California Press, 2004).

48 Bishop, *Artificial Hells: Participatory Art and the Politics of Spectatorship*, op cit.

49 Maria Lind, "The Collaborative Turn", in *Taking Matter into Common Hands: On Contemporary Art and Collaborative Practices*, ed. Johanna Billing, Maria Lind & Lars Nilsson (London: Black Dog, 2007).

50 Nato Thompson, "Articulations of Artist-initiated Organizations," in Mengual & Douroux 2017.

view of cooperation clashes with the demands of private companies and the state for increased profitability and efficiency."[51]

The second point concerns the relationship with public art. It is clear that art, which extends beyond the traditional art venue, will engage other spaces, thus also approaching the domains of public art. Dialogue-based art has emerged here as a critique of the way public art has been utilized. So problematic was public art seen to be that Suzanne Lacy coined the term *New Genre Public Art* for art that sought to actively engage in public spaces. "Unlike much of what has been called public art to date, 'new genre public art' – art in both traditional and non-traditional media that communicates and interacts with a broad and diverse audience on issues directly relevant to their lives – is based on engagement."[52] In a discussion that was also conducted in a broader field, Rosalyn Deutsche, for example, repeatedly problematized the role of art in the context of gentrification.[53]

As can be seen from the discussion of the emergence of an "alternative" public art, much of its self-understanding is based, from the outset, on a social commitment where there is also an ongoing discussion about how to avoid instrumentalization by external forces. It is also a question of occupying new areas and engaging participants, even if the artistic expression may be "traditional." Social engagement is often the driving force – artists strive to overcome the shortcomings and bridge the gaps that arise between producer and consumer in commercial culture.

This discussion broadens when we consider the participatory cultures that blossomed in the context of digital media. Henry Jenkins has repeatedly pointed to a shift in the creation of what he calls convergence cultures, showing how consumers take over the role and become co-creators, even re-creators of the work.[54] The word "participation" as used here and as the authors of the book Deltagarkultur (*Participatory Culture)* note, has become a positive word because it suggests a "democratic structure where everyone is offered co-determination," but at the same time, it states that this ideal is something that is

---

51 Lind "The Collaborative Turn," op.cit. , p. 20.
52 Suzanne Lacy, "Cultural Pilgrimage and Metaphoric Journeys", in *Mapping the Terrain: New Genre Public Art*, Eds. Suzanne Lacy (Seattle, Washington: Bay Press, 1995).
53 Rosalyn Deutsche, *Evictions: Art and Spatial Politics* (Cambridge, Massachusetts: MIT Press, 1996).
54 Jenkins, *Convergence Culture*, op.cit.

seldom realized.[55] Their view of participation is based on all involved parties being aware of what they are partcipating in and on a dialogue between them: "Participatory culture presupposes *reciprocal* communication between subjects within the context of a work, a medium or a social situation."[56] These are ideals that are not always so easy to live up to (if they are even desirable) in the case of artistic activity, where the issue is perhaps better formulated in terms of responsibility. The artist has a responsibility to the intended viewers, but the viewer also has a responsibility in this exchange.

As the above example shows, participatory art and the discussion surrounding it began in the United States in the 1980s and took over in Europe a decade later. Discursively, the same discussion revolved in relation to questions of *communities* and cultural consumption in general and in net art, in particular. All this forms a clear backdrop against which contemporary art's interest in dialogue-based processes emerges. The question that remains, however, is what relevance it has for understanding the emergence and function of temporary art in "public" public art. Can art be activist and still pass through all the processes associated with its anchorage in a specific municipality?

Perhaps the latter question is not asked the right way, or maybe it is a bit anachronistic. The conditions that shaped "new genre public art" are quite different from the conditions that prevail today. After three decades, process-based art has transformed the art world and with it the perception of public art as such. Public art has become more professionalized, and insights into the available modes of expression and shortcomings are much more salient today than they were just ten years ago. This does not mean that issues related to instrumentalization, or gentrification are a thing of the past, but there is a growing awareness of these issues among stakeholders.

The work with dialogue-based art commissioned by the public and placed in the public space can be described as a kind of convergence. Convergence, Jenkins writes, is a process driven from both the top down and bottom up.[57] From the top comes various *dispositifs* in the form of agendas, steering documents and organizational structures. From the bottom comes the will to access space and finances to work for a kind of art that activates its participants. Where the art

---

55   Haggren, *Deltagarkultur (Participatory Culture)*, op.cit. , p. 32.
56   Ibid, p.43 (my italics).
57   Jenkins, *Convergence Culture*, op.cit. , p. 28.

is forced to submit to increasing bureaucratization to enable public commissions, the institutions of public art must change too. Not only does this apply to their educational responsibility, but also to a review of their own structures so that they respond to the needs of art. In the responses from the 20 largest municipalities in Sweden, we see that such work is underway.

Appendix
Questions for municipalities

First, a few questions about structure, budget and initiatives.

- Do you aim to incorporate temporary and/or process-oriented/dialogue-based art as part of public art?
- How long have you been working with this kind of art?
- If so, what does this initiative look like? For example, do you need to deliver a "product" in order to fund the project? That is to say, can you work with process-based/dialogue-based art if it also leads to a physical manifestation?[1]
- Do you work with performance and other temporary artworks? If so, how and when?
- What role does the municipal art gallery/museum play in the development of public art in general and temporary art in particular?
- To what extent does your investment in public art consist of projects like these (e.g., as a proportion of the total budget or in actual numbers)? I understand that in some cases the budgets are quite different, and I understand that in some cases it is difficult to use 1% funds (if any) for temporary works. Therefore, I would be grateful if you could elaborate on this answer a bit. My goal is not to create an exact picture of how funds are distributed, but an idea of the bigger picture. (I also do not evaluate the answers; for me this is not a question of which art should be rewarded.)
- I understand that many art projects in the country are owned/funded by multiple stakeholders, such as the municipality, region and state in joint funding. Can you describe what it looks like for you?
- Do you think you can implement as many temporary works as you would like? If not, what would you like the distribution to be?

---

1   As the careful reader will note, there is no "only" here, so it should read "can you only work." But the recipients of the survey noted that omission as well.

Finally, some broader, more speculative questions. I understand if they are difficult to answer.

- Why do you want to work with temporary and/or process-oriented art? What value does it add that permanent art does not?
- What do you think is causing the shift towards temporary art (if there is one)?
- How do your counterparts/commissioners (e.g., construction companies) view the funding of temporary works instead of permanent works?
- Do you note any differences among recipients between how permanent and temporary art is received?

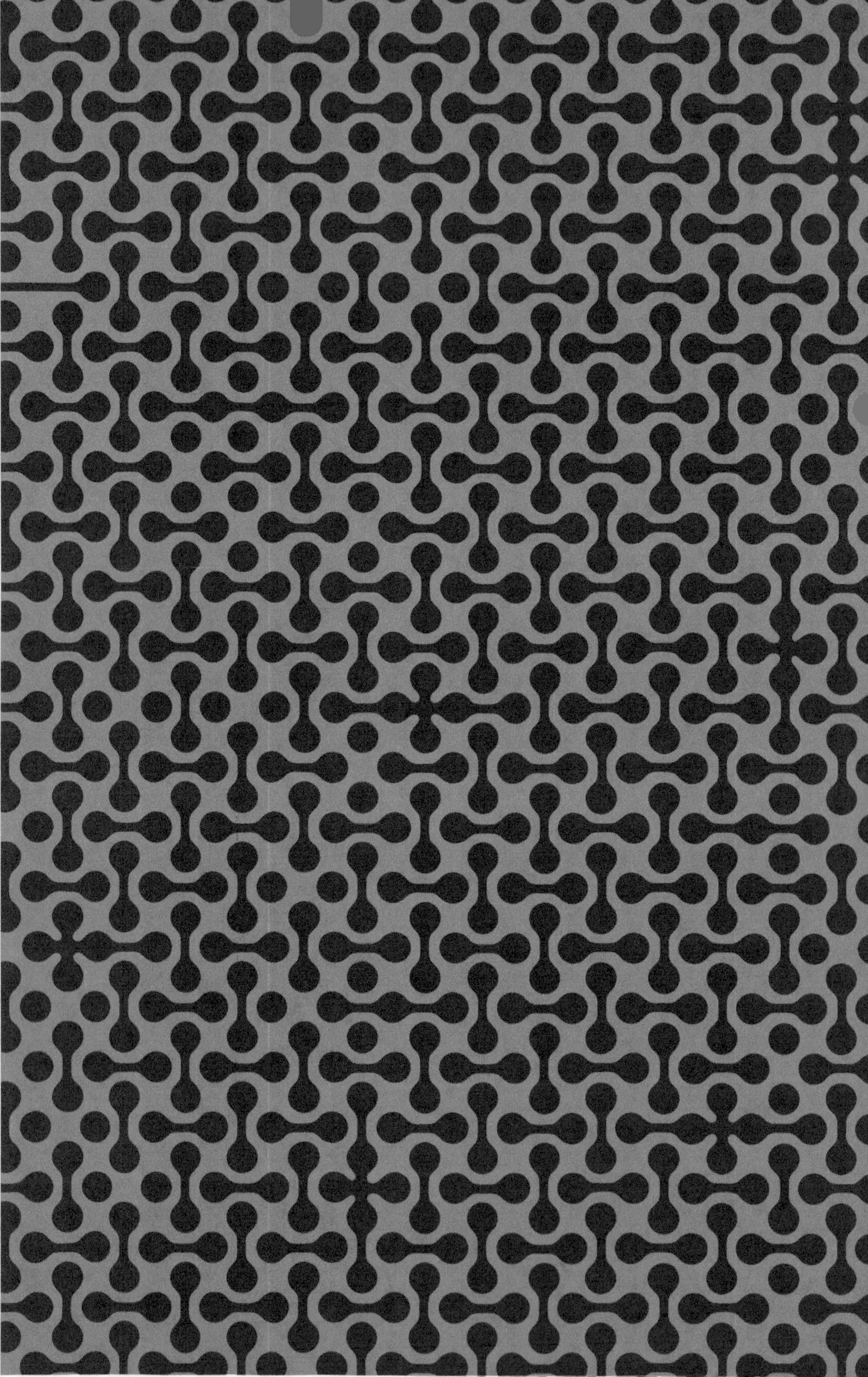

www.ingramcontent.com/pod-product-compliance
Lightning Source LLC
LaVergne TN
LVHW021316200726
843509LV00002B/58